Rewriting
the Victorians

Rewriting the Victorians

Modes of Literary Engagement with the 19th Century

ANDREA KIRCHKNOPF

McFarland & Company, Inc., Publishers
Jefferson, North Carolina, and London

Library of Congress Cataloguing-in-Publication Data

Kirchknopf, Andrea, 1974–
    Rewriting the Victorians : modes of literary engagement with the 19th century / Andrea Kirchknopf.
        p.   cm.
    Includes bibliographical references and index.

    ISBN 978-0-7864-7134-8
    softcover : acid free paper ∞

    1. English fiction — 20th century — History and criticism.
    2. English literature — 19th century — Influence.   3. Literature, Modern — 20th century — History and criticism.   I. Title.
    PR881.K56 2013
    823'.9109 — dc23   2013008265

British Library cataloguing data are available

© 2013 Andrea Kirchknopf. All rights reserved

No part of this book may be reproduced or transmitted in any form or by any means, electronic or mechanical, including photocopying or recording, or by any information storage and retrieval system, without permission in writing from the publisher.

On the cover: Charles Dickens giving public reading (Photos.com/Thinkstock); steampunk laboratory bottle (Hemera/Thinkstock); ornate antique globe (Stockbyte/Thinkstock); smiling girl (Zoonar/Thinkstock); age-old mechanical clock, brass bowl, clock spring and gear jewelry, cloud puffs, metal chain, rough sea, steampunk typewriter, top hat, torso (all iStockphoto/Thinkstock)

Manufactured in the United States of America

McFarland & Company, Inc., Publishers
    Box 611, Jefferson, North Carolina 28640
        www.mcfarlandpub.com

Table of Contents

Acknowledgments   vii
Preface   1
Introduction to Post-Victorian Fiction: State of the Art   5

1. From *Victorian* to *Post-Victorian*: Definitions, Terminology and Contexts   17
2. Post-Victorian Fiction and the Literary Scene   48
3. Post-Victorian Fiction in Its Political and Social Context   77
4. *Jane Eyre* Tailor-Made: A Case Study of the *Jane Eyre, Wide Sargasso Sea, Charlotte* Adaptive Chain of Novels   107
5. The Way We Adapt Now: Endings, Novel Series and Adaptive Maps   147

Conclusion: Ways Forward in Researching Post-Victorian Fiction   186
Chapter Notes   193
Works Cited   202
Index   215

Acknowledgments

I am especially indebted to Tamás Bényei for his extensive comments on an earlier version of this monograph and Judit Friedrich for providing exemplary critical support during the whole writing process.

I am also grateful for the conference events "Neo-Victorianism: The Politics and Aesthetics of Appropriation" at the University of Exeter in September 2007; "Adapting the Nineteenth Century: Revisiting, Revising and Rewriting the Past" at the University of Wales, Lampeter, in August 2008; "British Literature and Cultural Memory" at ELTE, Budapest, in September 2010; and "The Other Dickens" at the University of Portsmouth in July 2012. All these allowed me to share my research with other scholars. Special thanks to the European Society for the Study of English and Central European University for making these exchanges possible.

The conferences inspired publications that appeared elsewhere as early versions of sections of chapters in this book. Material from "(Re)workings of Nineteenth-Century Fiction: Definitions, Terminology, Contexts," originally published in *Neo-Victorian Studies* 1:1 (Autumn 2008): 53–80, is reprinted by permission of *Neo-Victorian Studies*. Material from "The Future of the Post-Victorian Novel: A Speculation in Genre," originally published in the *Hungarian Journal of English and American Studies (HJEAS)* 17:2 (2011): 351–70, is reprinted by permission of *HJEAS*. Material from "Post-Victorian Narratives of the Crystal Palace: The Case of Peter Carey's *Oscar and Lucinda*," originally published in *Confrontations and Interactions: Essays on Cultural Memory* (2011): 393–407, is reprinted by permission of *Confrontations and Interactions: Essays on Cultural Memory*. Material from "Adapting Dickens in Post-Victorian Fiction," originally published in *HUSSE 10 Lit Cult* (2011): 127–135, is reprinted by permission of *HUSSE 10 Lit Cult*.

Finally, I also wish to express my gratitude to Ivett Molnár and György Bézsenyi for assisting me in all sorts of ways toward completion of this project.

And to my son, Tádé Bézsenyi, who patiently postponed his birth until I finished the manuscript. This book is dedicated to him.

Preface

Why is the Victorian age still exciting today? How does this interest become translated into contemporary literature? What aspects of the past receive attention and in whose favor do they get reformulated? In what ways may these rewritings influence various sites of cultural production from theoretical thought to marketing strategies? In this book I survey such questions with a special focus on novelistic refashionings of the nineteenth century as a significant trend in present-day literature. The study of post–Victorian fiction has recently become an important field of research connecting various disciplines and gaining influence in university syllabi. It has been very exciting to follow the process of mapping out the post–Victorian phenomenon from the first conferences resulting in the establishment of subject-specific journals, through the enlivening debates about the scope and methods of research, to the numerous studies and books devoted to particular areas and aspects of the field. The inspiration for this book comes from the conviction that while research on post–Victorian fiction is becoming increasingly popular, there is a lack of literature which makes it accessible to a wider circle of students and professionals.

Therefore, my objective in this book is to provide a comprehensive overview of reading post–Victorian responses to Victorian texts. I focus on theoretical discourses, social and political contexts, and genres and modes of rewriting. I devote considerable space to defining the body of novels in question and outlining its research context because I believe this is a crucial step to take when a new field of research is in the making. In my contextualization of post–Victorian fiction I do not consider in detail areas like trauma, haunting and spectrality, or cultural memory, as they have exhaustively been discussed by other authors. I rather examine the literary scene and narratives of identity because these topics are not centralized in critical surveys, yet they seem crucial in understanding rewritings. Likewise, in the discussion of genres my primary aim is not to scrutinize the most fashionable ones, such as crime, detective and Gothic fiction, or steampunk, but to index generic choices to social and political contexts. This allows a closer look at biographical novels responding to the literary scene and island fiction portraying narratives of identity. In order to sustain both a synchronic and a diachronic perspective in my analysis, I study an adaptive chain of three historically consecutive texts as well as an adaptive map of simultaneous thematizations of a Victorian subject as different modes of reproducing earlier texts. So that the survey reaches a wider audience than current subject-specific research examining non-mainstream works, my work is based on case studies of mostly well-known novels, prioritizing close reading techniques. I also refer to film adaptations, cultural mementoes and theme parks, maintaining an interdisciplinary analytical perspective. Such an account is of interest to scholars and students familiarizing themselves with post/neo–Victorian studies as well as to researchers in cultural memory, heritage, adaptation and cultural studies. Readers surveying intertextuality and the postmodern or pursuing English literary and cultural studies with nineteenth, twentieth and twenty-first-century foci may also find this work useful.

When planning this book, I wanted its chapters to logically follow one another, which is extremely difficult in the case of such a complex field. Finally, I have settled for maintaining a structure that shows how a project aiming to outline a new field of research develops. The first chapter clarifies the terminology and background of reading post–Victorian fiction, in order to establish the scope and discourses utilized in the rest of my survey. The second and third chapters introduce prevalent ideological structures for discussing current fictional revisions, followed by case studies of texts of the genre that best express these frameworks. The literary scene framing the production and reception of refashionings of the nineteenth century is illustrated by the analysis of some Henry James adaptations specifically concerned with the author, literary criticism and the reading public; while the social and political context of such rewritings is exemplified by some island novels, amended by Peter Carey's *Oscar and Lucinda* and its film adaptation as well as the cultural memento of the Crystal Palace, sensitive to postimperial and postcolonial narratives of identity. The fourth chapter is a historical survey of an adaptive chain of novels inspired by Charlotte Brontë's *Jane Eyre*, employing the concepts approaches mainly depending on the chronological and topical foci of the novels. Interestingly, the analysis of such texts has acquired a position in recent histories of Victorian literature, usually towards the end of such collections, like the last two papers in *Writing and Victorianism*, edited by J. B. Bullen (1997) as well as in *Rereading Victorian Fiction*, edited by Alice Jenkins and Juliet John (2000). This proves both that some nineteenth-century texts are hardly read without their twentieth and twenty-first-century revisions and that fiction has become a legitimate tool of interpretation functioning interspersed with other modes of critical analysis.[4] One such additional analytical context for Victorian fiction appears to be film and media studies, as illustrated by the last paper in *A Companion to the Victorian Novel* (2005) edited by Patrick Brantlinger and William B. Thesing, where contemporary film and television adaptations of Victorian novels enhance the understanding of the source texts. Indeed, Victorianists trying to make sense of current rewritings of nineteenth-century material understand such undertakings as various new entry points into Victorianism, not establishing a new field of research but stretching the boundaries of the existing one of Victorian studies (Llewellyn 2008: 165, 168). Seeing a danger of favoritism towards the nineteenth century at the expense of the present, this approach is criticized as reductionist, positioning the body of current rewritings as "a secondary and derivative artifact" (Carroll 2010: 179).

Victorian Turns, NeoVictorian Returns: Essays on Fiction and Culture (2008), edited by Penny Gay, Judith Johnston, and Catherine Waters, marks a recent attempt to discuss Victorian novels together with their rewritings, promoting the coexistence of nineteenth-century and contemporary perspectives of reading: "In bringing together essays that address both Victorian writings and their afterlives, this volume differs from the other recent collections devoted to Victorian afterlives alone" (Johnston and Waters 2008: 10). Yet, this effort seems to fail here as there is a lack of correspondence between the two, quite disproportionate, parts of the collection, leaving largely untapped the potential of the establishment of topical relationships, as well as a possible dialogue between the chronologically opposite approaches. One of the underlying reasons behind this failure may be an apparent uncertainty of audience, whether the collection is intended for Victorianist or contemporary readers, or both. The problem of not paying proper attention to defining readership and the resulting inconsistent provision of contextual information is also pointed out by another critic (Llewellyn 2008/2009: 158), writing for *Neo-Victorian Studies*, a recently established e-journal devoted to clarifying "possible generic, chronological, and aesthetic boundaries" (Kohlke 2008: 2) of research; in other words, dealing with the problem specified. A more balanced endeavor at addressing both the Victorian and the present-day context is Louisa Hadley's *Neo-Victorian Fiction and Historical Narrative: The Victorians and Us* (2010). The author conceptualizes her readings of present-day refashionings based on Victorian tenets and structures her chapters accordingly: she first describes a set of nineteenth-century conventions of historical narratives, and then discusses how its various aspects function in today's rewrites. Identifying themselves as Victorianists and analyzing the post–Victorian output of the first decade of the twenty-first century in their *Neo-Victorianism: The Victorians in the Twenty-First Century, 1999–2009* (2010), Ann Heilmann and Mark Llewellyn also emphasize the importance of connecting Victorian studies with the "New Victorians" (Heilmann and Llewellyn 32).

In addition to attaching current revisions of nineteenth-century fiction to accounts of the Victorian novel and to establishing a dialogue between Victorian and contemporary works, there is a third widespread critical angle of surveying today's fictional responses to Victorian texts, and that is postmodernism, utilizing a number of discourses. In his *Nostalgic Postmodernism: The Victorian Tradition and the Contemporary British Novel* (2001), Christian Gutleben tackles novels exclusively and categorizes them as a specific subgenre of postmodern fiction, a status they claim to have achieved in the field of contemporary literary studies. Other collections of essays discuss fictional texts within a wider spectrum of cultural production and reproduction. In *Refracting the Canon in Contemporary British Literature and Film* (2004), edited by Susana Onega and Christian Gutleben, and in Cora Kaplan's *Victoriana: Histories, Fictions, Criticism* (2007) heritage film also features as a component in discussing (re)canonization; while *Victorian Afterlife: Postmodern Culture Rewrites the Nineteenth Century* (2000), edited by John Kucich and Dianne F. Sadoff; *Functions of Victorian Culture at the Present Time* (2002), edited by Christine L. Krueger; Jay Clayton's *Charles Dickens in Cyberspace: The Afterlife of the Nineteenth Century in Postmodern Culture* (2003); and Simon Joyce's *The Victorians in the Rearview Mirror* (2007) include theater, photography, architecture, teaching, science, technology, digital media, popular culture and different forms of living as further frameworks in which the Victorian influence on our times can be discussed. The variety of discourses applied to the phenomenon of readdressing nineteenth-century texts indicates its popularity as well as its present-day theoretical relevance.

Reading the issues of *Neo-Victorian Studies* (*NVS*), the already mentioned forum devoted to the discussion of current creative and critical material on revising the nineteenth century, provides an insight into how this emerging field has been developing over the years. Its alternating general and specific thematic numbers record scholarly engagements, from establishing and mapping out areas of inquiry, through keeping track of and responding to the abundance of new publications on the market, to identifying particular topical concerns towards which scholarship is branching out. These moves are connected to conferences with similar foci and monographs as well as collections of essays expanding their scope of research in the same directions. *NVS* 1.1 and 2.2, and *Literature Interpretation Theory* 20.1–2, document how the field was set up, the latter two being proceedings of the respective conferences "Adapting the Nineteenth Century: Revisiting, Revising and Rewriting the Past," that took place at the University of Wales, Lampeter, in August 2008, and "Neo-Victorianism: The Politics and Aesthetics of Appropriation," held at the University of Exeter in September 2007. At the moment, specific subfields of post–Victorian scholarship receive detailed attention, such as cultural memory in Kate Mitchell's *History and Cultural Memory in Neo-Victorian Fiction: Victorian Afterimages* (2010), as well as other forms of dramatizing the duality of how the present relates to the past, such as spectrality in *Haunting and Spectrality in Neo-Victorian Fiction: Possessing the Past* (2010), edited by Rosario Arias and Patricia Pulham; trauma in *Neo-Victorian Tropes of Trauma: The Politics of Bearing After-Witness to Nineteenth-Century Suffering* (2010), edited by Marie-Luise Kohlke and Christian Gutleben; Gothic in *Neo-Victorian Gothic: Horror, Violence, and Degeneration in the Re-Imagined 19th Century*, forthcoming by the same editors; and criminality in *NVS* 2.1.[5]

While scholarly work on such particular aspects of post–Victorian fiction is regularly published, there is a shortage of books comprehensively discussing the dimensions of current refashionings of Victorian narratives and the critical apparatus for reviewing them, making post/neo–Victorian studies accessible to a wider research audience. My book aims to fill this gap, also integrating the thematic monographs and collections of essays mentioned above, by systematizing the existing knowledge about the subject in the following way. First, I juxtapose competing theoretical perspectives available for the contextualization of current fictional responses to Victorian texts (Chapter 1). Second, I discuss the major ideological frameworks according to which these novels are produced and received, focusing on the literary scene (Chapter 2) as well as the contemporary political and social contexts (Chapter 3). Third, I survey how these discourses have functioned historically and what implications they have for the present, through a case study of a novelistic chain of three closely linked texts (Chapter 4). Fourth, I examine how Victorian source texts are written into post–Victorian novel series or adaptive maps (Chapter 5). By simultaneously providing a theoretical, chronological, and case study–oriented analysis of post–Victorian fiction, my work supplies a critical history of such novels and their discourses in a multifaceted way. It offers an extensive analytical section on terminological nuances and contextual clarifications regarding post–Victorian fiction, which is vital for forming and developing the discourse of rewriting the nineteenth century. In addition to orienting readers among prevalent notional and topical approaches to the field, I also survey frameworks and modes of adaptation. In order to add a diachronic overview of the development of the post–Victorian canon and its criticism as well, my book includes an analysis of a chain of novels spanning three centuries. This case-study model including a Victorian, a twentieth-century and a twenty-first-century text constitutes a unique feature of the book. I utilize critical material incorporating field-specific studies as well as a number of fictional examples for illustrative, intertextual or close reading purposes. In contrast to the recent research trend mapping out less popular novels for analyzing aspects of post–Victorian fiction, I have intentionally chosen texts that are better known, so that the close readings reach a greater circle of professionals familiarizing itself with this area of scholarship.

Chapter 1, "From *Victorian* to *Post-Victorian*: Definitions, Terminology and Contexts," is dedicated to the clarification of the theoretical background of the field of research, helping to provide both a narrower and a wider context for contemporary novelistic responses to the Victorian age. I juxtapose and analyze the competing concepts and definitions used to describe such rewritings. The exploration starts with the denotative and connotative aspects of the core term *Victorian*, which is often applied without taking into consideration its complex semantic field. Then, I scrutinize various appropriations of the core word to denote current texts, and inquire into the meaning and implications of the terms *Victoriana, Victoriographies,* and *retro–, neo–* and *post–Victorian fiction*. I argue that to date *post–Victorian fiction* appears to be the most appropriate term to characterize this specific group of texts as a separate entity within the larger body of historical novels to which it belongs, due to its intersection with postmodernist discourses and literary practices. A survey of contexts and discourses of post-Victorian fiction follows, reviewing literature on the subject in the fields of literary, film, adaptation and cultural studies, pointing towards the interdisciplinarity of research. I maintain that mainstream post-Victorian fiction ties in with the synthesizing tendencies of postmodernism, by fostering a co-existence of its paradoxes, as the intermingling of traditional and experimental uses of Victorian fiction in such rewritings proves. Since post-Victorian novels are closely concerned with the past and politics, I scrutinize how post-Victorian scholars working in the fields of cultural memory and trauma studies juxtapose these works with postmodernist perceptions of history and ethics, and establish that though they acknowledge the impossibility of attaining historical knowledge and drawing ethical consequences from it, they still insist on finding ways to access nineteenth-century events and narratives.

The authorship and readership of post-Victorian fiction often overlap, resulting in self-conscious criticism. Therefore, the literary landscape in which this body of works is set deserves a closer examination, which constitutes Chapter 2: "Post-Victorian Fiction and the Literary Scene." I study actors of the literary marketplace, including the author, the reader and criticism. In the market of post-Victorian fiction the author, both as a novelistic function and as a real-life celebrity, reacquires his or her nineteenth-century status, thereby reactivating the author-reader relationship on various platforms of the meet the author culture as well. I describe post-Victorian book cover designs and how literary criticism tackles this intersection of literature and visual culture, and point out that in the process of producing and receiving post-Victorian novels the existing split between literary journalism and academia may increasingly be remedied by employing cultural studies as an interpretive framework. The prominence of authorship together with its ensuing discourses of authority, authenticity, mystification and cult takes place in similar ways as was customary in the nineteenth century and has lead to the flourishing of post-Victorian literary biographies. I survey five Henry James adaptations published around the same time: Emma Tennant's *Felony* (2002), Colm Tóibín's *The Master* (2004), David Lodge's *Author, Author* (2004), Alan Hollinghurst's *The Line of Beauty* (2004), and Michiel Heyns's *The Typewriter's Tale* (2005). These works, as well as the subsequent authorial and critical reactions, show the interaction of literary biographies and criticism concerning the writing process, the limits of artistic compromise, the consequences of intellectual theft and ghostwriting historical authors, literary reception, and reactions to literary reception. This juncture, called biofiction, offers a joint interpretive site for fiction, theory and criticism.

The emphasis on history in post–Victorian novels foregrounds the issue of how contemporary Britain faces its colonial and imperial legacies, forging identities (self, national and cultural) in the eighties, nineties and the present. Therefore, in Chapter 3, "Post-Victorian Fiction in Its Political and Social Context," I read some post–Victorian novels of the past thirty years together with instances of cultural criticism, to see how various narratives of identity have evolved in a climate of changing political rhetoric. My analysis of Peter Carey's *Oscar and Lucinda* (1988) exposes how the postcolonial reading of the novel and cultural memory accounts of the Crystal Palace amend one another. The initial critical focus on how the imperial mission and national pride inspired by the Crystal Palace reverberate in heritage narratives of the eighties, shifted to how the Millennium Dome functioned as a repetition of the Victorian construction in the nineties' political rhetoric. At present, scholars survey cultural subtexts characterizing the nineteenth-century Crystal Palace and their effects on its current readings. I identify island novels as a specific subgenre within post–Victorian fiction that offers dislocation and travel, also characteristic of the adaptation process itself, as constructive tools assisting in the reconceptualization of current postimperial and postcolonial identities. I study Caryl Phillips's *Cambridge* (1991) and Matthew Kneale's *English Passengers* (2000) by juxtaposing concepts of eighteenth-century discovery narratives, nineteenth-century travelogues, and Simon Gikandi's trope of travel (1996). These novels reveal contemporary existential anxieties of loss of home and identity resulting from Britain's insularity and isolation, through exposing interisland journeys of ownership within the empire as failures.

Applying the contextual frameworks of the previous chapters and connecting the Victorian and the contemporary perspectives, in Chapter 4, "*Jane Eyre* Tailor-Made: A Case Study of the *Jane Eyre*, *Wide Sargasso Sea*, *Charlotte* Adaptive Chain of Novels," a critical historical analysis is provided of Brontë's Victorian cult text and two of its adaptations. First, based on the discussion of the literary scene in Chapter 2, I examine issues related to authorship, establishing that, with the proliferation of celebrity culture, the notions of author, narrator and character are increasingly interrelated in all three texts and in their criticism. Through this interconnection, the concepts of originality, authenticity and plagiarism also resurface in connection with post–Victorian fiction. The authorial anxieties of capitalizing on Charlotte Brontë's nineteenth-century cult text that Jean Rhys voices turn into public accusations of plagiarism and exploitation of the literary market in receptions of D. M. Thomas's *Charlotte*, a postmodern metacommentary about ventriloquizing earlier authors. Second, I inquire into narratives of identity in line with their theorization in Chapter 3, establishing that the questions of self and home are closely related in all three texts. Utilizing the discourses of postcolonialism, postimperialism and feminism, I pursue how characters' dislocation determines shifts in their self, national and cultural-identifications. While the success of Jane's identity quest in *Jane Eyre* is debatable, Antoinette's interculturation process in *Wide Sargasso Sea* emerges as a failure, deconstructing stable categories of identity. Miranda's double narrative in *Charlotte* comprises these two nineteenth-century figures as projections of her identity crisis, which she channels into fictional selves traveling between England and the West Indies. She finally finds her home in a similarly questionable space as Jane in Brontë's novel and with a similarly disintegrated self as Antoinette in Rhys's text.

Chapter 5, "The Way We Adapt Now: Endings, Novel Series and Adaptive Maps," surveys how various contemporary rewritings of nineteenth-century fiction embrace the sequelization and serialization of novelistic texts. This affects the classification of post–Victorian responses to Victorian texts, especially in terms of establishing their relationship to their sources. Terminology includes categories like *fluidity, literary continuum* and *aftering* to characterize the nature of these connections, in addition to temporal denominations like *prequel, sequel, midquel, parallelquel* and *adaptive series* or *adaptive chains* that depict refashionings of the same source text in terms of chronological order. Here I survey how the controversial plot resolution and character treatment of *Jane Eyre* inspires endings that confirm, amend or completely rewrite their source text, fitting into one or more of the above categories. I devote special attention to Jasper Fforde's *The Eyre Affair* (2001), which at the same time features as a sequel to Brontë's *Jane Eyre* and as the first item in a novel series following the adventures of a literary detective called Thursday Next. Confirming as well as revising the Victorian original at the same time, Fforde's novel simultaneously reinforces and shifts the romance-realism debate about the ending of *Jane Eyre* towards the economic realm of commodity culture. Finally, I scrutinize various refashionings of Dickens's life and work, commonly called Dickensiana. This multiplicity of contested interferences of novels, films and theme parks is best depicted by the term *adaptive map*. I focus on Peter Carey's *Jack Maggs* (1997) and Lloyd Jones's *Mister Pip* (2006), texts that both rewrite the same original, Charles Dickens's *Great Expectations* (1861). Authorship, identity and imperial legacies interconnect in these refashionings, according diverse functions to *Great Expectations*, from inspiring narratives of escape and empowerment to causing conflicts and wars.

Like the whole post–Victorian event, this monograph is interdisciplinary, a feature that naturally affects its methodology. My main focus is post–Victorian fiction, but, since I address concerns of both literary and cultural studies, instances of close reading of novels alternate with analyses of cultural objects or sections of cultural criticism where fiction assumes only a support function to reading cultural narratives, an approach specifically characteristic of the last three chapters. The project's interdisciplinarity entails the necessary limitation that certain areas of study, such as history, political science and media studies, are only briefly addressed, and so are relatively new research fields that feature in various disciplines and the critical apparatus of which is still in the making, such as trauma studies or cultural memory; nevertheless, I consider their inclusion crucial for the understanding of the complexity and extent of post–Victorianism. In this way, my account in some sections of the first two chapters becomes a metacritical text rather than an analytical one, drawing on various narratives with the purpose of indicating the web of connections within certain topics instead of surveying particular cases in detail and applying their frameworks or theses to others. The reason for this working method is that such an attitude seems to provide more revealing results in the case of an area of study for which the premises are still being delineated, leaving room for new definitions and terminology to emerge. Alternatively, it may turn out that this eclectic narrative inquiry becomes a legitimate interpretive strategy as it is, allowing for the adoption of a more holistic perspective on connections between the post–Victorian phenomenon, fiction, culture and criticism rather than delimiting their reading to separate categories, modes of interpretation and disciplines.

With this book I hope to contribute to an understanding of post–Victorian fiction as a vital and constantly growing part of the contemporary novelistic output in English. The body of novels I introduce and analyze indicates contemporary theoretical concerns with notions like authorship, through the intermingling of critical discourses, to the future of humanities, at the same time as voicing political, social and ideological anxieties connected to questions of identity and remembering. By addressing these concerns, post–Victorian novels reactivate and rewrite nineteenth-century cultural discourses that are currently in need of readjustment, due to the unearthing of more textual material as well as the changes in the critical perception of narrative empowerment and canonization which prompt rereading in the first place. Therefore, these texts not only serve as illustrations of today's problems, but may also supply means to possible solutions. Through following the interaction of the production of and critical responses to historical fiction, we can detect tendencies in interpreting present events that resonate with the past. Raising awareness of these affinities influences our perceptions of history and contemporaneity at the same time.

1

From *Victorian* to *Post-Victorian*: Definitions, Terminology and Contexts[1]

> "*He invented an entire period and made its imagination his own: no one had properly understood the medieval world until Chatterton summoned it into existence. The poet does not merely recreate or describe the world. He actually creates it.*"— Peter Ackroyd, *Chatterton* (1987)

In the event of a new (sub)discipline forming around the twentieth- and twenty-first-century refashioning of the nineteenth century, there are some basic tenets that need clarification. Profound scholarship concerning the definition and terminology applied to contemporary fiction rewriting the Victorian novel and the possible discourses in which it can be contextualized is still scarce. Therefore, the chapter begins by surveying the meanings attached to the term *Victorian*, to foster the historical understanding of its semantic field. This is followed by an analysis of the existing denotations and definitions categorizing current rewrites of Victorian fiction, mostly based on various appropriations of the term *Victorian*. The aim of this terminological query is to raise awareness of the variety of approaches to, and possibly enliven the debate of, designating this group of texts both chronologically and aesthetically, and ultimately find a suitable term and definition for them. The final part of the inquiry, examining the discursive contexts in which these novels appear, is intended to provide an informative background for the ensuing discussion, pointing towards the interdisciplinarity of the field.

Appropriating Victorian*: The Meanings of* Victorian *and Terming Contemporary Rewrites*

Do we know what we mean by *Victorian*? Does the term refer to an age, a set of conventions, or an image of both based on a limited and biased selection of sources? And what should we call the rewrites of the era: historical novels, post–Victorian fiction or adaptations? And how to specify the differences between them? Why are there so many terms and so few definitions? In their introduction to *Rereading Victorian Fiction* (2000), Alice Jenkins and Juliet John identify *Victorian* as a difficult term, without making any further attempts at defining it. They only point out the fact that *Victorian* can be understood chronologically and non-chronologically, and they welcome the resulting diversity of readings as a constructive means to avoid interpretations that frame the Victorian period in various totalizing myths (Jenkins and John 2000: 2). Such a broad understanding of the word seems to be a common attitude at present, and it is easy to agree with the emphasis on the plurality of readings the term invites. However, there is another side to this flexibility in employing the phrase. Simon Joyce recognizes this as its instability, namely, that it can be appropriated to express a wide range of interests, too (Joyce 2007: 168), which may serve opposing agendas. Therefore, a closer scrutiny of its definitional nuances would be useful, especially since "Victorian," a chronically indefinable denomination, carries complexities that also unfold in the attempt to classify its current refashionings.

Referring to Queen Victoria, as sovereign, *Victorian* (like Elizabethan) holds a denotative meaning that self-evidently marks that historical person's period of reign; however, since it also specifies characteristics of an era, its chronological boundaries often get further extended. Various disciplines also utilize the term at their convenience. In literary studies it has literary historical, literary theoretical, and/or aesthetic applications. Additionally, *Victorian* also triggers connotative readings. Respective deployments of the term depend on the school of thought emphasizing its different aspects, as well as on the way eras following the Victorian, such as modernism or postmodernism, review the nineteenth-century period in question. Hence feminist, postcolonial and other cultural revisions of the term *Victorian* prove crucial for a better understanding of how the present takes issue with the nineteenth century. Furthermore, all these considerations also influence the terminological choice for twentieth-century refashionings, including novelistic ones.

In current critical usage, the so-called *Victorian* referents of twentieth-century rewritings range from Jane Austen through Thomas Hardy to Virginia Woolf, so the periodization including all the reworkings gets construed aesthetically rather than historically. This way the concept of the *Victorian* comprises romantic and pre–World War I fiction and ignores historical data like "the life of its monarch" or "the beginning and end of her century" (Green-Lewis 2000: 30). The explanation for perceptions of such extended chronologies lies in the temporally and otherwise limiting nature of the term (Kohlke 2008: 2),[2] as well as the in-betweenness of the Victorian era dominated by the greater periods of romanticism and modernism (Armstrong 1993: 1). Still, this premise seems very dangerous to begin with, since, if taken seriously, a system of common aesthetic denominators would have to be determined for fiction written between the mid-eighteenth and the early twentieth centuries, against which we would then compare the late-twentieth and early–twenty-first-century corpus of texts.[3] To my knowledge, no such endeavor has taken place so far, which, considering the dubiousness of the task, is not surprising. Thus, in what follows, the term "Victorian," used in a temporal sense (and not italicized), denotes the specific historical period of Queen Victoria's reign from 1837 to 1901, while *Victorian* (italicized) is reserved for specific references to the term itself.

The connotative meaning of *Victorian*, emerging in parallel with the denotative one immediately after the death of Queen Victoria, was first employed to separate Edwardian attitudes from Victorian ones, where "'Victorian values' took on an almost oedipal quality," partly still retained today (Bullen 1997: 2). An anthropomorphic historiography of the term expands this by now established view, claiming that by the 1950s the threatening fatherly nature of *Victorian* gives way to a more tender grand- or great-grandfatherly remoteness, and then becomes increasingly intimate, sisterly and brotherly from the eighties onwards (Bullen 1997: 1–3). Note how the terminological categorization is fueled by a Darwinist need to establish familial correspondences. A more progressive critical history of the term argues that binaries not only exist between Victorianism and each historical era it is contrasted with, but that these oppositions also appear within every particular era that rereads the Victorian (Joyce 2002: 7).

Such connotative meanings of *Victorian* receive further scrutiny in the context of the postmodern. In the sixties, two conflicting attitudes to Victorianism emerged through the discourse of sexuality: on the one hand,

Victorian referred to everything that stood in the way of sexual freedom; on the other hand, due to the increasing temporal distance from the era, the deconstruction and reassessment of the coherence of the Victorians' supposed sexual repression began to take place (Kaplan 2007: 85–86). If the same duality is framed within the political context of the eighties, the Thatcherite (mis)interpretation of "Victorian values" can be juxtaposed with the Kinnockian one: in order to promote the ideology of their own politics, the conservatives employed key words like progress and prosperity, while labor opposed these by the likes of drudgery and squalor to describe the same concept (Joyce 2002: 3–4). Hence, while historicizing the term *Victorian*, the construction of binary oppositions surfaces in both the discourses of sexuality and politics, the former pointing out the moment when the term started to acquire contradictory interpretations and the latter reflecting a stage when it was already deconstructed.

All the above connotations come into play in Alasdair Gray's *Poor Things* (1992). The text is both a biography and autobiography of two characters, that of Archibald McCandless followed by the heroine Bella Baxter/Victoria McCandless' narrative, framed by the author's introduction and closing critical and historical notes. The competing narrative voices reveal different attitudes to the Victorian age. Giving an account of the couple's courtship and marriage, the establishment of a family and their careers, the happy ending of Archibald's nineteenth-century diary sounds very much like the closing chapter of *Jane Eyre*. This account is successively revised by Bella/Victoria, who requires the reader to believe her story instead of Archibald's, describing her distaste for the previous narrative in detail:

> As I said before, to my nostrils the book stinks of Victorianism. It is as shamgothic as the Scott Monument, Glasgow University, St. Pancras Station and the Houses of Parliament. I hate such structures. Their useless over-ornamentation was paid for out of needlessly high profits: profits squeezed from the stunted lives of children, women and men working more than twelve hours a day, six days a week in NEEDLESSLY filthy factories; for by the nineteenth century we had the knowledge to make things cleanly. We did not use it. The huge profits of the owning classes were too sacred to be questioned [Gray 2002: 275].

Fictitiously written in 1914, this highly critical reaction to the Victorian age betrays a typically modernist refusal in a distinctly oedipal tone. The concerns voiced about Victorian economic and social policies echo the Kinnockian view of the era as one of ignorance, poverty and social inequality, countering the Thatcherite interpretation depicting the period as an age of general progress, enrichment and prosperity. Bella/Victoria's assertive feminist narrative finally meets correction by the implied author's closing notes to the novel. The authorial commentary attempts to reinstate Archibald's version of the story by means of patriarchal revision, claiming that the heroine could show her talent only because her husband let her do so, and that, in reality, she was quite mad (again, a reiteration of *Jane Eyre*'s madwoman topos). Similarly to Bella/Victoria's earlier attack on her husband, the author indirectly blames his character for being too Victorian, citing a purported earlier commentator from 1920, namely, the socialist reformer and economist Beatrice Webb: "She is now quite sex-mad — an erotomaniac, to use the older term — and tries to hide it under prim language which shows she is still, at heart, a subject of Queen Victoria" (308). This remark sheds light on the controversial rhetoric and perception of Victorian sexuality as an issue of modernist as well as postmodernist criticism. The fact that she has two names — "Bella," used for referring to her own person, and "Victoria," employed by some other characters to identify her — further complicates the interpretation of this sentence, and of the heroine's role in the novel on the whole, generating allusions to the much-discussed figure of Queen Victoria herself.[4]

To return to the previously raised notion of binary oppositions, some contemporary readings of *Victorian* in our own time are similarly ideological and structuralist in nature. If *Victorian* is read as "a dialectical condensation of [...] contrary tendencies" (Joyce 2002: 7), we always have to be conscious of our own investment in the interpretation process (15).[5] In my view, the current investment mainly involves a drive to unearth — or invent — material that is not part of the official historiography of the nineteenth century, and to utilize this material to reinterpret the Victorians: witness the ever-growing number of literary biographies, such as Peter Ackroyd's *Dickens* (1990) or Colm Tóibín's *The Master* (2004), narratives of Charles Dickens and Henry James, respectively. Matthew Sweet's *Inventing the Victorians* (2001) seems a successful critical venture in reinstating the Victorians: following a discussion of many sources that counter the cliché-like understanding of the Victorians as repressed, oppressed and dull, the author reminds us in good Foucauldian spirit that "Victorian culture was as rich and difficult and complex and pleasurable as our own" (Sweet 2001: xxiii). Hence, he suggests not only that we are more Victorian than the Victorians, but also that we *are* the Victorians. On the one hand, we increasingly begin to acknowledge that "they [the Victorians] moulded our culture, defined our sensibilities, built a world for us to live in" (231);

on the other hand, we continue to deny our affinities with them, delimiting ourselves against the Victorians, thus acting as repressively and dully as we accuse them of having done. The title of Sweet's book, *Inventing the Victorians*, shows an awareness of the enormous creative input entailed in (re)interpreting an era and its conventions, which echoes the fictionalized George Meredith's praise of Chatterton, quoted in the motto of this chapter: "He *invented* an entire period and made its imagination his own [...]. The poet does not merely *recreate* or describe the world. He actually *creates* it" (Ackroyd 1987: 157, emphasis added).

By presenting these current attempts at differentiation within *Victorian*, I intended to emphasize the plurality of our possible relationships with the Victorian era.[6] Accordingly, the term, acquiring diverse possible readings in the sixties, in the eighties and nineties, and at present, summons a diachronic understanding, simultaneously inviting a synchronic one of multiple interpretations. Therefore, these different approaches can be read together, rather than against one another. Consequently, attitudes to current reworkings seem to be determined by a synthesis of the denotative and connotative meanings of the term *Victorian*. This, at the moment, allows for quite a number of possible interpretations, which readily shows in the abundance of terms used for rewrites, discussed next.

Is it *Victoriana, Victoriographies, retro–, neo–* or *post–Victorian novels* we encounter when we read rewritings of the Victorian era? Shall we adhere to the already well-rehearsed term *historiographic metafiction* or simply call them all *historical novels*? Could we categorize them as *adaptations, prequels* or *sequels* of Victorian texts, disguised as nineteenth-century novels, but in fact consider them postmodern variations of these novels? Are they instances of *pseudo–Victorian* or *pseudo-historical novels*? Why so many terms? Why so many different perspectives? Two broad approaches to terming contemporary fictional reworkings of the Victorian era can be distinguished: one makes the literary critical terminology of the novel, such as *historical fiction* or *historiographic metafiction*, its foundation, while the other takes the historically or culturally perceived term *Victorian* as a basis and attaches prefixes or suffixes to it, thus constructing *neo–, retro–, post–Victorian* or *Victoriana*, in order to recontextualize current rewrites in different ideological discourses. Some attempts synthesize the two and create hybridized terms like *Victoriography* to define the group of texts in question.

Historical fiction, itself a term constantly redefined, proves to be the broadest possible category applied to current rewrites. In the spirit of Hayden White's *Metahistory,* Linda Hutcheon coined the term *historiographic metafiction* to depict a postmodern subgenre of the novel that interacts with history and, at the same time, questions the possibility of such a venture.[7] As part of a general ideological discussion about whether we presently experience the end of history or a new beginning of it,[8] these two subcategories of fiction, *historiographic metafiction* and *historical fiction,* engage in a dialogue. On the one hand, they compete, since the annexation of either by the other can be reasoned for (*historiographic metafiction* being just a postmodern subcategory of *historical fiction,* or *historiographic metafiction* debunking *historical fiction* as its identical category); on the other hand, their ongoing mutual modification may end in their merging or, perhaps, giving birth to a third category integrating both of them.[9] Whichever way we interpret the terms, the present stage of the dialogue yields denominations like *pseudo-historical fiction* or *contemporary historical fiction* (Bormann 2002: 75). Both are employed to describe contemporary rewrites of the Victorian era as well but, as Brian W. Shaffer also argues, it is always contemporary history with which the novel engages (Shaffer 2006: 32). The term *pseudo–Victorian fiction* (Gutleben 2001: 50, 56; Letissier 2004: 111) refines the classification further by also indicating the revisions' convergence with, and divergence from, their source. However, since history has by now been deconstructed as, at least partly, narrative in essence, depriving the term *pseudo-historical* of any heuristic power, the same prognosis could be given to the term *pseudo–Victorian,*[10] especially since it is precisely its contemporary rewrites that take an active part in the deconstruction of the Victorian novel, naturally affecting the term *Victorian* itself.

Thus, numerous scholars propose that, since rewrites of Victorian texts fit the definition, that is to say, they engage with history in a paradoxical way, they should be grouped as *historiographic metafiction.*[11] The use of this terminology is justified since it leaves room for many different types of rewrites, encouraging a comparison of the postmodern understanding of Victorian texts and of rewrites of Renaissance, romantic or modernist ones. Nevertheless, if only for heuristic purposes, a more specific terminology for reworkings of Victorian texts, rather than texts of any/all earlier periods per se, could be revealing in its descriptive power. Accordingly, the alternative term *Victoriography* presents itself as an option. Julian Wolfreys's book on contemporary rewrites bears this title,[12] and he employs the same term for one of his university courses, defining *Victoriographies* as "cultural writing formed out of interpretations and translations of the high ground of nineteenth-century culture" (Wolfreys "Victoriographies: Inventing the Nineteenth Century" 2001). Both his book and the survey course apparently relate mainly to fiction, thus this definition, inclusive of all kinds of rewritings of the Victorian era, literary and otherwise, not to mention the wider interpretation of text as product, sounds somewhat broad. However, *Victoriography* appears to be a useful term for establishing an intersection of reworkings of Victorian texts and the already established postmodern discourse of historiographic metafiction, and it helpfully also includes the sound pattern of the word *historiography*.

The suffix -*a* has also become an increasingly popular ending attached to the term *Victorian*, hence the word *Victoriana* to name contemporary rewritings of Victorian texts. Originally, the term was restricted to an exclusively material definition, denoting objects from the Victorian era. If employed in this sense, it lacks an explanation given its etymology (see, for example, Kucich and Sadoff 2000: xxii). Cora Kaplan, whose 2007 book bears *Victoriana* as its title, applies the word differently. She provides its historiographic context in her introduction, revealing a gradual expansion of the semantic field of the term. Although in the 1960s *Victoriana* may still have referred to material remains of the nineteenth century, by the end of the seventies it was extended to a "miscellany of evocations and recyclings" of the age, to finally broaden its meaning to practically all "representations and reproductions for which the Victorian [...] is the common referent" (Kaplan 2007: 3). This periodization sounds convincing and explains Kaplan's choice of the same term for current rewritings of the age, although she does not offer examples to illustrate this observation. Examples would be especially welcome because those who use the term in its original sense feel the need to add a qualifier to make it fit contemporary (con)texts. Hence the term *postmodern Victoriana*, which depicts products of a postmodern Victorian mode (such as literary, screen or stage adaptations of Victorian novels or artistic objects inspired by the era), considering the postmodern as the Victorian's historical "other" (Kucich and Sadoff 2000: x, xi).[13]

In his *Science in the Neo-Victorian Novel: A Poetics (And Two Case-Studies)* (2002), Daniel Bormann consciously combines the two approaches of defining contemporary fictional rewrites of Victorian texts, those of novelistic discourse and cultural-historical criticism. Discussing the aspect of literary terminology, he first adopts Ansgar Nünning's definition of historical fiction,[14] which applies to novels based on the tension between past and present, dealing with subject matters that belong to history, historiography and the philosophy of history on all narrative levels and discourses (Bormann 2002: 55). Following Nünning's typology, Bormann then selects some subtypes of historical novels to limit his analysis to the discussion of *contemporary historical fiction*, a term referring to the broader category of novels in question, distinct from traditional or classic historical fiction (56–59). As a second step, he gives a brief account of existing definitions based on the term *Victorian*, specifying different cultural-historical understandings of current rewrites of Victorian fiction. He finally arrives at his own choice, the term *neo–Victorian novel*, which he defines by applying the adopted definition of the historical novel to contemporary reworkings of Victorian texts (61–62). This connection of the two approaches, specifying the second as part of the broader context of the first, proves to be an important move. Although Bormann does not develop an in-depth terminological historiography, he identifies the lack of a consensual and well-argued definition as a serious research gap in the field (18). Before exploring his preferred definition further, a short detour of other applications of the terms *retro–* and *neo–Victorian novel* seems appropriate.

In her article "Natural History: The Retro-Victorian Novel" (1998), Sally Shuttleworth coins the titular term *retro–Victorian novel*, which she uses interchangeably with the expression *Victorian-centered novel*. She identifies *retro–Victorian fiction* as a type of historical novel, and explains that the category of historical novel is broadly understood and thus inclusive of historiographic metafiction (Shuttleworth 1998: 254). The author delimits her analysis to a specific subset of *retro–Victorian novels*—explicitly nostalgic texts that engage with the discourse of natural history (253)—but does not provide any further definition. Similarly, Dana Shiller's seminal paper "The Redemptive Past in the Neo-Victorian Novel" (1997) introduces the term *neo–Victorian novel* "as at once characteristic of postmodernism and imbued with a historicity reminiscent of the nineteenth-century novel" (Shiller 1997: 538), though once again a more accurate definition fails to emerge.[15] Both authors attempt to disprove Fredric Jameson's critique of our current "historical deafness" (Jameson 1996: xi), by demonstrating that retro– or neo–Victorian novels reveal a profound engagement with history (Shuttleworth 1998: 266) and considerably enrich the postmodern present (Shiller 1997: 558). While such an apology for the artistic merit of contemporary rewrites has validity, the argument for the current value of history and historicity may remain trapped within the Jamesonian framework of recuperative practices towards the past (Jameson

1996: x–xi), unless a greater emphasis is accorded to these novels' specific relationship to the postmodern context.

In his *Nostalgic Postmodernism: The Victorian Tradition and the Contemporary British Novel* (2001), Christian Gutleben identifies a similar fracture between nostalgically inclined and innovative strategies of novelistic texts approaching history, which seems to raise terminological problems as well. Initially, he adopts Shuttleworth's term *retro–Victorian fiction*, which he uses interchangeably with *neo–Victorian*, interpreting it as "a new literary movement whose very essence consist[s] in re-thinking and rewriting Victorian myth and stories" (Gutleben 2001: 5). Surveying the body of novels labeled by these terms, the author later revisits the terminology and pinpoints a paradoxical state where "the most famous neo–Victorian novels are the least typical" (164). This means that apart from some well-known examples which comply with postmodernist conventions, like John Fowles's *The French Lieutenant's Woman*, numerous novels in the group, like Beryl Bainbridge's *Master Georgie*, resist them and "seem to partake of Habermas's category of *neo–Conservative fiction*" (ibid.). Although the discrepancy between the heterogeneity of texts and their categorization as *retro–Victorian novels* receives some attention, in the end the original terminology is retained. Bormann proposes that *neo–* and *retro–Victorian fiction* both denote the same group of texts only differing in focus: *retro–* emphasizes the past and *neo–* the future (Bormann 2002: 61). Their interchangeability was a general consensual but unreflected critical practice at the beginning of the twenty-first century, which has by now shifted into slowly abandoning *retro–* precisely for its emphasis on looking backward, and favoring *neo–* whose correspondence to the present is easier to establish. Therefore, in recent scholarly attempts at defining rewritings, if mentioned, the term *retro–Victorian* is usually discarded as overtly nostalgic or ahistorical, and thus not serving a critical purpose (Heilmann and Llewellyn 2010: 5, Hadley 2010: 18). Hence, the relationship between the texts rewriting the nineteenth century and the current context implicit in these prefixes needs more elaboration.

Repairing this shortage of elaborate descriptions of *retro–* and *neo–Victorian fiction*, Bormann takes Nünning's typology of historical fiction detailed above, applies it to the term *neo–Victorian novel*, and constructs the following definition:

> [A] neo–Victorian novel is a fictional text which creates meaning from the background of awareness of time as flowing and as poised uneasily between *the Victorian* past and the present; which secondly deals dominantly with topics which

belong to the field of history, historiography and/or the philosophy of history *in dialogue with a Victorian past*; and which thirdly can do so at all narrative levels and in any possible discursive form, be it through the narration of action, through static description, argumentative exposition or stream-of-consciousness techniques [Bormann 2002: 62].

This definition contextualizes current rewrites as a specific group within historical fiction, establishing a relationship between history and fiction with a particular relevance to the Victorian age, yet it opens up the possibility of further delimitation. How exactly should "meaning" be understood that emerges from the intermingling of the Victorian past and the present? And which (sub)genres, narrative types and stratifications get reactivated by neo–Victorian fiction and why? In addition, the way the author makes his terminological choice implies certain dissatisfaction with the existing possibilities: "If I will adopt Shiller's *neo–Victorian novel*, it is only because it resembles other approaches to contemporary literary phenomena [...] and because, indeed, this kind of contemporary Victorian novel is a new —*neo*— phenomenon" (61).

Thinking along these lines, the newness of a movement that has been in vogue for at least fifty years deserves further periodization, however useful it proves to call it (still) new. This process necessarily involves a closer scrutiny of the nature of these texts' relationship with different aspects of the present, especially those of postmodernism, which they largely intersect with, substantiating the implied expectation of freshness and novelty. Similarly, a detailed analysis of the parallels between neo–Victorian and other movements with the same prefix, like the neo–Renaissance or the neo–Gothic, could expand Bormann's reasoning. One useful step in this respect has been a footnote remark in the introduction to the collection *Victorian Turns, NeoVictorian Returns: Essays on Fiction and Culture* (2008), where the political implications of the prefix *neo–* are separated from its generic ones. Hence, when added to words like fascism or Victorianism in the sense of a political movement, it "implies a desire to return to the political beliefs of that movement's past"; while "used in conjunction with a genre, the implication is rather a new, modified, or more modern style," as in neo–Gothic or neo–Victorian (Johnston and Waters 2008: 10–11 fn5). The *NVS* has also adopted the term *neo–Victorian*, and applies it in its widest possible sense:

so as to include the whole nineteenth century, its cultural discourses and products, and their abiding legacies, not just within British and British colonial contexts, and not necessarily coinciding with Queen Victoria's realm; that is, to interpret neo–Victorianism outside of the limiting nationalistic and temporal identifications that "Victorian," in itself or in conjunction with "neo–," conjures up for some critics [Kohlke 2008: 2].

More explicitly than Bormann's, this explanation juxtaposes the Victorian with the contemporary, so much so that another essay in the same volume of *NVS* regards the *neo–Victorian* as "new approaches to the Victorian period rather than an attempt to indulge in escapism masked as historical narrative" (Llewellyn 2008: 169). The inviting terminological flexibility, countering the dread of repeating old narratives as a detour from current uneasiness, presents itself in both definitions; yet, this way the boundaries of the research field seem to become unclear. Especially from the second remark, the *neo–Victorian* emerges as an addendum to the *Victorian*, which implies a scholarship primarily focusing on the nineteenth century and not the present.

Despite its controversial connotations, current critical usage seems to have settled on adopting the term *neo–Victorian*, as the titles of recent and forthcoming publications in the field indicate.[16] Among the scholars utilizing this denomination, Heilmann and Llewellyn seem to devote most critical thought to the question of terminology, hence my analysis of this choice mainly draws on their text. Authors who briefly outline the problem of definition admit that the *neo–Victorian* has so far been loosely defined (Heilmann and Llewellyn 2010: 4), and they keep on formulating flexible definitions: "[I]n order to encompass the range of fictional responses to the Victorians, I define neo–Victorian fiction in the broadest possible terms as contemporary fiction that engages with the Victorian era, at either the level of plot, structure, or both" (Hadley 2010: 4). Therefore, just as in the case of *Victoriana*, authors opting for the term *neo–Victorian* feel the need to further delimit it, in order to better highlight the specific aspects of research they engage in. The way to achieve this is to explain in more detail what *neo–Victorian* means, which happens not through amending the term but by adding a definite article to it, in order to identify the particular understanding of the *neo–Victorian* they subscribe to: "To be part of *the* neo–Victorianism we discuss in this book, texts (literary, filmic, audio/visual) must in some respect be *self-consciously engaged with the act of (re)interpretation, (re)discovery and (re)vision concerning the Victorians*" (Heilmann and Llewellyn 2010: 4, first emphasis added). Due to the specified metareflexive quality the examined corpus should possess, this categorization covers a much smaller body of texts than the flexible definition of *neo–Victorian* fiction quoted above. Such an emphasis on the "metahistoric and metacultural" (Heilmann and Llewellyn 2010: 6), "the need for critical inflection, metafictional play" (32) points towards a strong correspondence of this group of novels to postmodern literary practices, a connection other authors make explicit in their understanding of the term: "Neo-Victorian fiction serves not one but two masters: the 'neo' as well as the 'Victorian'; that is, homage to the Victorian era and its texts, but in combination with the 'new' in a postmodern revisionary critique" (Carroll 2010: 173). This combination is closely connected with postmodern writing techniques, such as the conventions of historiographic metafiction (Yates 2009/2010: 189–190, Carroll 2010: 180–182). Heilmann and Llewellyn introduce another restriction that brings the corpus defined as *neo–Victorian* even closer to postmodernism, namely, its separation from other historical fiction set in the nineteenth century that stereotypically recycles Victorian clichés. As their definition requiring neo–Victorian texts to be *"self-consciously engaged with the act of (re)interpretation, (re)discovery and (re)vision concerning the Victorians"* (Heilmann and Llewellyn 2010: 4) automatically excludes such novels, this demarcation would not be necessary, yet they consider it important, which suggests the still unclear critical usage of the term *neo–Victorian*. They cite a literary academic's ironic blog entry on the know-how of writing neo–Victorian novels and then, separating it from their understanding of neo–Victorianism, regard the blog description to be of value only for defining contemporary historical novels with nineteenth-century settings instead (Heilmann and Llewellyn 2010: 6–7).

Besides the delineation of the field of reference of *neo–Victorian* at the synchronic level, Heilmann and Llewellyn also aim for a diachronic concept of the term. Discussing the periodization of *neo–Victorian*, they establish that its chronological boundaries reach back to the beginning of the twentieth century (Heilmann and Llewellyn 2010: 8). Generally, criticism focuses on texts of the 1960s, the Thatcherite eighties, and post-millennial fiction, since these are the times when such rewritings became prevalent and formed their own discourses and traditions. Nevertheless, from a historical, cultural, and, last but not least, a terminological point of view, it is worth looking back somewhat further to survey late Victorian and modernist authors' relationship to Victorianism through their texts. Joyce does this in his *The Victorians in the Rearview Mirror* (2007), where he examines the complex and often conflicting modernist and postmodernist reactions to the nineteenth century, beginning his analysis with a deconstructive reading of the Bloomsbury group's attitude to the Victorian era from 1901 onwards. The difficulty of establishing a starting point of neo–Victorianism manifests itself already in the title of another such study, Cheryl A. Wilson's "(Neo-) Victorian Fatigue: Getting Tired of the Victorians in Conrad's *The Secret Agent*." In the case of this essay, which contrasts the hype around Queen Victoria's Golden Jubilee and the increasing frustration with such aspects of Victorianism described in Joseph Conrad's 1907 novel, the starting point would still be within the Victorian period (Wilson 2008: 19–40). Matthew Beaumont looks at Agatha Christie's *Murder on the Orient Express* and Max Ernst's *Une Semaine de bonté*, both of 1934, as responses to Victorianism between the two world wars. The author categorizes these modernist texts as *neo–Victorian*, though they do not seem to correspond with the recent understanding of this term. He finds that they exhibit two contrasting versions of *neo–Victorianism*: Christie's is iconographic or conservative, rehabilitating nineteenth-century social values, while Ernst's is iconoclastic or avant-gardist, devouring the same (Beaumont 2009: 12–26). This difference appears problematic from a terminological point of view, especially concerning Ernst's more critical work, so Beaumont insists that in the case of *Une Semaine de bonté* "the prefix 'neo' in 'neo–Victorian' acquires a polemical overtone" (24). The same difficulty could arise with reference to Christie's recuperative *Murder on the Orient Express* as well: while it can be accommodated with Beaumont's perception of *neo–Victorian*, if one adopts Heilmann and Llewellyn's narrower definition of the term, the novel does not fit into this category. As we can see, there is a discrepancy of understanding *neo–Victorian* even among those who periodize it the same way.

To sum up, even if it has become consensual critical practice to utilize the term *neo–Victorian fiction* for novelistic responses to the Victorian age, there are numerous problems with this usage, inherently as well as resulting from its largely unreflected employment. As I have shown, *neo–Victorian* is generally used in its widest sense, a reference that has repeatedly proved too broad and thus unsatisfactory, either in terms of its political versus generic connotations, or due to its incorporation of other, non-reflexive historical fiction than the body of novels scrutinized by critics. Consequently, scholars make extra efforts to further delimit their research focus, which is labeled but not appropriately demarcated by this term. These attempts have various results, some of them leading to additional complications. One such issue seems to be the difference in surveying *neo–Victorian fiction* with the eyes of a Victorianist, looking at ways this new research focus can possibly reinvigorate Victorian studies, or viewing it through a more contemporary lens, and designating it as a new area of scholarship in its own right called neo–Victorian studies, or framing it from a postmodernist perspective, and grouping it as a subset of postmodernist fiction. A problem closely connected to whether researchers opt for one of these approaches or a mixture of them is their often missing, or only tangential, critical elaboration of the relationship between neo–Victorian novels and the postmodern context. This causes difficulties in delimiting neo–Victorian texts less critical of the Victorian age from those that are more revisionary, as well as in distinguishing neo–Victorian fiction written according to the conventions of the realist novelistic tradition from those that employ modernist or postmodernist writing techniques, all of which also affect their synchronic and diachronic categorization.

Though discarded by contemporary scholars for its possible ahistoricity (Heilmann and Llewellyn 2010: 5, Hadley 2010: 3), the term *post–Victorian fiction* that I advocate in this book appears to offer a solution to most of these difficulties, by instigating a more accurate delimitation of the body of novels in question. In contrast to *neo–Victorian fiction*, it incites a more explicit association with postmodernist discourses, and viewed from that context, similarly to the terms *postcolonial* or *postnational*, it expresses a purpose of reviewing rather than replicating earlier accounts and routines. Thus the depiction *post–Victorian* better expresses the intersection of current refashionings of the Victorian era with postmodernism, a connection the importance of which I promote in this study. Other scholars who also use the term *post–Victorian* stress the existing debate between the nostalgic and innovative aspects of *Victorian* (Kucich and Sadoff 2000) and raise awareness of its historicity (Letissier 2004). Additionally, rather than having either the Victorian or the postmodern as the focus of their analysis, they usually examine them together.[17] Viewing contemporary rewrites from a late postmodernist angle, John Kucich and Dianne F. Sadoff define *post–Victorian* as "a term that conveys paradoxes of historical continuity and disruption" (Kucich and Sadoff 2000: xiii). Georges Letissier also adopts the term *post–Victorian*, explaining his choice by suggesting that, contrary to *retro–*, *neo–* or *pseudo–Victorian*, *post–Victorian* "conflates *post*-modernism and *Victorianism*, highlighting the paradoxes of historical continuity and disruption that underpin the *post–Victorian* cultural movements" (Letissier 2004: 111). Letissier implicitly suggests an important point in favor of opting for *post–Victorian* amongst competing possible terms, namely, that it may be understood as a term connotatively blending the Victorian, the modernist and the postmodernist eras (Kirchknopf 2008: 64),[18] which can also be of assistance in the periodization of post–Victorian novels, especially in terms of designating a starting point for such rewritings. This current integrativity of postmodernism demonstrates a substantial move away from the exclusive nature it exhibited in the seventies: "Postmodernism became more and more an inclusive term that gathered to itself all literary and cultural phenomena that could not be classified as either Realist or Modernist" (Bertens 1986: 25).

A closer scrutiny of the meanings of the prefix *post-* in *postmodern* and *post–Victorian* may further strengthen my argument for the utilization of *post–Victorian fiction* to term contemporary rewritings of the nineteenth century. Interpreting the prefix *post-* of *postmodern*, Brian McHale points out the complexity of the relationship between these two eras encompassed by the term: it includes a temporal posteriority, with postmodernism coming *after* modernism, and it also implies a logical or historical consequentiality, meaning that the postmodern follows *from* modernism (McHale 1999: 5). By analogy, the prefix *post-* in the term *post–Victorian* may be read in at least two senses: first, as a modifier of *Victorian*, underlining the presence of the Victorian tradition in everything that comes after,[19] and second, as the first part of the compound *postmodern*, signaling that contemporary practices are perceived to stem more from the Victorian than the modernist era. In fact, the argument Jameson advances in his rejection of the term *postmodernism*, namely, that surveys under that heading do not yield substantial results concerning the postmodern but inform us of modernism instead (Jameson 1996: 66), can be fruitfully adapted to the analysis of *post–Victorian*. Since *Victorian* itself still lacks a comprehensive referent, the utilization of *post–Victorian* to approach contemporary (re)interpretations of Victorian material may similarly provide substantial knowledge of the *Victorian*. Consequently, if the meaning of *post-* is contextualized in the postmodern debate, used both to depict whatever comes after modernism or structuralism and to signify a subversion of these trends, its reading can be harmonized with that of *Victorian*: both terms have a temporal as well as an aesthetic perspective. Regarded this way, the term *post–Victorian* cannot be discarded as a purely chronological denomination.

The fact that the body of novels mostly analyzed by scholars utilizes postmodern literary practices, and can thus be brought into close proximity with postmodernist discourses, also points towards the application of *post–Victorian fiction* to term it. As cited earlier, researchers who are in favor of the term *neo–Victorian* have also underlined that a critical reading of the past (Mitchell 2010b: 3), metafictional writing techniques (Yates 2009/2010: 189–190, Carroll 2010: 180–182), and metareflexive qualities (Heilmann and Llewellyn 2010: 6, 32) count as crucial constituents of these texts. Therefore, instead of putting additional effort into separating a narrower definition of the *neo–Victorian* from other types of neo-Victorianisms (Heilmann and Llewellyn 2010: 1–32), or to argue for the (re)integration of postmodernist revisionism into *neo–Victorian fiction* by "Putting the 'Neo' Back into Neo-Victorian" (Carroll 2010: 172–205), it would be easier to adopt the term *post–Victorian* to delimit the body of novels referred to. This way, the difficulty of having to apply a term that, in a broad sense, incorporates texts (meta)critically reflecting on the Victorian era as well as conventional, conservative or reproductive rewritings of the nineteenth century, including historical novels and romances, could be avoided.

Besides offering a solution at the synchronic level, the employment of *post–Victorian* could also be functional diachronically. When introducing a historical dimension into their categorization, Heilmann and Llewellyn make a distinction between *neo–* and *post–Victorian*: "It is necessary to remember that the birth of the genre [neo–Victorianism] in its broadest definition was itself almost simultaneous with the end of Queen Victoria's reign in 1901. Indeed, chronologically speaking *everything after that key date is in an essential manner post–Victorian (though not neo–Victorian)*" (8, emphasis added). This implies that *post–Victorian* is only understood in a temporal sense, whereas *neo–Victorian*, accounting for all critical material that comes after the Victorian era, is employed in a chronological as well as an aesthetic sense. In contrast to this, I argue that, analogously to McHale's contextualization of the prefix *post-* in *postmodernist* as one possessing both a temporal and an aesthetic semantic field, *post–Victorian* also implies both these features. Thus not only can the term *post–Victorian* be positioned at an equal level with *neo–Victorian*, which has been employed this way so far, but, due to its intersections with postmodernism as well as its integrative qualities in looking back at earlier times, *post–Victorian* may even replace *neo–Victorian*. Surveying the beginnings of critical rewritings of the Victorian age from a postmodernist framework provides a clearer critical perspective for the selection of the corpus and the establishment of a post–Victorian canon. Reading this canon with a contemporary understanding of realist, modernist and postmodernist writing techniques would also facilitate the interrogation of its conscious poetic and political relationship with the nineteenth century.

I consider it worthwhile to tease out the assumptions behind this terminological debate, since it may be informative regarding the process of rethinking current theoretical and ideological constructs. We can learn from which perspective and with what biases scholars attempt to approach the literary, historical, and cultural phenomena analyzed, thus this polemic could be equally revealing at a metacritical level. As it emerges from the above inquiry, all denominations competing to label the category of contemporary adaptations responding to the Victorian era are controversial in some respect, yet for the reasons outlined below, I opt for the term *post-Victorian fiction* in this monograph. Modified or on its own, the term *Victoriana*, just like *Victoriographies*, invites a broader frame of reference than just the fictional, since it relates to various representations of the nineteenth century, not only novels. Terms like *historical novel* or *historiographic metafiction* prove to be necessary in a generic sense, since they account for the heterogeneity of texts adapting previous historical eras and the ways these eras are addressed, but they do not specify the age that is being refashioned. Most works analyzed in this book can be characterized as pastiches, that is, reprises of Victorian fiction writing which display a relationship to the present and often use metafictional techniques as well. However, numerous novels engage with the Victorian age without having such connections to the postmodern. These belong to the traditional genres of the *historical novel* or romance.[20] Categorization may be further complicated by having to account for texts that use postmodern novelistic techniques and establish an explicit connection with the present by corresponding timelines, so they do qualify as *historiographic metafiction*, yet the era they rewrite is not the Victorian one. A representative example of this would be the novel *Hawksmoor* (1985) by Peter Ackroyd, which is set in the eighteenth and the twentieth centuries.

This contextual information reveals important aspects to consider when choosing the term that best describes the addressed corpus of rewritings. Not only should novelistic revisions of the Victorian age and its conventions be distinguished from texts refashioning other eras, which makes the term *Victorian* a crucial part of the denomination, but also fiction tackling the Victorian age by following nineteenth-century conventions has to be separated from texts that establish a dialogue with those conventions through their intersection with postmodernist discourses and practices. The terms *neo-* and *retro-Victorian fiction* designate the era but lack an emphasis of the postmodernist influence in these texts, and, as we have seen, need to be further explicated and delimited if such connections are to be securely established. Therefore, at the moment, the term *post–Victorian novel* offers itself as the most suitable to denote contemporary reworkings of Victorian texts for the following reasons. Firstly, just like *Victorian*, it displays nuances in both the historical and the aesthetic realms. Secondly, *post–Victorian* comprises historical settings without immediately taking a stance on the hierarchy of the eras. Thirdly, similarly to the terms *postcolonial* or *postimperial*, it expresses an intention of revision rather than repetition of earlier narratives. Fourthly, *post–Victorian* implies overlaps with numerous postmodernist theoretical concerns and literary tools. Since I aim to contextualize late–twentieth-century and early–twenty-first-century creative responses to the Victorian era in current critical discourses, my work largely concentrates on adaptations written in the past thirty years, in addition to including one Victorian and one modernist-postmodernist text in its historical section. These foci are best incorporated by the term *post–Victorian*, as it may embrace the Victorian, the modernist, and the postmodernist eras, which is a final argument in favor of applying this denomination. This integrative nature of the term blends in with the interdisciplinarity of research into the post–Victorian phenomenon, examined next.

Contexts and Critical Discourses of Post-Victorian Fiction

Being a relatively new research field, the framework of post–Victorian studies is still in the making. This section aims to review the disciplines and discourses that reflect on the post–Victorian phenomenon, in particular the post–Victorian novel. Literary criticism constitutes the most obvious context in which to look for discussions on the subject. Some studies, such as Gutleben's *Nostalgic Postmodernism: The Victorian Tradition and the Contemporary British Novel* (2001) are exclusively devoted to examining how the post–Victorian phenomenon interacts with fiction or, approached from the reverse, as Hadley's *Neo-Victorian Fiction and Historical Narrative: The Victorians and Us* (2010) does, how historical narrative forms resurface in contemporary novels; while others, focusing more generally on literary history or the novel, increasingly dedicate space to the analysis of rewritings, usually by way of a separate chapter towards the end of the collection.[21] Hence, it seems that we can hardly address Victorian texts without reflecting on their rewritings too, and likewise the discussion of the novel as a genre proves difficult without considering the influence that literary adaptation has on its reception. The perception of Victoriana as an inventor and colonizer of genres (Kaplan 2007: 4) or the view that the "[t]he Retro-Victorian novel is not a new genre, it is the novel of all genres, the composite novel of its epoch, which highlights the cannibalizing, ever-broader, all-encompassing and all-assimilating nature of the novel" (Gutleben 2001: 223) illustrates how scholars perceive the effect post–Victorian fiction has on literary conventions. As the above observations show, the concept of rewriting definitely influences our perception of the novel. Novelistic texts are always in discussion with other texts, repeating old stories and existing conventions, so that the novel inherently reveals itself as a genre of rewriting and thus a postmodern project (Humpherys 2005: 444–445). In this framework, post–Victorian texts engaging with their nineteenth-century predecessors indicate both generic and thematic repetitions in fiction, best visible in novels with a double plot, such as A. S. Byatt's *Possession* (1990) or Graham Swift's *Ever After* (1992).

Literary interpretations are increasingly joined by discussions of various media adaptations of Victorian texts and contexts, extending the research focus of studying post–Victorianism. One chapter in Kaplan's *Victoriana: Histories, Fictions, Criticism* (2007) explores how a variety of nineteenth-century novels and subtexts add up to an adaptive complex in a single movie.[22] Clearly positing the intersection of literature and film, the Oxford journal *Adaptation*, established simultaneously with *NVS* in 2008, and edited by Timothy Corrigan, Deborah Cartmell, and Imelda Whelehan, expresses an interest in book-to-screen as well as screen-to-book adaptation, aiming "to theorise and interrogate the phenomenon of literature on screen from both a literary and film studies perspective" (*Adaptation* "About the Journal"). The collections *Refracting the Canon in Contemporary British Literature and Film* (2004) and *Victorian Turns, NeoVictorian Returns: Essays on Fiction and Culture* (2008) both feature surveys on screen and stage revisions of literary works, in which critics intermingle reading tools of literary and film/theatre studies.[23] Extending this focus of refashionings, Heilmann and Llewellyn's *Neo-Victorianism: The Victorians in the Twenty-First Century, 1999–2009* (2010) also introduces more popular forms of adaptation, such as television and the theme park. *Janespotting and Beyond: British Heritage Retrovisions Since the Mid-1990s* (2004) edited by Eckart Voigts-Virchow, and Dianne F. Sadoff's *Victorian Vogue: British Novels on Screen* (2009) underline the importance of the transnational and cross-cultural aspects of mediating nineteenth-century texts. Voigts-Virchow devotes a whole section to essays exploring how visualizing the past affects teaching practices, especially in an Austro-German context, while Sadoff emphasizes the hybrid aesthetics that result from the global "travels" of British texts adapted to film, in particular, to Hollywood and Bollywood.[24] In her seminal work, *A Theory of Adaptation* (2006), Linda Hutcheon not only highlights adaptation's transcultural nature, but also puts it into a historical perspective, thus connecting the Victorian and the post–Victorian perspectives: "The Victorians had a habit of adapting just about everything — and in just about every possible direction; the stories of poems, novels, plays operas, paintings, songs, dances, and *tableaux vivants* were constantly being adapted from one medium to another and then back again. We postmoderns have clearly inherited this same habit" (Hutcheon 2006: xi). The author further expands the contemporary spectrum of adaptive media, including, among others, video games, websites, song covers and operas, as well as refining the definition of adaptation, by separating the process and the product labeled by the same term.

The launching and title of the journal *Adaptation* and the fact that key theorists like Hutcheon have started to frame its discourse show how adaptation and adaptation studies, the research forming around it, are becoming an increasingly important field of inquiry. Adaptation studies provides a good example of the emerging interdisciplinarity of research invited by the post–Victorian phenomenon, where the templates for cinematic readings of canonical novels developed by Deborah Cartmell and Imelda Whelehan, in their *Adaptations: From Text to Screen, Screen to Text* (1999), are widely applied in film studies but also imported back into discussions of literary adaptation. Julie Sanders does this in her *Adaptation and Appropriation* (2006), establishing that in the case of adaptation a source text is always identifiable, whereas in that of appropriation it may either not be obvious or not exist at all (Sanders 2006: 26). Thus, in her comparative analysis of these two literary processes of rewriting, appropriation emerges as more independent and more critical than adaptation. In the context of this ongoing adaptation fever — with multiple post–Victorian perspectives available on the story of *Jane Eyre*, for example — might it eventually become impossible for readers ignorant of the texts' first publication dates to establish whether Jean Rhys's *Wide Sargasso Sea* (1966) or D. M. Thomas's *Charlotte* (2000) was written first? And, in the future, might nonacademic readers even lose track of the *original* text? If this turns out to be the case, following Sanders's definitions, all adaptations may be in danger (or luck?) of becoming appropriations. After long years of the fidelity debate, this opposition has apparently been collapsed in film studies, as Whelehan's remark shows: "We are adapting adaptations not source texts any more" (Whelehan 2008). In literary research, this problem goes back to the different value judgments attached to creation and invention. Robert Macfarlane examines the oscillation of the importance of these two faculties from one era to the other with a specific focus on the second half of the nineteenth century in his *Original Copy: Plagiarism and Originality in Nineteenth-Century Literature* (2007). He claims that the transition from the primacy of creation or originality, characteristic of romanticism, to the prevalence of invention and plagiarism, fashionable in the twentieth century, was well under way from as early as the 1860s. This explicitly reversed the hierarchy of first- and secondhand texts by the last decades of the nineteenth century, leading to the superiority of rewriting from the beginning of the twentieth century (Macfarlane 2007: 210–211). On the basis of these critiques, one would expect the controversies related to originality, fidelity and plagiarism to be largely resolved, however, this does not seem to be the case. Recent collections of essays in media studies still engage with the problems of "an adaptationist or 'fidelity'-approach" (Voigts-Virchow 2004: 25),[25] and literary criticism, too, expresses occasional concerns related to plagiarism, as in connection with D. M. Thomas's novels, not to mention the anxiety of authorship voiced by the authors themselves, as did Jean Rhys, both explored in more detail in Chapter 4.

Apart from literary, film and adaptation studies, cultural criticism involving multiple disciplines also represents a fruitful platform for discussions of the post–Victorian event. In fact, Jay Clayton regards this "[f]orging alliances among disciplines" as the only realistic approach to today's globalized world, and opposes it to a naïve understanding of a synthesis of all disciplines as well as a pessimistic one of accepting the hegemony of science over all other discourses (Clayton 2003: 212–213). Thus in his *Charles Dickens in Cyberspace: The Afterlife of the Nineteenth Century in Postmodern Culture* (2003), Clayton examines, alongside with literature and film, contemporary discourses of information technology and genetics in parallel with the Victorian engineering and scientific accomplishments they developed from, declaring the restoration of the nineteenth-century link between literature and science as one of his main aims (Clayton 2003: 5). Likewise cautious about possible oversimplifications of interpreting our nineteenth-century cultural inheritance, Joyce tackles Victorian and post–Victorian correspondences from a social and political angle, with a particular interest in questions like the relationship of the individual and the state, examining the Victorian roots of modern welfare policies and its economic repercussions (Joyce 2007: 13–14). The essays in Kucich and Sadoff's *Victorian Afterlife: Postmodern Culture Rewrites the Nineteenth Century* (2000) reflect on a range of art forms and technologies from photography to computing, connecting social and political ideologies with economic production and reproduction; while the ones in Christine L. Krueger's *Functions of Victorian Culture at the Present Time* (2002), as its title also suggests, examine how nineteenth-century cultural paradigms resurface in some of today's sciences, such as pedagogy, psychology and law, as well as on a wide spectrum of material culture, including clothing and furniture. The relationship between such areas of commodity culture and literary production constitutes the main subject of Christoph Lindner's *Fictions of Commodity Culture: From the Victorian to the Postmodern* (2003), where novelistic responses to commodification are surveyed by reading nineteenth- and twentieth-century texts together. Here fiction is not read for its own sake but to demonstrate social responses to economic changes, in other words, as texts for illustrating contexts. The author's argument that the nineteenth-century roots of commodity mainly lying in production have by now shifted to consumption (Lindner 2003: 15) can be associated with a seemingly parallel move in the field of literature, namely, the one from writing to rewriting, that is, from the production of literary works to their reception and reproduction. Similarly, the *NVS* journal also emphasizes "remembrance, revision, and reconstruction" in its call for submissions, which is advertised in a variety of fields, from arts and humanities to medicine, psychology, sexology, and studies in cultural memory, surveying the dialogue of the Victorian and post–Victorian eras (*NVS* "Aims and Scope").

This expansion of interest in rewriting and reinterpreting the Victorian has also interacted with some changes in postmodern theories of thought and political movements in the fields of feminism, postcolonialism, neocolonialism or nationalism studies, affecting sexual, racial, economic and social policies. This was accompanied by practical cultural and political influences, like the mass production and consumption of Victoriana, or the Thatcherite appropriation of Victorianism the political practice ever since. The extent to which post–Victorian fiction is intertwined with current changes in the discourses of the postmodern is, perhaps, best illustrated by the fact that the same prefixes of *post-*, *reverse-*, or *neo-* that are affixed to contemporary rewritings of Victorian fiction are also attached to words like feminism, colonialism, imperialism, nation, state or culture in the process of their reinterpretation. Hence, rather than either exploring current novelistic refashionings from the perspective of Victorianism or as a subset of postmodernist fiction, I look into post–Victorian fiction mostly through its intersection with postmodernism. In order to examine the exact nature of this juncture, I first situate post–Victorian novels in the tradition of novels in English in terms of writing techniques, which, as we have seen, largely affects the denotation, definition and categorization of these texts. Since they have close ties with the past and politics, I then survey the place of these works in the context of postmodernist perceptions of history and ethics. In the course of this inquiry, I concentrate more on introducing areas of research in which other scholars have recently theorized post–Victorian fiction, such as cultural memory, trauma studies and spectrality, and focus less on authorship and questions of identity, because I investigate the latter two in more detail in the rest of this monograph. Nevertheless, as it emerges from the query, the connections between the post–Victorian and the postmodern produce interdisciplinary research models that intermingle these fields of scholarship.

The chronology of the postmodern period until now could be constructed as follows: it witnessed a revolutionary phase in the sixties, then conventionalized these changes during the eighties, to reach its present phase with a tendency to juxtapose its own paradoxes. In his *Postmodernist Fiction* (1987), McHale outlines one of the central theses of postmodernism, claiming that while modernist fiction foregrounds epistemological issues, the dominant concerns of postmodernism are ontological (McHale 1999: 9–11). Alexander Marguerite questions this proposition in the early nineties, pointing out that a number of late–twentieth-century British novels resist this distinction (Marguerite 1990: 22–23), and Gutleben explicitly disproves it in the case of post–Victorian texts (Gutleben 2001: 50–51). Rather than arguing for the opposition of epistemological and ontological features in today's artistic products, scholars suggest more of a compromise between such traits (Butler 2002: 125–127, Hutcheon 1995: 50), which may eventually lead to another "condition," named syncretism, which amalgamates previous aesthetic traditions and synthesizes opposing ideologies (Gutleben 2001: 220–223). If synthesis is too far-fetched, a coexistence of opposites can be envisioned, which is the way the postmodern processes of adaptation and appropriation are interpreted as well: they develop in the vein of Darwin and Derrida (Sanders 2006: 160), in other words, they are both evolutionary[26] and revolutionary, de- and reconstructionist. The restoration of the link between experimental writing and the tradition of realism provides an example of the current synthesizing tendencies in postmodernism, as the literary critic Andrzej Gasiorek argues:

> Any simple distinction between experimental and traditional writing has long ceased to be pertinent. What marks the fiction assessed here [examples of postwar British fiction] is precisely the interanimation of forms, styles and techniques. Attention to language's constitutive role, the doubleness inherent in fictional representation, and the impossibility of unmediated access to the real, are everywhere apparent [Gasiorek 1995: 19].[27]

Mainstream post–Victorian fiction utilizing nineteenth-century realist novelistic conventions together with twentieth and twenty-first-century experimental and metareflexive writing techniques also reflects such a conjoining of traditions, and thus concurs with this view of postmodern fiction in English in critical discourse.

A similarly determining aspect of postmodernism, which has also shown its significance in the generic categorization of post–Victorian fiction, is its relationship to history. Jameson explicitly denies the existence of such a relationship, claiming that "the past itself has disappeared (along with the well-known 'sense of the past' or historicity and collective memory). Where its buildings still remain renovation and restoration allow them to be transferred to the present in their entirety as those other, very different and postmodern things called *simulacra*" (Jameson 1996: 309). Hutcheon considers such a reduction of reference to simulacrum (which is an adoption of Baudrillard's theory of simulation; see Baudrillard *Simulacra & Simulations* 1981) just as simplistic as the traditional interpretation of reference as something transparent (Hutcheon 1995: 229). Instead, she argues that the postmodern problematizes the representation of reality, searching for means of understanding it (223) by intermingling the historical and the self-reflexive (225). This is exactly the way post–Victorian fiction responds to the past, which explains the fact that it is grouped under historiographic metafiction. Hutcheon underlines that the historical knowledge these novels produce is constructed (89, 99); in other words, information is always mediated through various systems that we are always part of as well, which puts the knowability of history in question.

Though recent critiques of post–Victorian fiction acknowledge this paradox inherent in our access to the past, nevertheless they stay committed to somehow grasping history and aim for finding entry points into it. From this perspective, the post–Victorian novel becomes an important epistemological tool (Onega and Gutleben 2004: 14), written as an endeavor to decipher how human consciousness reacts to epistemological challenges (Letissier 2010: 95). Formulated in less extreme terms, these novels are "more concerned with the ways in which fiction *can* lay claim to the past [...], rather than the ways it can not" (Mitchell 2010b: 3), for example, by "offering it as cultural memory" (Mitchell 2010b: 7), or asserting "the reality of past suffering and the importance of *making it known*" (Kohlke and Gutleben 2010: 28). These interpretive perspectives connect contemporary rewriting with remembering and trauma, two contexts which at present mostly engage with postcolonial and postimperial issues. Thus post–Victorian fiction takes a crucial part in narrating historical memory and influencing political attitudes beyond Britain's former empire (Kaplan 2007: 162). These influences affect changes in various cultural and material perceptions, from trends in marketing and consumerism, to literary prize distribution and concepts of identity (all examined in more detail in the next two chapters), raising awareness of the importance of the critical capacities of novelistic texts in framing contemporary historical reality. Hence, these novels also function as memory texts[28] or memory objects,[29] similarly to commodities or other relevant sites of material culture, which provides a fruitful research subject for cultural memory and trauma studies.

Studying cultural memory in contemporary fiction, Kate Mitchell also understands post–Victorian works as memory texts and as acts of memory (Mitchell 2010b: 4), which remember and re-member — in other words, recollect as well as reconstruct — the dis(re)membered parts of the nineteenth-century period, in order to examine which aspects and images of the past are reconstituted with what aims and implications (7). In addition to textual modes of remembering, the author also includes nontextual ones, and thus juxtaposes oral histories, geographies, cartographies, paintings, photographs and bodies with diaries, letters, poems, novels and historical archives (ibid.), and maps out connections between history, cultural memory and fiction as interdependent discourses of historical representation (178–179). While Mitchell mainly concentrates on personal and collective memory by integrating essays of various theories of thought, Lena Steveker utilizes Aleida and Jan Assmann's seminal works in cultural memory studies, and discusses how individual identity gets constituted by way of cultural strategies provided by fiction. She argues that by (re)considering the past of the other, the self could be better perceived in the present (Steveker 2009: 143). Surveying identity and cultural memory in A. S. Byatt's fiction, Steveker approaches memory as a productive asset of the human mind with the ability to creatively (re)construct the past, and posits the function of literature as that of a medium of cultural memory (4–5). Similarly, Tamás Bényei reads the contemporary historical novel, to which post–Victorian fiction belongs as well, as one of the praxes of cultural memory that assumes a mediating function between personal identity and collective memory (Bényei 2005: 37–38). He argues that, for example, the symptomatic nature of postmodern amnesia, structured according to the nonlinear temporality of trauma, illustrates how the cultural understanding of history has changed, in this case into a painful relationship to the past (40–41). As it emerges from these accounts, the notions and concepts related to remembering, (re)reading and (re)writing the nineteenth century are strongly interrelated and relevant for the interdisciplinary research the post–Victorian encounter involves, therefore these intersections should be fostered so that they produce meaningful insights. Clayton adopts a comparable view by advocating that we should pursue ways in which "literature can aid the project of historical cultural studies" (Clayton 2003: 17). He regards literature as a model for responding to often incompatible cultural imports in diverse modes via multiple perspectives, with an awareness of temporal and spatial differences as well as intertextuality, which constitutes important meaning-making strategies for the discourse of cultural studies (19, 24).

The relationship of the postmodern to ethics, a likewise controversial issue as its connection to history, gains relevance when post–Victorian fiction is read in such interdisciplinary frameworks, including discursive contexts like cultural memory and trauma studies. In his introduction to *Postmodernity, Ethics and the Novels* (1999), Andrew Gibson summarizes the contentious issues in ethical criticism at the end of the 1990s (Gibson 1999: 1–21), and argues that in English literary criticism the new positivism and the "politics of English" have caused an undue neglect of ethics. The author is in agreement with Leavisites on the ethical importance of novels, but rejects their moralizing study of literature based on the liberal humanist tradition, and grounds his argument on the Levinasian understanding of ethics instead. Thus debating with David Parker and Wayne Booth's adoption of a more classical tradition of ethical criticism of the novel, Gibson follows the footsteps of Adam Zachary Newton and Zygmunt Bauman and works with the concept of postmodern ethics that is aware of "moralities as myriad, groundless, incommensurable and interminable"

(14). Post-Victorian scholars equally emphasize the need to reinforce the ethical exploration of contemporary fiction, however, they are anxious to avoid the extreme deconstructionist perception of ethics for fear of completely discrediting the notion, which would lead to the possible view of postmodernism as a "post-ethical" movement (Onega and Gutleben 2004: 14). Arguing against such moves, researchers rather advocate a fundamental return of ethics: "Far from being delegitimated as an axiological trace of Enlightenment, ethics, then, is restored to the central place of the narrative apparatus in neo–Victorian fiction, doubly so in contemporary narratives of trauma" (Gutleben and Wolfreys 2010: 65).

Indeed, it is trauma studies, defined as "a strand of cultural and memory studies indebted to psychoanalytical, poststructuralist, and postcolonial, as well as literary theory" (Kohlke and Gutleben 2010: 1), that currently mostly engages with the ethical in literature and criticism. For example, Susana Onega's trauma studies project running since 2008, "Ethics and Trauma in Contemporary Narrative in English," specifically surveys contemporary fiction in English in this framework (Onega "Ethics and Trauma in Contemporary Narrative in English"). In the introduction to the first issue of *NVS*, also launched in 2008, general editor Marie-Luise Kohlke underlines the increasing importance and impact of adapting such an analytical perspective of reading post–Victorian fiction, claiming that, similarly to the nineteenth century, our own age is also characterized by a number of traumas asking for urgent memory work[30] (Kohlke 2008: 7). Areas of concern range from the politics of the empire gaining new relevance with the attacks of 9/11, as far as a growing environmental consciousness hostile towards industrialization due to ecological disasters caused by human irresponsibility (7–8). This initiative receives further publicity in the post–Victorian trauma studies collection, where post–Victorian fiction is surveyed as a means of working through nineteenth-century as well as present-day traumas (Kohlke and Gutleben 2010: 3). The editors point out the transgenerational repercussions of trauma, and relate the postmodern self and the Victorian other as the *self-as-other* rather than two opposing entities, meaning that today's traumatized subject pre/rediscovers *itself* in its nineteenth-century others (13–14). The ethical dilemma involved in this self-discovery is the question of recreating historical traumas by way of bearing after-witness, as the collection's title also suggests, which is necessarily a secondary, appropriated, and possibly misrepresented experience (7, 14–23). This puzzle gets resolved by the claim that "representing the other's trauma is *not* unethical in itself and that neo–

Victorian fiction *can* assume an ethical function in 'speaking-for-the-other'" (22). The first essay of the collection, "Postmodernism Revisited: The Ethical Drive of Postmodern Trauma in Neo-Victorian Fiction" further elaborates this issue, explaining the attention the postmodern pays to the Victorian within the framework of trauma studies and emphasizing the return of ethics into fiction and criticism, this time as "an ethical concern for otherness" (Gutleben and Wolfreys 2010: 56).

The critical awareness of traumas in our times implies an understanding of the present as a moment of crisis, the narrativization of which also leads back to the Victorian age, especially its last years. As Frank Kermode argues, "for most of us the best known outbreak of *fin de siècle* phenomena occurred at the end of the nineteenth century; at any rate, it was in that century that the expression became current" (Kermode 1966: 96). He maintains that this "sense of an ending" still dominates our lives, enhancing narratives of decadence as well as renovation (98–100). So much so that the first publications on the post–Victorian phenomenon, namely, Kucich and Sadoff's *Victorian Afterlife* (2000) and Gutleben's *Nostalgic Postmodernism* (2001) are structured accordingly, calling the section discussing decadence "mystifications" and "fascination" and the one analyzing renovation "engagements" and "revisitation," respectively. Both works assume that the allure of rewriting the nineteenth century resides precisely in this possibility of producing double-faced narratives. The tropes of haunting and spectrality foreground such a dialogue between the past and the present, emphasizing that both parties constantly influence each other. Linking Derrida's hauntology and Freud's uncanny, Rosario Arias and Patricia Pulham envision the influence of the Victorian age on the present through the image of the ghost, whose "liminal existence, neither present nor absent, functions as a powerful metaphor for the dynamic relationship maintained between Victorianism and neo–Victorianism" (Arias and Pulham 2010: xxv). The editors emphasize the importance of various forms of repetition in conveying this connection between the past and the present from nostalgia to ghostwriting (xi–xxvi). These notions also centralize the problem of the narrator and the narrative voice, which Tatiana Kontou examines in more detail in her *Spiritualism and Women's Writing: From the Fin de Siécle to the Neo-Victorian* (2009). Specializing in the female medium, the author surveys the mutual impact of the Victorian séance and our contemporary understanding of mediumship and the medium as writer, and reads post–Victorian novels as "a mediumistic continuation of spiritualism's own narrative structures" (Kontou 2009:

201). Writing in the apocalyptic spirit of an expected ending (of life on earth, a century or the Gutenberg galaxy), recentralizes sensationalist approaches, such as the reinvigoration of dubious historical or fictional characters, events and controversial practices, as well as the adaptation of corresponding earlier genres such as crime, detective, sensation and Gothic fiction, to experiment with them in a contemporary context.

The examined contexts and debates in literary, film, adaptation, and cultural studies, and postmodernist theories of thought show that the post–Victorian phenomenon constitutes fruitful discursive sites for diverse ideological schools, which may also account for the popularity of post–Victorian fiction. The common motivating factor for researchers of the described disciplines and discourses engaging with this field seems to be precisely its immense range and potential, which they identify and explain in different but overlapping ways. There seems to be a debate between those who regard post–Victorianism as a misrepresentation of history and historical knowledge and those who see its potential in its progressive contributions to rereading history (Kucich and Sadoff 2000: xxv). The former point of view echoes Jameson's attitude to historical fictions as a compensation for our present-day impotence to facilitate historical changes (Jameson 1996: 369), whereas the latter approach is a more constructive application of our knowledge of Victorianism in a post–Victorian environment, namely, by using Victorian narratives to work out ways of being in the future (McGowan 2000: 24, Carroll 2010: 195–199). This second approach, which I also align with in my monograph, seems to have become dominant in current post–Victorian research, reflecting the understanding that the juxtaposition of Victorian and contemporary texts and contexts may lead to new ways of understanding history or offering alternative solutions to current sociopolitical issues. Some even claim that the act of rewriting (understood in its widest sense including [re]interpretation) is a moral imperative, so that we can live up to current cultural realities and their manifestations in critical thinking (Bryant 2002: 177, Flint 1997: 302). The perception of post–Victorian novels as texts empowered by such an explanatory force already serves as a reason in itself for the production and consumption of such works. Research into rewriting gives hope to scholars that a certain lost social potential can thus be restored to the study of literature, strengthening the discipline (Lefevere 1992: 9), while the current effort to save literary studies by reiterating and reforming the canon can soon work in another way, too, namely, by pushing literature towards criticism. Due to their self-reflexive qualities and the critical consciousness in their reading, post–Victorian novels are prone to functioning as literary critical sources as well. This way post–Victorianism may become not only a theoretical, but also a more applied field of research, exemplifying how humanities can assist in the explanation and prediction of social and cultural changes. Whichever way it goes, at present, the research into post–Victorian fiction is clearly accomplished in an increasingly interdisciplinary framework.

2

Post-Victorian Fiction and the Literary Scene

> *"Well, you know these writers. They'll steal any..."* And her voice trailed off as she looked down at her trembling hands.
> *"Anything, that's right."* He leant back in his chair, and smiled benevolently in her general direction. *"It's called the anxiety of influence."*...
> *"And of course it must be true of novelists, too."* She paused, and licked her lips. *"No doubt,"* she went on, *"there are resemblances between my books and those of other writers."*— Peter Ackroyd, *Chatterton* (1987)

After setting the terminological framework and establishing the literary theoretical relevance of the post–Victorian novel, in the next two chapters I survey the literary, social, political and economic environment in which post–Victorian texts have been produced and received. The generic choices I make for contextualizing this background are determined by the dominant genres that can be indexed to specific topics: I have a closer look at how biographical novels respond to the literary scene and how island fiction portrays narratives of identity.

In what follows, I first survey the literary scene focusing on authorship, readership, literary criticism and the market. The discussion includes the refocalization of the author and the context of celebrity culture connecting reader and writer by the establishment and maintenance of various meet the author forums. Important reading techniques, such as self-reflexivity, affective and plot-centered comprehension, as well as the requirement of double reading specifically summoned by historical texts, are also taken into consideration. This is followed by a brief survey of market-oriented book cover designs also reflected on by literary criticism, leading to a discussion of the split between the academia and literary journalism also present in the production and reception of post–Victorian fiction, and endorsing cultural studies as a framework that may assist in remedying this problem. Finally, I contextualize one of the most prestigious literary awards often distributed to authors of post–Victorian novels, the Man Booker Prize, as a site where all discussed participants of the literary scene, from authors, readers, and critics, to the book market, interact. In the second section, I examine how biographilia and the literary scene interact. I highlight the prevalence of biofiction by scrutinizing some Henry James adaptations published in 2004, and the series of authorial and critical responses to these works. The venture of rewriting the late Victorian author in Emma Tennant's *Felony* (2002), Colm Tóibín's *The Master* (2004), David Lodge's *Author, Author* (2004), Alan Hollinghurst's *The Line of Beauty* (2004), and Michiel Heyns's *The Typewriter's Tale* (2005) could itself be read as a symbolic move of restoring authorship into the central position it assumed in the nineteenth century. Through the evolving chain of texts, tackling the processes of (re)writing and (re)reading as well as questions of literary production and reception, I explore how the fictionalization of historical authors and their art influences attitudes to authorship and literary biographies.

Authors, Readers, Criticism and the Market

In line with the less experimental and more referential, less text- and more author-based phase of postmodernism that mainstream post–Victorian fiction intersects with, the notion of the death of the author, introduced by Roland Barthes in the 1960s and promoted ever since, seems to gradually be fading away. At the end of the eighties, David Lodge, who has always been a strong supporter of realist fiction, takes a stance against text-based criticism (Lodge 1990: 14–21). Arguing against Barthes's notion of the death of the author and de Man's denial of a relationship between text and reality, Lodge makes a strong case for the author-centeredness of novelistic production and reception, emphasizing the perspective of the writer: "The foregrounding of the act of authorship within the boundaries of the text, which is such a common feature of contemporary fiction, is a defensive response, either conscious or intuitive, to the questioning of the idea of the author and of the mimetic function of fiction by modern critical theory" (19). In his book *The Death and Return of the Author* (1992), Seán Burke traces how the absence of the author is theorized in anti-authorial discourses, through conducting a close reading of texts by Barthes, Foucault and Derrida. He argues that the exclusion of the author by textual criticism is problematic per se. Authorial subjectivity cannot be theorized in such a framework, although it is impossible to expel it from criticism, which makes (the question of) the author an "unquiet presence" in theory. Among others, he lists authorial intention, influence and revision as important authorial functions that cannot be circumvented when analyzing texts (Burke 1993: 173–174). Similarly, Linda Hutcheon underlines that in adaptation theory, naturally involving influence and revision, the role of intentionality should be seriously considered, "even if this means rethinking the role of intentionality in our critical thinking about art in general" (Hutcheon 2006: 95).

As it emerges from these critical works as well, authorship is being reinstated together with its ensuing discourses of authority, authenticity, mystification and cult,[1] acquiring a similar degree of popularity by which it was characterized in the nineteenth century. Many scholars draw parallels between Victorian and present-day manifestations of the central position of the author in public literary discourse. After Jane Gaines, James F. English and John Frow argue that values attached to nineteenth-century authorship resurface in different terms in today's context: thus the Victorian signature and copyright respectively have become a brand name and an exchangeable trademark of the present (English and Frow 2006: 48–49). As the authors claim, the fame of Charles Dickens and Oscar Wilde is comparable with that of J. K. Rowling and Jeanette Winterson (39–40). Although his main focus lies in the Victorian scene, Bradley Deane similarly makes a direct connection of the past with the present, already in his introduction: "Yet the legacy of the nineteenth-century author refuses to be laid to rest. In the twenty-first-century literary marketplace, authorial cults of personality continue to drive production and consumption" (Deane 2003: ix). The ongoing revival of Charles Dickens and his works, which I discuss in the last section of this book, is a good example for this.

This myth surrounding authorship has both economic and sociopolitical implications. If an author publishes a work that wins a literary prize, inspires a movie adaptation, or evokes sensationalist reactions, s/he acquires a celebrity position which puts her/him on the market. This position and the accompanying market value vary according to the real or assumed interest of the audience; as Richard Todd phrases it "contemporary fiction is retail-driven" (Todd 2006: 20). Therefore, authorship becomes a corporate marketable item, fueled by media-based brand management (English and Frow 2006: 41). Interpreting authorship in similarly economic terms, John Sutherland claims that the myth of the author is often largely manipulated by the market. He provides the example of two contemporary campus novel writers and critics with parallel careers, David Lodge and Malcolm Bradbury, whose identities were blurred as part of a guessing game emploted for the entertainment of the audience, which resulted in perceiving them for a long time as one and the same person (Sutherland 2006: 122). From such moves the myth of authorship emerges as a cultural effort of collaboration rather than individual endeavors.

The sociopolitical potential of authorship that gained strength in the nineteenth century has currently also been reemphasized. Deane characterizes authorship as a site of projection of hopes and anxieties of Victorian society (Deane 2003: xi), which function eventually led to a pragmatic social influence that nineteenth-century writers were endowed with (29). In an age that lacks social and political models, this renewed authorization of writers as public figures is not surprising. In Britain this may be especially true, since, besides the manipulated winners of reality shows or games aspiring to the status of social heroes,[2] and the politicians who keep losing face in the continuously uncovered instances of corruption, the scandals of the nineties have also curtailed the authority of the royal family.[3] In this context the speculative question arises whether the post–Victorian reaching back to famous Victorian authors, texts and conventions could spring from similar considerations: Do contemporary authors reinvigorate well-known historical material to make up for the missing models of current times in order to become famous? Could the publishing of post–Victorian fiction then be perceived as a market-driven move today's authors make for self-fashioning? Or does the act of rewriting enhance the reinstatement of (the prestige of) authorship? Having acquired a celebrity status, writers enter the now again fashionable "meet the author culture" (Todd 2006: 29), where they can contact their audiences on various forums, from television appearances through reading tours to online chat rooms (Todd 2006: 34–36, English and Frow 2006: 50). Not only does such a public presence assist in marketing their products, but by attaching themselves to various causes, they also fulfill important social and political functions.

This context of celebrity culture developing around the novelist's person encourages a positive reception of his/her work as well. The establishment or encouragement of reading groups for debating on various pieces serves as an effective means to increase the popularity of writers' work (English and Frow 2006: 46–47). This strategy nicely ties in with reintroducing the sequelization of literary texts, as the digestion of installments appears to be easier than that of whole novels, and their discussion in groups also proves more straightforward. In some cases the actual publications provide questions to guide the audience in such discussions. The 2003 Harvest edition of Michel Faber's *The Crimson Petal and the White*, for example, closes with a list of questions under the heading "Reading Group Guide" (Faber 2003: 901–905),[4] followed by an advertisement of three novellas to be published by the same author, ensuring the visibility of the writer as well as the possible attachment of the readers to the same author. This chain shows how the concepts of the series and sequels prove to be effective means of production "generated by the cultural and material conditions of authorship" (Budra and Schellenberg 1998: 15). Reading groups are also viewed as current means to save the Gutenberg galaxy, forums ensuring the future of reading. Books maintain their popularity not only because of their materiality, making the connection with the text more immediate and practical, but also for their privacy, not allowing any mediation into the private act of reading, such as tracking or recording that takes place when using the internet (Sutherland 2006: 31–41). Apart from adjusting to current reading practices, reading groups also maintain the important social function of community-building, enabling the formation of discussion groups with common issues of interest.

However, in terms of cultural studies, following the Althusserian and Foucauldian tradition of perceiving literature as an ideology-forming institution, post–Victorian fiction also functions as an educational device. As such, it may change social and political attitudes, as well as affect reading habits. For the understanding of a twentieth-century or later rewriting of a nineteenth-century text, depending on the focus, readers need to familiarize themselves with actual Victorian authors, texts, events or conventions. This means that post–Victorian fiction requires a certain level of double reading: "The reader must interpret two texts at once" (Humpherys 2005: 445), which constitutes a much greater challenge than traditional ways of reading. Readers learn about nineteenth-century and contemporary culture simultaneously, not to mention the rewriting of these they experience at the same time, which appears especially well-plotted in John Fowles's *The French Lieutenant's Woman* (1969). In this novel the (author-)

narrator has a mediatory function, facilitating reader access to both ages, by using twentieth-century references and bases of comparison for the explanations and interrogations of his nineteenth-century text-construction. For this purpose, he utilizes various texts from a wide range of disciplines of both ages, and integrates them in diverse modes of writing, from metacomments within his Victorian narrative, to devoting a whole analytical, essay-like chapter (Chapter 35) written in the style of a hundred years later, including footnote remarks. Such a double reading method also affects the canon: new items rewriting history and theory may be added to it, in parallel to the recanonization of historical texts that have been omitted or forgotten. André Lefevere also emphasizes that the canon-forming importance of rewriting earlier texts invests cultures with power (Lefevere 1985: 241).

The fact that the authorship and readership of post–Victorian novels frequently coincide means that there is a very close connection between writing and reading these novels, which may even resurface at a textual level. A. S. Byatt's *Possession* (1990), the plot of which is based on twentieth-century scholars interpreting nineteenth-century texts, provides a good example of self-conscious criticism of literary scholarship, as well as an emblem of the critical reading process per se. The novel lines up various literary scholars representing a range of theoretical schools of scientific value. In the process of deciphering the nineteenth-century texts, all these researchers become implicated in their readings, putting the solely rational basis of their stream of critical thought in question. James Blackadder "thought often, in his dim place, of how a man becomes his job" (Byatt 2002: 33); Mortimer Cropper muses on his relationship to Ash, feeling "as though he had no existence, no separate existence of his own" (118), and underlines how much of an indissoluble part "the shadowy biographer is of his subject's life" (417); and, forced to give up on Ash, immersed in his wife's journals, Beatrice Nest "became implicated, began to share Ellen's long days of prostration in darkened rooms" (128). These scholars adjust their view of their subjects, as their inquiry into the liaison of the historical couple Randolph Henry Ash and Christabel LaMotte unfolds: Blackadder and Cropper reconsider their perception of Ash and their own selves as strongly masculine characters, and Nest reemerges from forgetfulness and experiences herself as well as her research on Ellen Ash as useful. The most unlikely change happens to Leonora Stern's self-perception: she revisits her research on the repressed lesbian relationship between Christabel LaMotte and Blanche Glover that resulted in Blanche's tragic suicide, and reconceives LaMotte's and her own identity from a lesbian to a possibly heterosexual one.[5]

As it emerges from these insights, the identities of the scholars are deeply interwoven with their research subjects. Lena Steveker even argues that the initial reason for starting their biographical research projects is the scholars' lack of self-identity, which they acquire only through their engagement with the nineteenth-century characters (Steveker 2009: 135). The reading competition for the "true" interpretation of the Victorian poets is, so to say, won by the two leading characters whose research is also emotionally invested. As Bo Lundén points out, *Possession* shows the limitedness of mere intellectual endeavors, offering a plot resolution through the activation of affective capacities only. Roland has a possibility to become a famous researcher because he follows the impulse to steal a manuscript, but he emerges as a future poet instead, concentrating on his own emotions; similarly, the coldness of Maud, the other scholar, recedes once she discovers family ties with the historical author Christabel LaMotte. This awakens the feeling of belonging, and she finds happiness in her promise of a harmonious relationship with Roland (Lundén 1999: 113–125). Lundén underlines that one cannot neglect the insistence of such novels on "(re)educating their readers by suggesting alternative modes of knowing as a way to confront intellectual practice" (132).[6] Thus a turn towards the emotional versus the rational seems to be another way of enhancing reader response. Other researchers also emphasize the "politics of affect" as a feature strongly influencing mass culture, which can thus capitalize on readerly desire, specifically stressing sensational fiction as its main forum (Jaffe 2005: 438).

Utilizing emotion for plot resolution is likely to incite changes in generic choices when rewriting Victorian fiction as well, with a preference for genres like steampunk, science fiction, romance, Gothic, crime and detective novels, and even graphic novels. *Possession* belongs to the most popular ones of the listed genres: it shows features of the Gothic, romance, sensation and detective fiction alike. The desire that motivates reader demands for sequels of earlier figures or stories may thus overlap with reasons for authorial inspiration to rewrite them, namely, "[a] fascination with the character, a storyline, or a world which has been created, or even a desire to rewrite a story that has proven unsatisfactory" (Gillies 1998: 132). In *Possession* most of these seem to be on offer: the nineteenth-century text construction is inspired by a fascination with the texts and secret lives of Victorian poets resembling the Brownings and Christina Rossetti, driven by the quest for truth, knowledge, love, and identity. Such sensibilities also get activated in the twentieth-century plotline, but the possibility of arriving at any reasonable result through their utilization is strongly denied. Yet, the theories feeding this denial are gradually deconstructed, and the impersonal and emotionless present finally changes into a promise of the imagined past rich in affect and creativity. This provides a representative example of how cultural revision takes place by refashioning source texts, topoi or historical eras to serve contemporary audiences, as Steveker phrases it in terms of memory studies, "Literature is a medium of cultural memory insofar as it provides cultural strategies to understand and, therefore, to access the past of the other, thus leading to an improved understanding of the self in the present" (Steveker 2009: 143).

The sensation invited by the strategies of double and affective reading also materializes in devising and marketing book covers that incite and respond to readerly desires governing commodity culture. Such emotional appeals emerge in the context of refashioning, with an awareness of and attachment to substantial remains of nineteenth-century social and cultural structures, architectural designs, and various other objects, collectively called Victorian mementoes, which equally legitimize the centrality of post–Victorian fiction (Sutherland 2007). Matthew Sweet goes out of his way to give credit to the Victorians for many more innovations and inventions than we are aware of, from housing estates through free education and investigative journalism to fish and chips and the fax machine, just to mention random examples (Sweet 2001: xii), and others also emphasize the popularizing impact of the fact that we are surrounded by nineteenth-century material culture (Krueger 2000: xv). This effect of Victoriana on contemporary audiences is widely exploited, not only in selling and exhibiting historical objects and their remakes, but also in the publishing industry, especially concerning marketing strategies for new editions of Victorian fiction or newly appearing post–Victorian fiction, from book cover designs to associations with films of the same subject. Thus, in addition to influencing the cultural objects themselves, such market schemes equally manipulate the representation of these objects. In other words, "commodities in postmodernity not only inhabit the material world, but have also colonized the realm of representation" (Linder 2003: 12).

In accordance with these developments in the literary market and material culture, post–Victorian fiction is often published with Victorian imagery on its cover. This connection of the nineteenth with the following centuries corresponds with readerly expectations, and thus usually proves to be promising in terms of sales figures as well. For example, a very popular cover image of post–Victorian novels seems to be the figure of a Victorian woman, a much-discussed and controversial trope in literary criticism, and an equally fruitful subject for film adaptations, as well as reading club discussions. Instead of featuring a full-size image of the female protagonist of the post–Victorian text, mostly only part of her body or a thinly clad woman is visible to the reader, indicating a mysterious story involving issues of womanhood and sexuality. Tindal's edition of Gaynor Arnold's *Girl in a Blue Dress* (2008) features a nineteenth-century lady half hidden by a flowery drapery, and seated in an armchair ready to tell her story, while the 2009 McClelland & Stewart edition has her figure seated in a study, her head on the desk buried in her arms, which also implies the nature of her story. On the 2003 Harvest edition cover of Michel Faber's *The Crimson Petal and the White*, the white bedsheets and red curtains entail the heroine's progress from innocence to experience, or girlhood to womanhood, which becomes a much more overtly suggestive image of a half-naked woman from behind on the 2010 Canongate release. The fascination with storytelling and the book as its medium are similarly popular features on post–Victorian publications. The motif on Belinda Starling's 2007 and 2008 Bloomsbury editions of *The Journal of Dora Damage* imitates a journal sealed by a bookbinder, the image of which also includes a corset; on the front cover of Jane Harris's Faber & Faber–published *The Observations* (2006), a Victorian woman is sitting holding a book or diary, while on its 2007 Penguin cover, there is an image of a woman in undergarments getting dressed behind a page of a diary. These designs imply narrative (and sexual) revelations, which the 2007 Faber & Faber edition of Harris's work further emphasizes by featuring a sealed envelope and a key on top of it, much akin to Jasper Fforde's *The Eyre Affair*, published by Penguin in 2003, which has a book with a huge lock and a key on its cover. Two additional Penguin editions hint more closely at the mysteries to uncover in Fforde's text related to reading, writing and publishing: the 2002 Viking edition has a clock and a woman making her way through a book, and another 2003 edition features a woman climbing out of the novel *Jane Eyre*. These designs indicate the excitement and intriguing possibilities in time and book travel, both of which take place in the novel.

 The publication history of Emma Tennant's *Adèle* sets a special case, as the cover designs change with the titles of later editions, probably because a wider audience is targeted. Maia Books published the novel under the title *The French Dancer's Bastard: The Story of Adèle from Jane Eyre* (2006), featuring a woman's waist in corset, not showing but implying the rest of the dancer's (or her daughter's?) uncovered body, obviously playing more heavily on the first part of the title and the excitement it may cause. *Thornfield Hall: Jane Eyre's Hidden Story* (2007), released by Harper, exchanged the name of the narrator of the first publication (*Adèle: Jane Eyre's Hidden Story*) to that of the location of the plot, and the image of Thornfield Hall on the cover of the 2003 edition to the image of a Victorian woman peeping out of the window, who most likely represents the narrator, Adèle. The reasons for these alterations may be manifold, yet *Jane Eyre* is a common point of reference in all three titles, and Adèle also needs a more effective identification, either by emphasizing her dubious origin in the title, or by putting her on the cover to be identified with the teller of Jane's hidden story, to help the reader place her in the original story. Some scholars even treat such different editions of the same text as a type of rewriting, calling them versions, based on the claim that variation in layouts and prints creates a difference in meaning as well (Bryant 2002: 66). Accordingly, the assumption behind the different titles of these two latter editions of *Adèle* may be a cultural one, namely, that the British audience, for whom the 2006 edition was intended, has more proximity to the original text, and responds adequately to the narrator figure and the French connection, whereas a non–British audience, for whom the 2007 version was prepared, can relate more to the geographical location aided by historical visuals. Similarly, in the case of novels adapted onto the screen, cultural differences on the recipients' side seem to be a motivating factor for designing diverse editions of such items. Besides stylized Victorian ones depicting a historical painting or other figurative art, these texts usually also have editions that feature the movie poster image of well-known actors who impersonate protagonists of post–Victorian texts, which is probably aimed at audiences that have seen the motion picture and may subsequently turn to the book version. For example, the 1997 Vintage edition of Peter Carey's *Oscar and Lucinda* features Ralph Fiennes and Cate Blanchett, who play the two leading characters in the screen adaptation of the novel,[7] and the 2002 Vintage edition of A. S. Byatt's *Possession* also has the two leads of the movie version of the novel on its cover page, Gwyneth Paltrow and Aaron Eckhart.[8] Not only the film version of novels or vice versa, but also a male author adapting a female author's piece, or an American film director revising an Australian or British writer's work, means a change of cultural context and ensuing market demands (Hutcheon 2006: 28).

This brief description of marketing strategies employed in designing book covers shows how the publishing industry can exploit visual material. Recently, post–Victorian scholars have also become aware of the critical potentials in the intersection of literature and visual culture. Ann Heilmann and Mark Llewellyn call attention to the implicatedness of the readers in sensationalizing Victorian literature through their appropriating gaze that objectifies and commodifies the nineteenth century. Focusing on post–Victorian fiction written about and by women, the authors argue that the essence of the exploitation women experience when the male/imperial or otherwise possessive gaze becomes obsessive can be collected into an emblematic image. Some book covers display such images, reminding the reader of nineteenth-century freak shows as well as today's peep shows that establish sexual relationships determined by medical, scientific and pornographic discourses. (Heilmann and Llewellyn 2010: 106–142). The book covers to which the authors refer as featuring "incomplete" women are the early editions of Belinda Starling's *The Journal of Dora Damage* and Jane Harris's *The Observations*, described above. In their analysis of the designs, the scholars imply the complicity of the reader in unmasking the Victorian age. In the case of Starling's novel, "the act of opening and reading the book is thus pictorially associated with the loosening of the laces and the stripping of a faceless woman's body of her clothed 'bindings'" (Heilmann and Llewellyn 2010: 108); and the cover image with the loose sheets of the diary and the title of Harris's work indicate both the processes of reading and writing, "while at the same time destabilizing the position of the reader-as-observer, hinting at the subversive possibilities of returning the gaze" (Heilmann and Llewellyn 2010: 111). A similar reading could apply to the cover design of Michel Faber's *The Crimson Petal and the White* (2003), which appropriates Fragonard's eighteenth-century painting *The Bolt*. Interestingly, the couple on the right-hand side of the painting about to make love does not appear on the book cover; only the image of the empty but suggestive bed gets adopted. This emphasizes the novel's subversive qualities. As Bényei also observes, the topic of the novel is the female body and its narratives, decipherable from the abundance of body metaphors all through the text (Bényei, 2006: 28), and thus from the cover image as well. Surveying the nature of scholarly engagement in its relations to the past, Marie-Louise Kohlke reads the frontispieces of critical publications on the post–Victorian encounter. Among others, she refers to the cover of Christine L. Krueger's *Functions of Victorian Culture at the Present Time* (2002), which features a historical painting in a wooden frame with the image of Queen Victoria staring at her own reflection in a computer screen; and the front of John Kucich and Dianne F. Sadoff's *Victorian Afterlife* (2000), where the torso of a fully dressed Victorian figure is visible hiding her/his face behind her/his clothing. Kohlke concludes that the obscure imagery of most of these publications may be symptomatic of our using the Victorians as a site of our own projections, instead of properly defining and delimiting the critical praxes involved in current research (Kohlke 2008: 11–13). Hence, as all these critiques confirm, the visuals included into literary research prove to be fruitful illustrations of various cultural processes, from theoretical and ideological discourses within disciplines to more interdisciplinary approaches, intertwining authorial moves, readerly expectations, publication strategies and market values.[9]

Such intermingling of various aspects of criticism has in some respect become a controversy in contemporary literary criticism. Scholars argue that the increasingly professional and theoretical nature of critical discourse has widened the gap between the academia and literary journalism (Easthope 1999: 118, Bényei 2003: 39). The same split survives into the present in Rónán McDonald's book tellingly titled *The Death of the Critic* (2007), where the academic detachment of literary criticism is contrasted with other university disciplines like art and film which have managed to maintain their expertise on the public market as well. Social critics tend to blame the ivory tower that literary criticism has become on exclusively text-based approaches to reading, especially those of New Criticism and deconstruction, which disregard referential interpretive frameworks. As a result, literary studies has been losing its cultural relevance from the seventies onwards (Ashcroft 2001: 13). This isolation of literary studies within educational institutions, identified by some critics as early as the beginning of the nineties (Lefevere 1992: 10), may have accelerated its slow disappearance as a self-standing academic discipline. Antony Easthope prognosticates the collapse of the paradigm of literature on the basis of Thomas Kuhn's theory of scientific revolutions, claiming that when a paradigm gets confused about its premises and becomes too theoretical, it dissolves and a new paradigm comes into being, which is how, as the author maintains, literary has been replaced by cultural studies (Easthope 1991: 3). Perhaps the notion of replacement appears slightly radical: examining recent literary companions of various literary historical eras, the critical foci of literary and cultural studies rather seem to be in the process of merging. Patrick Brantlinger and William B. Thesing's *A Companion to the Victorian Novel* (2005) is, for instance, a collection divided into three main parts: the first one examines historical and cultural issues, the second focuses on various novelistic forms, and the third part is theoretical, mainly oriented at reception and adaptation, also introducing twentieth-century remakes of nineteenth-century fiction. James F. English's edition of *A Concise Companion to Contemporary British Fiction* (2006) also has three main sections with similar divisions but slightly different emphases: the first part is devoted to some aspects of the literary market, the second examines how changes to the empire have influenced postmodern British fiction, and the third one surveys emerging novelistic genres.

Post-Victorian scholarship seems to respond to these changes in the critical discourse by attempting to synthesize elitist and non-elitist aspects of reading, which, as outlined in the previous chapter, is achieved by utilizing a variety of interpretive frameworks along with academic literary criticism, including that of cultural studies. This is also apparent from the range of topics discussed in the collections devoted to the study of post–Victorian novels, the premises laid in the introductions of those analyses, not to mention their titles, which more often than not include the term *culture* (Kucich and Sadoff 2000, Krueger 2002, Clayton 2003, Gay, Johnston, and Waters 2008). In these books, the post–Victorian novel is already often regarded as both a cultural document and a form of criticism, which may imply how literary criticism intermingles with cultural studies. The criticism of the Victorian novel is claimed to have played a significant part in the shift from literary to cultural studies (Jaffe 2005: 425); moreover, the Victorian era is regarded as an especially appealing point of reference for rewriting in terms of inciting cultural changes (McGowan 2000, Clayton 2003). This move towards reading literature as culture is accompanied by a change in identity discourses, which also influences the critical approach to interpreting novels. Fiction and criticism are both closely related to national identity, the discursive roots of which are traced back to empiricism (Easthope 1999) and liberal humanism (Schwarz 1986). Therefore, changes in national identity triggered by the decline of the empire also produced narratives of the decline of the novel (Bényei 2003: 69). As historical and political circumstances change, there seems to be a shift from the insistence on national identity to attempts at defining cultural identity (Easthope 1999: 228). Bill Ashcroft traces the transformation of English into cultural studies in the framework of postcolonial theory, claiming that postcolonial literatures in English have assumed a major role in this process. In the last century, English departments promoting

British cultural values were established in colonial settings as assertions of imperial hegemony (Ashcroft 2003: 2). The discipline in this form has been deconstructed, by allowing both a wider range of cultural material, including more popular texts, as well as highly inventive postcolonial fiction, to complement or even outlaw the high culture associated with the English literary canon (7–8).

Hence, the change in the discourses of identity translates into disciplinary renewals as well: cultural studies and cultural memory are gradually emerging as fields of teaching and research, and, through their interdisciplinary nature, they enhance the production and reception of new sites and narratives of identification, in which post–Victorian fiction and its criticism actively participate. This reintroduction of the concept of culture into the center of critical discourse has made cultural revision into a critical premise as well as a political act: the revisions of texts are revisions of culture which require new analytical skills and new "critical thinking based on difference, variation, approximation, intention, power, and change" that will, hopefully, lead us to democracy (Bryant 2002: 177). As this remark shows, revision is perceived as a crucial tool in shaping our culture, implying that both fiction and criticism engaging in the act of revision have ethical responsibility. In terms of criticism, this means a possible revisiting of authorial intention, which may well follow the reinstatement of authorship already in process. Bryant lists a number of critical notions to rethink, which is an attitude shared by Hutcheon, who likewise urges for a scrutiny of political and historical intentionality in rewriting (Hutcheon 2006: 94). Post-Victorian fiction is by definition based on revision. Consequently, it assumes a major role in such possible reshaping of critical praxes. Scholarly terminology that delineates the angle of revision, including terms like *postcolonial*, *(post)feminist*, *postimperial*, or *postmodern*, all prefixed by *post-*, presupposes a previous state of affairs just like *post–Victorian* does, thus the historical and political analysis of discourses of authorship and identity formation in post–Victorian texts may have implications for adjustments in the language of research as well.

Changes in Britain's cultural and national self-definition also affect the literary scene, therefore I provide a brief survey of the changing perception of, perhaps, the most representative award of the British literary world, the (Man) Booker Prize. This award, simultaneously engaging authors, readers, critics, and the market, indicates the thoroughly politicized nature of literature and literary criticism: from the postcolonial point of view, the prize represents the history of colonization and decolonization

(Shaffer 2006: 15–30); viewed from a postimperial perspective, it has evolved from symbolizing the nation into an icon of the multiple identities of culture (Strongman 2002: 221–237). Regarding the marketing aspects of selling literature, the award "drives publishers mad with hope, booksellers mad with greed, judges mad with power, winners mad with pride, and losers (the unsuccessful short-listees plus every other novelist in the country) mad with envy and disappointment" (Barnes 1987: 21), and considering it with the mindset of the self-made literary outcast, "the only sensible attitude to the Booker is to treat it as posh bingo" (ibid.). The intersection between post–Victorian fiction and the Man Booker Prize appears to be their mutual concern with narratives of identity, also addressed in relevant critical literature, such as Richard Todd's *Consuming Fictions: The Booker Prize and Fiction in Britain Today* (1996), or Luke Strongman's *The Booker Prize and the Legacy of Empire* (2002), so it is worth providing a brief outline of how post–Victorian novels can be characterized through this overlap. The eighties and the nineties, which were the time when the British seriously started redefining their identity, are also considered peak periods in the production of post–Victorian novels, two of which were awarded the Booker Prize. The two texts, *Oscar and Lucinda* and *Possession*, strongly engage in negotiating postcolonial, postimperial and individual identities by juxtaposing various nineteenth-century texts and memory objects with twentieth-century attempts at identity formation. The novels have triggered an enormous and ongoing critical interest, at the same time generating a boom in the market, increasing sales figures, and prompting film adaptations largely as a consequence of receiving the literary award which has thus fed into a permanent reflection on the evolving discourses of identity.[10]

As identity-shaping and reflecting devices, both post–Victorian fiction and the Man Booker Prize encounter an inherent ambivalence concerning problems of location and inclusion. As the discourse of the center and periphery between the colonizer and the colonized fades away in the name of literary globalism, the Man Booker Prize is still based in and handed out from London (Strongman 2002: xi), and the language of fiction is that of the dominant culture, English. In addition, despite the fact that it also produces literature in English, the U.S. is not allowed to enter the competition, so American fiction is still perceived as something threatening against which the British has to define itself (Todd 1996: 77–83), not to mention that the more experimental local fiction is just as much out of the prize's scope as American writing (Easthope 1999: 203–204). Similarly, in both prize-winning novels, *Oscar and Lucinda* and *Possession,* the English are conscious of their "other," and employ the strategies of self-battering and self-protection, respectively, to define themselves in the new context, yet holding on to the narrative lead, they do not allow these "others" much space for self-expression. Regarded through the lens of the perceptions of the literary award, these two post–Victorian classics seem to indicate the following ambivalence: the controversial revival of Victorianism, serving the redefinition of national and cultural identities, produces new self-definitions by keeping the traditional ethos of the English novel alive.

Such complexities can also be observed in the case of the identities of authors of post–Victorian fiction. Many of the writers who address postcolonial issues in their texts themselves have a postcolonial identity, such as the Australians Gail Jones and Peter Carey, or Lloyd Jones, who comes from New Zealand. Others with a postimperial identity write back to the English from within the UK, as does the Scottish Alasdair Gray and the English-born Welsh Jasper Fforde. Interestingly, the authors whose novels feature the fear of reverse colonization effected by the U.S., such as campus novels by David Lodge and A.S. Byatt, are English and have a traditional educational background, graduating from the best universities of London and Oxbridge. And then there are those authors whose origin or identity is multifarious, influencing the range of topics they address in their writing. A common characteristic of these writers seems to be the fact that they have traveled extensively, like the Welsh-Dominican Jean Rhys, who lived in various places from the Caribbean to Europe; Matthew Kneale, who was educated in England but worked in Japan, and at present resides in Rome; or the Dutch-born Michel Faber, who grew up in Australia and now writes in Scotland. Without drawing farfetched conclusions from these data, I think it is important to note that the rewriting of the Victorian era with a particular focus on identity formation seems especially appealing to authors of marginal, uncertain or multifaceted identities. This underlines the political potential of post–Victorian fiction in emphasizing the hybridity of identities.

In the first decade of the twenty-first century, there still appears to be a balance kept between England-based and external authors in the Man Booker prize distribution, and the plots of the winning novels mostly oscillate between postimperial and postcolonial settings. Post-Victorian texts conceptualizing legacies of the empire got as far as the short list. Matthew Kneale's *English Passengers* debunks the English colonial mission to

Tasmania as disorganized, opportunistic, and corrupt, becoming instantly dangerous and hilariously grotesque as soon as powers are reversed and the passengers themselves become the objects exhibited to the natives. This indicates the emergence of a freshly humorous tone after the gloomy accounts of the previous two decades. Lloyd Jones's *Mister Pip* reveals new sensibilities in constructing multiple identities from the point of view of the self, of the nation and of culture. This is achieved by utilizing correspondences between the nineteenth-century and the present (post)colonial and postimperial spaces of travel and a literary object that assumes the function of an agent of cultural discourse. The recent focus in post–Victorian fiction seems to have shifted to a more individual authoring of selves. Literary biographies offering alternative perceptions of nineteenth-century authors, and paying special attention to authorship and authorial legacies, regularly acquire a place on the long and short lists of the Man Booker Prize. *Mister Pip* and Gaynor Arnold's *Girl in a Blue Dress* prolong the list of Dickensiana, Julian Barnes's *Arthur and George* (2005) fictionalizes Sir Arthur Conan Doyle's career, while Colm Tóibín's *The Master* and Alan Hollinghurst's *The Line of Beauty* (which won the Prize in 2004)[11] thematize the life and writing of Henry James. The fact that since Hollinghurst's text no novel belonging to the category of post–Victorian fiction has won the prize may provide a good chance for the manifestation of subversive voices in this genre, and possibly lead to its diversification.

Biofiction: Reinventing Henry James[12]

As argued above, at present we experience the return of the author on many levels: the author as celebrity, the author as the responsible creator of a literary text, and authorship as a concept to be readdressed by literary criticism. This renewed attention to the author results in recentering and increasingly involving the author as a public figure in the literary market, renewing discourses of authority, authenticity, anxiety and cult. This also brings the genre of literary biographies to attention, providing an important hallmark of how the historical dimension of empirical realities and social, political and ethical questions becomes refocused in the creative realm, explained by some scholars as a returning belief in the liberal humanist subject (Kaplan 2007: 79).[13] The gradual rise of authorship to a central determinant of the novel's literary value in the nineteenth century resurfaces in today's interest in reputations and status of worth for literary authors as celebrities (Deane 2003: ix–xvi, English and Frow 2006: 39–57), which can also be observed in most post–Victorian biographilia of the eighties and nineties. These reconstructions of nineteenth-century writers quite clearly distinguish between the authors' life and work, questioning the myths, both positive and negative, surrounding the former, and mostly maintaining praise for the latter. Thomas Hardy's chauvinism, as in Howard Jacobson's *Peeping Tom* (1984) or Emma Tennant's *Tess* (1993), and Oscar Wilde's homosexuality, as in Peter Ackroyd's *The Last Testament of Oscar Wilde* (1983), featured among the popular topics fictionalized. Peter Ackroyd specializes in writing fictional biographies of historical authors, his most famous one, overarching three centuries and providing the source of mottoes for the chapters of this book, being *Chatterton* (1987), and his most monumental being *Dickens* (1990), labeled as "Ackroyd's melodrama of Victorian authorship" (Kaplan 2007: 62). Julian Barnes, another author expressing interest in literary biographies, voices concerns related to the critical construction of historical authors in his *Flaubert's Parrot* (1984) already, to further engage with them in his massive *Arthur and George* (2005). Considering the cultic status of authors in the Victorian era, I think that the post–Victorian rewriting of nineteenth-century authors could also be read as a symbolic move of reinstating the importance of authorship.

After this period of reviving or debunking scandals around Victorian authors, a certain shift of interest can be observed towards the authors' lives and characters in connection with the writing process itself. The proliferation of Henry James biographilia provides a representative twenty-first-century example of this change. In the late Victorian era, James fought the contemporary trend of subordinating authorial principles to mass-market consumerism by constructing "an authoritative image of his integrity and mastery" (Deane 2003: xiv), manifest in the scant focus on social and political themes, as well as in presenting more self-reflexive forms of authorial consciousness (xv). In his seminal essay *Technique as Discovery*, the new critic Mark Schorer already defines the modern novelist as someone who rigorously peruses his medium and thereby discovers his subject matter, referring to James as a perfect example for this (Schorer 1972: 392). This view of the historical author prevails today as the following remark of one of his adaptors shows: "We after-comers nevertheless venerate James for the uncompromising subtlety and technical refinement of his writing. He was the first English novelist to insist on fiction-writing as an exacting art, the technique of which was available to scrutiny and analysis" (Heyns "The Curse of Henry James" 2004). Moreover, the adaptations surveyed below constitute a corpus, written in a similar spirit to James's "the portrait of the artist"–type novels, that discuss the artist, art and artistry.

Why so many works appear on the same author is a question open for speculation. It is commonly accepted that James's aversion to making his life public was sooner or later bound to excite some interest in his life and inspire attempts to fictionalize it (Kramer "The Secrets of the Master" 2008). Some even claim that James, a biographer himself, "tried to control his biography through the selective destruction of evidence" (Rollyson "James & the Zeitgeist" 2005). Others explain the rising interest in turning Henry James's life into fiction as a possible consequence of the reinvigorating scholarship on James, maintaining that contemporary practices focus on the subject and its current narratives of identification, which inspires life-writing (Kaplan 2007: 64). More specifically, they argue that biographical novels have directly developed out of the scholarship rethinking James's social contacts, especially his personal attachments to men and women (Saunders 2008: 123). Critical analyses, such as Eric Haralson's *Henry James and Queer Modernity* (2003), illustrate James's relevance for recent theoretical discourses and disciplines, for example, queer theory or gender studies. Ann Heilmann's "The Haunting of Henry James: Jealous Ghosts, Affinities, and *The Others*" attributes the nineteenth-century author's popularity to the multiplicity of instabilities in his work and recurring end-of-century crises (Heilmann 2010: 129), reflecting on James as "a writer whose experimentation with issues of authorship, identity and subjectivity reflects central literary and critical preoccupations of the turn of the millennium" (111).

James's transgressiveness does not only manifest itself in the author's uncertain sexual preferences and national or cultural belonging, but also in his in-betweenness concerning two literary historical eras: the Victorian and the modernist. Because he lived and wrote at the turn of the twentieth century, it is difficult to categorize him, as Sergio Perosa's attempt of putting Henry James into a literary historical context in "The Case of Henry James: From Victorianism to the Avant-Garde" (Perosa 1992: 61–77) shows. This problem of categorization is also echoed at the level of interpreting James's work. Heilmann reads the most recent appropriations of James's seminal novel, *The Turn of the Screw*, in the context of the protagonist's psyche, following its disintegration for not coping with social, sexual, and other boundaries (Heilmann 2010: 111–130). Even though he mainly wrote in the tradition of the modernist psychological novel, James still adhered to some kind of Victorian moral imperative in his art, which yields an intriguing combination for today's authors. Besides embodying a fruitful subject matter for current discourses of fluidity, "he also presents himself as a model: not for imitation or copying, but of an artistic ideal" (Heyns "The Curse of Henry James" 2004). In this survey, James's crisis as a writer in the 1890s receives central attention through the discussion of twenty-first-century adaptations, thus he fits into the post–Victorian category whose nineteenth-century point of reference, as already pinned down in Chapter 1, I understand as a chronological one.

By the year 2004, five novels featuring Henry James had lined up for literary acclaim: the paperback edition of *Felony: The Private History of The Aspern Papers* (2002) by Emma Tennant; Colm Tóibín's *The Master* (2004); Alan Hollinghurst's *The Line of Beauty* (2004); David Lodge's *Author, Author* (2004); and Michiel Heyns's *The Typewriter's Tale* (2005).[14] *Felony* was ahead of time, so in that respect it did not participate in the competition; publishers rejected *The Typewriter's Tale* because of a simultaneous overproduction of similar projects; and the other three all qualified for the Man Booker Prize of the year, *Author Author* not entering the long list, *The Master* making it to the short list and *The Line of Beauty* eventually winning the prize. These novels are related not only through their time of appearance, but also in their topic, indicated already in their titles. None of them actually names Henry James as a major character or point of reference, but they all relate to writing; Hollinghurst's text is associable with painting as well. Some of them echo their Victorian precursor's own pieces, and the use of words like *author, master, typewriter, papers, line, history,* and *tale* illustrates a preoccupation with authorship, the authority of author and text, and the life and art of storytelling, which serves as a nominal basis for most of the adaptations, albeit their respective foci, described in what follows.

"*Felony* is about the misdemeanours inherent in writing — theft, false memory, plagiarism and greed for celebrity," declares the blurb of the novel's first hardcover edition, setting the context for reading as well as articulating a critical interest in the process of writing. The appropriative chain, with Emma Tennant researching into the nineteenth-century Henry James inquiring into eighteenth-century romantic texts, gives an ironic twist to the Victorian author's fear and disgust of upcoming generations interfering with his private life. Making him a mouthpiece for warning celebrities with something to hide to beware of future publications of their scandals, further emphasizes the ridiculousness of this anxiety (Tennant 2002: 8), not to mention that James carries out the same notorious research for his *Aspern Papers* on romantic poets that his future biographer does on him. Critics interpret the James of *Felony* as a thief who does not refrain from any kind of stealing to be able to write his story (Rollyson "James & the Zeitgeist" 2005). From the perspective of James's authoress friend, Constance Fenimore Woolson, who gets a share of the narrative, this critique is carried further, contrasting the writer's supreme artistic achievement with his life as an undecided bachelor insensitive to the needs of those closest to him. She remembers a conversation in which she overheard him say that women write very badly, so she begins to suspect that he may not only be unable to understand women, but specifically dislikes women who write (Tennant 2002: 158–159). This point of view provides a more critical opinion, not only of James's talents as a writer, but also of his general ethical stance towards his sources and his female colleagues. Along the lines of Sandra M. Gilbert and Susan Gubar's reinterpretation of Harold Bloom's notion of the "anxiety of influence" attributed to male poets, as an "anxiety of authorship" experienced by female poets,[15] a feminist reading of Tennant's text could be developed that tackles aspects of this anxiety.

A male author devoting his life to high art, who features as the main character in James's "The Lesson of the Master" and gets compared to the nineteenth-century author himself in *Felony*, has also provided a source of inspiration for Tóibín's *The Master*. Published in February 2004, this work constitutes the next item in the chronology of Henry James biographilia. Tóibín gives a convincing portrait of how the author's focus on other people's lives that yield promising stories affects his own life and relationships. The subject of appropriating source material already addressed in *Felony* reappears here as intellectual theft, the best example of which is James stealing and publishing a tale Edmund Gosse tells him. This leads to frictions and Gosse's "objections to the art of fiction as a cheap raid on the real and the true" (Tóibín 2005: 76), which basically amounts to James's being humiliated with his own weapon. Critics also claim that this exclusive concentration on his fictional characters leaves no space for the articulation of the author's own desires: James behaves evasively in his conversations and does not appear more accessible for his own private self than for others (Rollyson "James & the Zeitgeist" 2005), which obviously results in loneliness. Due to the sensitive picturing of these vital conflicts interweaving James's life and art, *The Master* usually receives praise for its psychological richness, characterized as "a lovely portrait of the artist" (Cohen "The Quest for a Necessary Shell" 2004), the use of which category tunes in with these novels being *Künstlerromans*. Regarding the anxiety of authorship, especially in the case of an adaptor who has virtually moved into his predecessor's consciousness, one could agree with the observation that parallels James's relationship to the dead, that determines the narrative of *The Master,* with Tóibín's connection to James, whom he ventriloquizes (Saunders 2008: 131).

In his *The Line of Beauty*, which was published shortly after *The Master*, Alan Hollinghurst also ghost-writes the Victorian author. Lacking a nineteenth-century plotline and set in the 1980s gleam and gutter of Thatcherite Britain, the novel is yet denied the status of biofiction (Kaplan 2007: 74). Still, if one considers how nineteenth-century writers get transposed into contemporary settings in other types of post–Victorian fiction, *The Line of Beauty* can also be interpreted as a text expanding the boundaries of biofiction in the same way. Miranda in D. M. Thomas's *Charlotte* (2000), for example, provisionally assumes the identity of Charlotte Brontë in the West Indies, fantasizing about the kind of life Brontë might have had in the twentieth century, and Mr. Watts of Lloyd Jones's *Mister Pip* (2006) impersonates Charles Dickens in an equally postcolonial setting, interweaving his life story with that of Dickens's *Great Expectations*. These instances indicate alternative fates for historical authors, which imply further potentials in writing literary biographies. In this context, the protagonist of *The Line of Beauty*, a young homosexual, reads as a bold twentieth-century impersonation of Henry James. Nick Guest habitually interweaves James quotes with his own words, which he perceives as having a love affair with the historical author (Hollinghurst 2004: 208), and he often finds himself imitating James, for instance, when dictating long, complex sentences to his typist in his predecessor's fashion (396). The way Nick juxtaposes the discourse of his academic study on James with his sexual self-discovery, and the interpretation of his own experiences in the light of Henry James's texts yields an exciting recontextualization of the Jamesian life-art dichotomy. Nick's failure in adapting James's *The Spoils of Poynton* into a popular film script drives him to the limits of artistic compromise, which constitutes another parallel between Nick and James concerning their attitude to artistic production during their brief career as playwrights. Not being able to compromise, Nick rather starts working on a magazine called *Ogee*, which he dedicates to beauty. Picking up on the moral duplicity of the ogee curve echoing the title's "line of beauty," James Wood draws a comparison between Hollinghurst and James's approach to aestheticism. The critic concludes that by such a connection of beauty and morality, Hollinghurst's text "seems to be delivering itself of a critique only about the potential uses and abuses of aestheticism; whereas James suggests that aestheticism is intrinsically dangerous" (Wood "The Ogee Curve" 2004). The fact that such comparisons exist between the two writers emphasizes the level of proximity the Man Booker Prize-winning author has achieved in this work to his Victorian predecessor in refashioning late Victorian and early modernist concerns.

David Lodge's *Author, Author*, published as the last of the three James adaptations in the autumn of 2004, could not escape comparison with the previously appearing novels. Reviewers generally regard it as the weakest of the three, accusing the writer of too closely following historical data (Harrison "The Portrait of a Layabout" 2004, Wood "The Spoils" 2004). This kind of critical sensitivity implies an increasing concern with the generic differentiation between biography and biofiction, essential for the establishment of the latter as a distinct category. Similarly to *The Master*, *Author, Author* gives an account of James's crisis of authorship in his middle years, especially the failure of his play *Guy Domville*, but it focuses less on the loneliness of the artist split between his life and art and more on James's literary recognition, rejections and jealousies. Among his social connections, those that also bear importance professionally, relating to the author's artistic production, receive the most attention. For example, characterizing his relationship to Constance Fenimore Woolson, Henry James admits that he communicates more easily and honestly through fiction than in real-life situations (Lodge 2005: 169). At the end of the book, Lodge's implied author enters the narrative in the shape of a literary critic and expresses his reverence for the master, assuring him of his future as an "established classic, essential reading for anyone interested in modern English and American literature" (375). This intrusion further complicates *Author, Author* from the point of view of genre, because, besides biography and fiction, it also overtly includes literary criticism, resulting in an even more complex *hybrid form*.[16]

Michiel Heyns's *The Typewriter's Tale*, rejected in the "year of Henry James" and published in 2005 only, exhibits a similar authorial consciousness of writing biofiction as Lodge's text. In this novel, it is not the author but the narrator, James's secretary, who appropriates the position of the writer and attempts to compile her own novel based on stolen material from her employer. Frieda Wroth, modeled on James's last typist, Theodora Bosanquet, working in close proximity to the author as does Fenimore in *Felony*, notes that through his exclusive devotion to his art, James behaves in a largely insensitive way towards people around him, especially women: "He should lose himself in analyzing the structure of a story of a young woman affronting her destiny and disregard the daily presence of just such a young woman in his own house" (Heyns 2005: 76). He remains similarly unaware of Edith Wharton's possible affair with his admired William Morton Fullerton, which surfaces only through Frieda's narrative mediation of James's social contacts. Critics see her character as supplanting the readers hoping for some kind of real-life experience or recognition behind the intriguing prose (Kramer "The Secrets of the Master" 2008). With various instances of theft, likewise addressed in the other adaptations, and the assumption of an authorial self, this readerly identification immerses with a quasi-authorial one. Karen Scherzinger points out that besides a general inquiry into authorship, including the James-Frieda-Heyns appropriative chain, the novel also reveals a very apparent "fantasy of intimacy" with the historical author, not only by putting his textual originals to various uses, but also by employing mediums and telepathy to enhance sensual closeness to him (Scherzinger 2008: 15–16).

This abundance of novels devoted to the same subject summoned a number of responses, out of which the most interesting ones from the point of view of authorship are those articulated by some of the authors themselves. Writers on the losing side fostered a superstitious reading of the fate of these novels, suggesting that Henry James's curse on anyone interfering with his private life came true (Michiel Heyns even titled his essay devoted to the subject "The Curse of Henry James"): literary biographers closely engaging with the historical author's life experienced rejection or negative criticism (Heyns "The Curse of Henry James" 2004, Lodge 2006: 39). In his *The Year of Henry James: The Story of a Novel* (2006), recording the production and reception of *Author, Author*, David Lodge draws a parallel between James's efforts, frustrations and pains of rejection and his own similar endeavors (Lodge 2006: 54). His predecessor's difficulty of preserving readership without compromising his literary aims was a consideration Lodge equally had to face, when he switched from writing bestsellers serialized by television to creating *Author, Author*, a period novel about a celibate historical person in an elegiac tone (64).[17] Heyns takes this comparison further, in his essay (parts of which Lodge also quotes in *The Year of Henry James*), by presenting "James's lonely artistic integrity" as a model to his adaptors for dealing with such disappointments, as a "proof of a dedication that so much in the modern publishing industry conspires to discourage" (Heyns "The Curse of Henry James" 2004).

Though provoked by an unfortunate situation, Lodge's follow-up book could serve as a first step towards an inquiry into the creative process of literary adaptation, the understanding of which Hutcheon regards an absolute necessity for the appreciation of the popularity of rewritings (Hutcheon 2006: 107). In addition, this work offers a further means to investigate the return of the author. For the writer of *Author, Author*, the creative process centers on the joys of appropriating the nineteenth century, the research part of which also involves actual literary tourism. Such trips enable the writer to establish not only intertextual, but also quasi-inspirational relationships, by gaining insights through historical locations and objects. These, sometimes overlapping, visits[18] and the unexpected competition of the ensuing writings result in a type of literary rivalry not unknown to James himself and also fictionalized in most of the adaptations.[19] Lodge's account elaborates how authorial distress emerges in both of their subjects' and their own conflicts of personal life and the creative process of writing. Such conflicts sometimes make the twenty-first-century authors into the ghostwriters of their predecessor, which the writer-critic seems to interpret as one possible reason for the current popularity of biographilia, namely, "a positive and ingenious way of coping with the 'anxiety of influence'" (Lodge 2006: 10).[20] The motto of this chapter seems to echo this line of thought: though Harriet Scrope, a twentieth-century novelist who earns her living by plagiarizing Victorian and other authors, participates in the conversation on anxiety and plagiarism with some frailty as "her voice trailed off as she looked down at her trembling hands" (Ackroyd 1987: 100), her attitude to appropriating earlier writers' work suggests that she accepts it as a perfectly natural behavior: "No doubt," she went on, "there are resemblances between my books and those of other writers" (101). Charles Wychwood, her partner in the dialogue, accepts this view without objections—he even expands it in his preface to the book he writes on Chatterton: "Thomas Chatterton believed that he could explain the entire material and spiritual world in terms of imitation and forgery, and so sure was he of his own genius that he allowed it to flourish under other names" (126).

Following up the genesis of biographilia is thus enlightening, in terms of the question of how far we can delve into the life of historical individuals in the name of historical investigation, and how such inquiries affect the biographers and their subjects. Besides the authorial reactions, critical responses to the Henry James adaptations also signal telling sites of current engagements with biographical fiction. Kaplan, for example, reads three of the above five texts, *The Master, Author, Author,* and *The Line of Beauty*, with a focus on anxieties connected to masculinity, writing and authorship, concluding that the past and present exposure of these leads to the recognition of "a more paradoxical and contradictory masculine — and literary — subjectivity" (Kaplan 2007: 78). This view provides an important critical angle on the authors' self-reflexive comments on the anxiety of authorship. Max Saunders suspects a potential narcissistic drive behind fictional recreations of the dead author, whereby contemporary writers create their own authorial persona through engaging with similar concerns of their nineteenth-century predecessor (Saunders 2008: 127). This assumption sounds plausible, considering that James's contested biography yields a perfect locus for the projection of various authorial sensibilities. Lodge's, for example, invites comments on the basis of the title of his work, *Author, Author,* as one that aims for a cohabitation of the author position (Scherzinger 2008: 10), leading to the conclusion that adaptations of such kind will trigger a change in literary criticism toward "a participatory collaboration of reading, writing, theory and [...] scholarship" (19–20). The above-discussed authorial and critical reactions not only emphasize collaborative authorship, but also aptly show how the genres of biofiction and literary criticism interact in their engagement with the writing process, life and writing, representations of life and writing, and literary reception and reactions to literary reception, increasingly collapsing the boundaries of text and critique in the process.

On the basis of the above, it can be expected that the literary agency of authors and authors as fictional characters will become more extensively explored in the future. Barnes's *Arthur and George* (2005) indicates a longish example of such an exploration, where a parallel account of the lives and interaction of George Edalji, a wrongly sentenced Parsee solicitor, and Arthur Conan Doyle, the renowned writer who fights for Edalji's reinstatement, acquires relevance in connection with the creation process of the Sherlock Holmes series. Interestingly, in the very same year, another novel structured in a similar manner came out by the German author Daniel Kehlmann. His *Die Vermessung der Welt* (*Measuring the World*, 2005) also follows the career of two nineteenth-century celebrities, Alexander von Humboldt, explorer and naturalist, and Carl Friedrich Gauss, mathematician and scientist (not literary but natural science authors this time), by writing parallel narratives of their lives, thoughts and relationship with each other. Perhaps the idea of providing two intertwining fictional biographies is a more democratic way of presenting historical persona, as this means the qualification of one story by the other, putting them both into perspective. In addition, intellectual history or the broader cultural context can also be better understood if more accounts are juxtaposed, therefore this type of fictional biography seems to have an equally promising future. Also, two texts from the growing list of Henry James adaptations supply such extensive overviews of fin-de-siècle thinking and movements by fictionalizing more historical characters. Carol de Chellis Hill's *Henry James's Midnight Song* (1993) provides an intriguing picture of cosmopolitan Vienna at the turn of the twentieth century, including the Freud and the Jung families, Edith Wharton and, of course, Henry James, who is on a journey of self-knowledge in the midst of some murder mystery. Paula Marantz Cohen's *What Alice Knew: A Most Curious Tale of Henry James and Jack the Ripper* (2010) has a very similar detective novel setting, combining the perspectives of three historical characters, focusing on a very specific event: the chase of a mysterious serial killer, Jack the Ripper. The siblings Henry, William and Alice James team up to solve the puzzle of the Ripper murders, and through their lives a good glimpse of England's intellectual history at the turn of the twentieth century is offered, emphasizing art, psychology and the suffragist movement.

The fact that the most important characteristics of Henry James, namely, his passion for writing and his credo of the writer's profession, feature even in some of these more sensationalist texts, show how much the nineteenth-century author embodies issues related to authorship, production and reception of literary works. Chapter 39 of Cohen's novel, for example, starts like this: "Henry had been working on his novel, practically without pause, all week. It was like that with him. Everything else was embroidery and diversion; writing was the center and foundation of his life. *Bounded by a nutshell*, he sometimes thought during these intensive, almost maniacal periods" (Cohen 2010: 279). Cynthia Ozick, who is a well-known Henry James adaptor, confesses James's influence on the formation of her authorial persona as well as her writing, as early as 1982, comparing herself to the character of the young writer in James's "The Lesson of the Master." She also adopts this as the title of her essay, which, similarly to the novels analyzed earlier, is related to the crisis of the author, but Ozick uses the nineteenth-century writer's story to survey her own "middle years" (Ozick "The Lesson of the Master" 1982). In her *Dictation: A Quar-*

tet (2008), she fictionalizes a rivalry between Henry James and Joseph Conrad, which is also passed on to their typists, Theodora Bosanquet and Lilian Hallowes, a competition that is between attitudes to writing, art and ardor. Such a focus on authors and their writing process further questions posterity's authority over the life and texts of historical writers, especially considering the positivist implications of the referentiality of these post–Victorian *Künstlerromans*. Taking into account the trust the readership puts into historical facts, the prefaces of some of the discussed Henry James biographilia reverse the usual warning about the entirely fictitious nature of characters and advocate claims for the opposite, only allowing for fiction in the case of lack of facts leaving room for speculation (Lodge 2005: "Preface," Tennant 2002: "Author's Note"). Scholars argue for the keeping of a healthy balance between biography and fiction (Miller 2002: 169) or for the indissoluble difference between the two (Kaplan 2007: 65), yet the shift in terminology signifies the primacy of fiction: analogically to biopics in film studies, literary biography slowly transforms into biofiction.

It seems, then, that from being one type of biography, the subgenre of literary biography has gone a long way to making the biographical into one kind of fiction. In the nineteenth century, biographers recorded the biographee's life as precisely and truthfully as possible. These scientific attempts at documenting a historical person's moral and character development were written in the tradition of the realist novel, with first- or third-person omniscient narration aiming at immediacy and objectivity. Adhering to this perception of Victorian biographical writing and thus keeping the term *biography*, Louisa Hadley analyzes three post–Victorian refashionings of historical persons and fictional characters. She reads Peter Carey's *Jack Maggs* (1997), James Wilson's *Dark Clue* (2001) and Janice Galloway's *Clara* (2002) based on the "life and letters" type of biography, which works from compiled documentary evidence and maintains an indexical relationship to its subject, and claims that these adaptations are rooted in Victorian forms of biography. (Hadley 2010: 32–38). However, as I also show later in this book in the case of *Jack Maggs*, today's biographilia are more aware of their status as interpretations of a fictional figure or historical personality's life aimed at the contemporary reading public, which necessarily involves various levels of manipulating historical data. Lucasta Miller's *The Brontë Myth* provides a good example of a critique that processes this shift of biography towards the fictional. The scholar traces how Charlotte Brontë's biography and its fictional appropriations have been subject to various myths and critical schools of thought in the last two centuries. Depending on the disciplinary background of writing up the author's life, terms such as *life-writing* or *psychobiography* emerge that may prove useful in further elaborations of the genre of biofiction. Similarly, Saunders's constitution of biofiction as a four-part hybrid consisting of biography, autobiography, fiction and criticism (Saunders 2008: 126) exemplifies how the genre's terminological refinement has already begun. Finally, a service that contemporary biofiction can do for historical authors and their canonical works is to facilitate reconstruction by involving the readers in the game of literary detection and thus make them learn about the nineteenth century through its twenty-first-century rewritings, possibly leading them back to the sources.

3

Post-Victorian Fiction in Its Political and Social Context

"That was the problem. None of it seemed very real, but I suppose that's the trouble with history. It's the one thing we have to make up for ourselves."—Peter Ackroyd, *Chatterton* (1987)

In this chapter, I delineate historical changes in identity narratives, with special focus on those triggered by postcolonialism and postimperialism, through surveying the last thirty years' output of post–Victorian fiction. Since such novels engage in rereading the past by offering alternatives to existing narratives and achieve this, upholding historical continuity, by making Victorian times correspond with the present, they may serve as especially effective identity-forming devices. Graham Swift's *Waterland* (1983) provides an example of the intermingling of (post)colonial and (post)imperial narratives in search of a national identity, acknowledging colonial atrocities at the same time as escaping from them into accounts of natural history. The juxtaposition of readings of Peter Carey's *Oscar and Lucinda* (1988) proves how changes in the discourses of the nation and culture reverberate in various critical approaches to fiction. In particular, I discuss the contexts of the eighties' narrative of heritage and enterprise, the nineties' cultural policy culminating in the millennium celebrations, and the current trend of liberalizing political attitudes to remembering. *Island fiction* is a subgeneric category that is especially sensitive to narrating the past. In the second part of the chapter, I theorize *island fiction* as a contextualization of inventive attempts at expressing how Britain faces legacies of its historical empire. I read Matthew Kneale's *English Passengers* (2000) and Caryl Phillips's *Cambridge* (1991) by juxtaposing concepts of eighteenth-century discovery narratives, nineteenth-century travelogues and Simon Gikandi's trope of travel (1996). These novels engage with the concepts of insularity, travel and home from (post)imperial and (post)colonial perspectives. These concepts are distinguished by dislocation, a trait that also characterizes the adaptation process itself.

Narratives of Identity

As the novel is perceived as a tool of creating both identity and history, it takes a crucial part in working out discourses of the self, the nation and culture as well as the past. Victorianists commonly attributed the emergence and popularity of narrative fiction to the establishment of political democracy and the ensuing interest in the individual (Childers 2005: 414), which became a widely shared view in the twentieth century on the basis of Ian Watt's 1957 classic, *The Rise of the Novel*. Some contemporary scholars also maintain an association of the novel with various discourses of identity, narrowing their focus to postimperial and postcolonial developments. Patrick Parrinder closely relates the rise and decline of the English novel to the rise and decline of the British Empire (Parrinder 2006: 2), and foresees the twenty-first-century function of English fiction as an active participant in the ongoing process of negotiating national identity (414). Brian W. Shaffer reads the history of British fiction as the history of colonialism and decolonization and categorizes English-language novels accordingly (Shaffer 2006: 15–30). These contexts are closely intertwined with post–Victorian fiction, since in novels of this type questions of identity are addressed through rereading historical processes of the past with specific relevance to the present. Hence, adaptations are perceived as inherently critical acts (Bryant 2002: 110), correcting past narratives according to present needs, involving colonial and imperial legacies in particular. Also assuming the status of political acts, refashionings are particularly prone to expressing political alternatives to ones that have proved unsuccessful earlier (Sanders 2006: 97–98). Post-Victorian novels have the temporal continuity of more than two centuries of accumulated knowledge and an even longer history of means employed to express it. In fact, post–Victorian fiction has itself obtained an at least fifty-year history by now.

From the 1960s onwards, in parallel with the gradual loss of the empire, the ensuing devolution of British imperial power, and the movements of social and sexual liberation, questions related to redefining political power and integrating marginalized members of society became central in intellectual discourse. In terms of fictional responses to these changes, including those of post–Victorian literature, this meant an increase in novels resuscitating silenced voices writing back to their oppressors, as well as a number of texts admitting to British colonial follies of the past. In parallel, theories of feminism and postcolonialism were diversified and applied to the interpretation of such fiction. Generally considered as the first post–Victorian novel, Jean Rhys's *Wide Sargasso Sea* (1966) provides a genuine example of such a text, prompting a whole tradition of rewriting canonical Victorian novels and inspiring theoretical debates thereof. A more detailed discussion of this pioneering novel takes place in the next chapter, which is devoted to *Jane Eyre* adaptations. The other trendsetting work in the development of the post–Victorian tradition is John Fowles's *The French Lieutenant's Woman* (1969). This text thematizes most contradictory phenomena of the nineteenth century with inventive metafictional tools, thereby epitomizing the experimental novel of the sixties, not to mention the positive example it provides of the much debated viability of English fiction. The impressive inventory of Fowles's groundbreaking adaptation has since appealed to authors refashioning the same era both in terms of the topics addressed and the novelistic strategies employed. One of my main reasons for not conducting an in-depth analysis of this text is precisely its immense popularity and the ensuing overproduction of critical reactions to it. Consequently, its closer scrutiny would appropriate this book in a similar way as the novel itself cannibalized the whole Victorian age. Rather than providing an overview of this tableau of topics and conventions *The French Lieutenant's Woman* consists of, in the case-study chapters of my work, I aim to examine novelistic chains rewriting canonized Victorian texts and subgenres based on specific nineteenth-century authors or events.

Since the seventies were not very rich in post–Victorian fiction, my survey here focuses on the next wave of such novels, which came in the eighties and has persisted until the present. In this section I rely quite heavily on sociopolitical accounts of cultural events, as I mainly focus on various narratives of national and cultural identity, which are inherently politicized. Besides empowering hitherto neglected members of the empire, an additional need to theorize national identity emerged, which was, as Patricia Waugh points out, based on equaling nineteenth-century conceptualizations of the nation-state with contemporary global British power (Waugh 1995: 161). The political rhetoric of the eighties was dominated by the Thatcher administration's reintroduction of "Victorian values," which echoed in heritage fiction, specifically the genre called *natural history novel*, which was often associated with escapism, nostalgia and isolation. According to Sally Shuttleworth, who provided this generic label, the natural history novel is a subset of retro-Victorian novels, reconceptualizing the nineteenth-century religion-science dichotomy in the face of the conservative government's social Darwinism that was strongly present in the eighties (Shuttleworth 1998: 253–254, 260).[1] The interest post-Victorian fiction expresses for Darwinism seems more complex than just a reaction to specific social policies. Intersecting with ways ontological and epistemological concerns of the postmodern are synthesized, this group of novels addresses the issues of faith and human evolution in diverse ways, out of which the interaction of these questions with actual political and cultural narratives constitutes one aspect only.[2] The withdrawal to the pastoral celebration of rural England that the natural history novel could offer seemed an appropriate respatialization of the national narrative, in the process of coming to terms with territorial losses after the disintegration of the empire (Bényei 2003: 142–145). This strategy of internal colonization recalls nineteenth-century uses of the same approach. In her reading of Emily Brontë's *Wuthering Heights* (1847), Nancy Armstrong argues that the process of internal colonization, of which the Victorian novel can be regarded as part, was happening simultaneously to the formation of the modern British Empire in the middle of the nineteenth century. Drawing on Renato Rosaldo's concept of imperialist nostalgia, she theorizes internal colonization as an idealization of regional cultures that were becoming peripheral or demolished in the modernization process (Armstrong 1992: 446–447). Yet, while Victorian fiction mostly seems to romanticize the English countryside without paying much attention to the empire-building that destroys it, post–Victorian novels tend to appropriate this strongly nostalgic concept by more explicitly making it into imperialism's "other."

In Graham Swift's *Waterland* (1983), though it operates with a broader historical context than the post–Victorian one, the described narratives of identity are juxtaposed. Exclusively set in and centered around England, the novel attempts to construct a national identity for the country, by tracing its rural history and simultaneously deconstructing not only the glorious days of the empire, but also the twentieth-century rhetoric surrounding it, both of which are exposed as escapism from current prob-

3. Post-Victorian Fiction in Its Political and Social Context 81

lems, as the following two extracts of Thomas Crick's distressed narrative illustrate: "[Those in power] had fed the people with dreams of inflated and no longer tenable grandeur, intoxicated them with visions of Empire (which ought to have been clouded for ever by the disgraces of the South African War), thus diverting their minds from matters nearer home" (Swift 1983: 161); and "During a great Depression which returns to haunt us in our own unprosperous times, Empire Day was regularly celebrated with no small enthusiasm (and no reference to brewery fires)" (179).[3] It is notable that the dark side of empire-building so often criticized in the seventies and eighties is, in both quotations, referred to in parentheses only. This may be because of the commonplace nature of the argument, but possibly also to mark the unwillingness of those in power to face the less popular historical events they instigated, which is subverted by these sentence markers.

This simultaneously evasive and subversive strategy is further underlined by the fact that the account of British imperialism is mostly presented as some kind of bedtime story, not to be treated too seriously. What is serious, instead, is an exclusively English space, that of the fens and how man attempts to control the natural interaction of land and water. No coincidence that *Waterland* was so popular in the Netherlands (Todd 1996: 236). The natural history of the Fenland (its name implying this space as a possible country as well, if a national discourse was to require it) obviously overwrites all dominant conceptions of colonialism and the progress of culture, especially that of images of empires:

> There is this thing called progress. But it doesn't progress, it doesn't go anywhere. Because as progress progresses the world can slip away. It's progress if you can stop the world slipping away. My humble model for progress is the reclamation of land. Which is repeatedly, never-endingly retrieving what is lost. A dogged, vigilant business. A dull yet valuable business. A hard, inglorious business. But you shouldn't go mistaking the reclamation of land for the building of empires [Swift 1983: 336].

This passage is ideologically suspect, for it is highly metaphoric, if only the meaning of the term "world" is considered, which can practically be anything from the Fenland to any other external colony of the empire. The same is true for "slipping away," which may refer to land remaining unreclaimed just as well as to the losing of colonies, or for "progress," the meaning of which shifts between development, the passing of time, expansion and conserving existing expansion. In this context, the last sentence, which warns against the confusion of internal and external colonization, may also have a contrary effect. Thus, it may be claimed that though this passage is supposed to function as a counter-narrative to that of imperialism, yet, by the dubious application of the same imperialistic discourse it opposes, this intention is undermined.

A similar disappointment of the initial expectations of a revision and correction of colonial discourse takes place in Peter Carey's *Oscar and Lucinda* (1988).[4] This is also noted by its critics: "Carey shows in *Oscar and Lucinda* that what seems at first to be a broadening of cultural horizons, a re-addressing of the follies of a barbaric colonialism, is in fact the re-appropriation of the colonial impetus in a postcolonial form" (Strongman 2002: 95). The heroine, Lucinda, feels guilty being wealthy at the expense of the colonized: "This money did not belong to them [her parents], or to her either. The money was stolen from the land. The land was stolen from the blacks. She could not have it" (Carey 1997a: 104), yet, even if she has a bad conscience about this injustice, it does not stop her from becoming a gambler and a manufacturer, thus from partaking of the colonization process. The same ambivalence can be observed in the descriptions of the general behavior of the English as colonizers. Mr. Jeffris, directing an expedition that delivers a glass church to the colony, gets entangled in conflicts with the natives leading to murder, which he acknowledges as the dark side of the colonizing mission by statements like "Churches are not carried by choirboys" and "Neither has the Empire been built by angels" (401), yet he maintains his colonizing view of the natives, constructing them as the frightening dark "other":

> He was, himself, fearful of the blacks in the Manning and the Macleay. It was likely he would one day have to confront them himself. He attempted to explain their behaviour to Mrs Burrows [a woman whose husband was murdered by the black], not so much to calm her as to still, through explication, his own anxiety. These blacks, he said, were the most murderous of all, having been dispossessed of their lands and driven into the dense, tumbled country of the "Falls" [...]. She talked of calling out the army, of a final all-out war against the blacks [143].

All this is framed by the narrative of Oscar's descendant in the 1980s, attempting to reconstruct and understand the nineteenth-century events. In 1988, the novel received the Booker Prize as an acknowledgment of its attempt to adjust national self-perceptions to the legacies of the empire (Strongman 2002: ix). However, this effort of admitting the nation's imperial wrongdoings towards its colonized "other," attempting to define itself in the new context of the eighties, produces an ambivalent result, very much like the Booker Prize itself, which is accorded to authors from the ex-colonies but maintains the language and location of the imperial center. The novel's narrative lead remains with the colonizer throughout the text, not allowing the colonized space for self-expression except for a brief spell. In this section of the novel (Chapter 100), probably narrated by one of the natives, the sentences become shorter and the indigenous narrative perspective seems at once to be innocent and ironic, freshly and subtly illustrating the point of view of peoples about to be colonized:

> The white man came out of the clouds of Mount Darling. Our people had not seen white men before. We thought they were spirits. They came through the tea-trees, dragging their boxes and shouting. The birds set up a chatter. What a noise they all made. Like twenty goannas had come at once to raid their nests. Anyway, it was not nesting time [Carey 1997a: 395].

Although to a lesser degree than in *Waterland*, there are reminiscences of the natural history novel in *Oscar and Lucinda*, except that here the beauties of England are not experienced as a reality, but are presented in contrast to Australia as an imagined reality, by the London-based Oscar, the male protagonist:

> I am homesick for hedges and birds with pretty melody, for the lovely chalky blue sky of England. This colony seems so hard and new, all newly broken ground, much clay and sandstone, but nothing yet to make the soil friable. The birds are bright but raucous. Everything is lacking in gentility and care, and society as a whole (although better dressed than anyone in England could imagine) seems little concerned with the common good, only individual benefit [Carey 1997a: 273].

His lived reality is mostly that of industrialized London, which, compared to the more natural Australia, seems an uninhabitable place for Lucinda, who is based in the colony: "It was soon clear that this great sooty machine was not home at all" (168).

The mission of transporting a glass church to Australia for converting the natives to the imperial religion provides a convincing example of how cultural imperialism worked, and sometimes failed, in the colonizing process. The novel follows this project from beginning to end. Its conception was inspired by the Crystal Palace, the famous glass and iron structure built for the 1851 Great Exhibition, which features in so many other novelistic adaptations as well. In J. G. Farrell's *The Siege of Krishnapur*, both the event and its exhibited objects become the obsession of a character, while in Michel Faber's *The Crimson Petal and the White* (2002), the construction of the exhibition hall influences the building of the Rackham factories. In Carey's novel, it is not just the aesthetics of the Crystal Palace but also the ideology which should be transferred to the colonies. Transporting the church is a long and difficult process, just like the effort the twentieth-century narrator of the text has to make in order to understand the past. As Jay Clayton points out, *Oscar and Lucinda* awakes the Crystal Palace's nineteenth-century haunting presence in the colonial history of Australia, on the level of its nineteenth-century plotline at the same time as its legacy in the 1980s, influencing the identity of its narrator (Clayton 2003: 17). The fate of the glass church and questions arising on both the Victorian and the twentieth-century narrative levels supply an interesting parallel to current readings of the Millennium Dome as a reconstruction of the nineteenth-century Crystal Palace and its accompanying discourses of cultural imperialism and identity formation.

The beginnings of this parallel can be traced back as far as the 1980s, when the dominant cultural discourse managed to intermingle the fields of industry, economy, politics and culture, thus translating aesthetic values into material ones. This translation can best be seen in the official endeavor to interrelate the concepts of heritage and enterprise to serve the Thatcher administration's ideologies of national identity formation. John Corner and Sylvia Harvey explain how this connection of seemingly contradicting terms worked on different levels. Firstly, the idea of nostalgically constructing the nineteenth-century empire as a successful past triggered sensibilities for making the inherited idea of progress into a cultural and industrial enterprise of the present and the future. Secondly, this connection was not only a theoretical image-production, but also an intermingling of terms that implied practical results: the already industrialized promotion of national heritage was gradually integrated in enterprise as a cultural attitude and praxis. This materialized, for example, in an increase of private museums, achieved in the framework of privatization, with changes in their profile from being purely documentary and educational institutions, to becoming leisure-oriented theme parks and fun fairs attracting tourists and money (Corner and Harvey 1991: 45–49). As the authors argue, "In this sense, heritage and enterprise form together a key mythic couplet for preserving hegemonic equilibrium and momentum during a period of major national reorientation" (46).

Unfortunately, this political ideology proved problematic in many respects. Firstly, there was a discrepancy between the theory and practice of the principles advanced. In his essay "Mrs Thatcher and Victorian Values," Raphael Samuel provides an analysis of the Iron Lady's disregard of or outright attack on substantial Victorian legacies despite her rhetoric promoting the same. The author characterizes Thatcher's application of

"Victorian Values" as "double-coded, a programme for the future disguised as a narrative of the past" (Samuel 1999: 343).[5] Secondly, as Corner and Harvey maintain, this attempt at homogenizing the narratives of various interest groups took place at a time when national narratives were influenced by many factors, from the loss of the empire and the devolution of power to a greater diversity of ethnicity and class, all constituting a threat to the envisioned image of a consensually shared national identity. Marginalized groups who were theoretically included in the common narrative as owners of the "nation's values" actually experienced losses and exclusion (Corner and Harvey 1991: 61–73). Catherine Hall and Sonya Rose give a detailed account of the racial and ethnic dimensions of this exclusion that caused the postcolonial crisis in British intellectual discourse (Hall and Rose 2006: 8–22), and Robert Hewison reflects on how the implementation of Thatcherite cultural policies debarred lower classes from sharing cultural narratives with the middle-upper ones (Hewison 1991: 162–177). Hewison argues that, similarly to dominant narratives of the nineteenth-century (the most likely choice of ideological model for this era), Thatcherite policies were based on serving and preserving the assets of the ruling elite (175). He exemplifies this with the process of privatizing museums and integrating them in free-market economy, which caused the destruction and restructuring of many, entailing the loss of jobs, not to mention the rise of entrance fees, making culture an often unaffordable commodity for a considerable percentage of the population (162–173).

Examples of post–Victorian fiction contextualizing the Crystal Palace seem to be doing so from this background of inequalities and duplicity of communication, mainly emphatic of the issue of class. In Alasdair Gray's *Poor Things*, the female narrator compares the male narrator's diary to pompous Victorian narratives that covered up for less desirable empirical realities, including the exhibition space, in a simile: "To me this book stinks as the interior of a poor woman's crinoline must have stunk after a cheap weekend railway excursion to the Crystal Palace" (Gray 2002: 275). This image is fictionalized into the actual experience of the protagonist of Claire Boylan's *Emma Brown*. Emma travels to London by train, a journey on which she spends most of her money. When in London, she quickly becomes the victim of thieves and has to earn her living by begging. Her attire, which has become sweaty and sticks to her, hinders her in this activity, as it is too good for a homeless woman. She becomes feverish, faints in a church and is finally transferred to the workhouse infirmary.

On her way to London she conversed with a poor Irishman about the Great Exhibition:

> He had told her he meant to make his fortune at an exhibition of all the world's wealth and industry, which was to be displayed in a glasshouse. When she asked who would be so foolish as to place treasures in a house of glass to which every thief would have access, he answered that it was the scheme of a foreign gentleman married to a rich little woman who wore her diamonds on her head [Boylan 2004: 173–174].

This fear of stealing is echoed by middle–upper-class critics labeling the exhibition as "bivouac of all the vagabonds in London" and "one of the greatest humbugs, the greatest frauds, the greatest absurdities ever known" (215). An additional anxiety voiced by the same people relates to foreigners. The location of the exhibition that is to house industry in the green, aristocratic Belgravia is seen as an intrusion into national honor (214), and the display of products from all over the empire is understood as a venture internationalizing the country too obsessed with "its own nationhood" (216).

Thus the emblematic structure housing all the exhibits is an empty signifier, which has various qualities attached to it, as the heroine's enthusiasm in Carey's novel also shows: "The Crystal Palace, that building she admired more than any other, was nothing but a fancy of a kind, and there were ideas like this, the philosophical equivalent of great cathedrals of steel and glass, which were her passion" (Carey 1997a: 219–220). Inspired by the Crystal Palace, Lucinda imagines and creates her glass church. Oscar admires the object: "He understood that it was the gross material most nearly like the soul, or spirit (or how he would wish the soul or spirit to be), that it was free of imperfection, of dust, rust, that it was an avenue for glory" (317), and calls it a "kennel for God's angels" (318). The church is evaluated differently at its destination: "a miracle, a spider web, a broken thing, a tragedy, a dream like something constructed for George III and then assaulted in a fit of rage" (420). The Crystal Palace has indeed affected many artists and architects ever since its construction, triggering a series of similar projects from the nineteenth century onwards. The Glaswegian Kibble Palace constitutes one such example, whose glass and iron configuration was adapted for buildings of various functions, from botanic gardens and sports centers to railway stations. Another creation that shows some similarities with the interior of the Crystal Palace is the GUM in Moscow, which was erected in 1893 and opened as a department store in 1953, anticipating today's shopping malls with similar designs.

The movie *Oscar and Lucinda*, a Hollywood blockbuster featuring Ralph Fiennes and Cate Blanchett, came out in 1997 and provides a convincing case in point of how earlier political and cultural narratives were maintained in the 1990s. The film adaptation concentrates mainly on the mission of transporting the glass church to Australia, and accordingly the relevant sections of the novel are transferred into the script. The whole process of its construction is dominated by the aesthetic experience, leaving the economic and social value, and future cultural context of this object largely neglected, despite warnings to the contrary: "It is this which makes this church impossible [...]. The Australian sun will scorch your congregation as though they were in hell itself" (Carey 1997a: 360); "It will be hot [...] as hot as hell. The congregation will fry inside [...]. They will curse you. They will curse God's name" (362). The journey of the church is full of risks, including transportation difficulties due to its fragility, the fact that it almost falls prey to the gambling addiction of the protagonists, not to mention the warfare and lives it costs on the way. The natives are curiously omitted from the film adaptation, just as they are from the narrative, but for a brief fight scene and as threats to the arriving glass church. The actual and symbolic failure of this mission takes place after the arrival of the church to its destination when Oscar admits the prize paid for it:

> He begged God forgive him for the murder of the blacks which he, through his vanity, had brought about.
> He begged God forgive him for the death of Mr Stratton.
> He begged God forgive him for the murder of Mr Jeffris.
> He begged God forgive him for the seduction of Mrs Chadwick.
> He begged God forgive him for his complacency, his pride, his wilful ignorance. But even as he prayed he felt himself polluted almost beyond redemption [431].

So, at the end of the nineties, political anxieties still seem to circle around social and postcolonial aspects of national identity, which had surfaced again in the eighties rhetoric. There may be various reasons for this apparent conservation and continuation of the rhetoric of earlier years. They can be searched for in the general truth that cultural innovation takes place in sub- or counter-cultures, that is, political opposition, rather than as a result of official cultural policies (Worpole 2001: 246). Or, examined from an ideological background, the narrative of liberal thinking promoting cultural studies is based on similarly teleological tenets as the neoconservative one it counters (Clayton 2003: 23). This means that neoconservativism reads the present compared to Victorian times as a linear narrative of decline, narrating the nineteenth century as an age of bliss, whereas liberal endorsers of the past take the Victorian age to be the beginning of scholarly conceptualizations of culture through which the present can be interpreted. In the end they overlap since, "[d]espite their opposed agendas, both end up relying on similar conceptions of the historian's task, which they see as that of producing a continuous, unified account of how the present has emerged from the past" (ibid.).

For the commemoration of the turn of the twenty-first century, a new event was planned: Britain's millennium project. This idea was originally proposed by John Major's conservative government and, contrary to all expectations, Tony Blair adopted the project, converting its focus from the celebration of British private enterprise to symbolize "New Britain." The Millennium Festival is read in parallel to the Great Exhibition, even more so since the architect Richard Rogers made it clear that Joseph Paxton's nineteenth-century creation served as his model. Critics Ken Worpole and Ronald R. Thomas regard the two ventures as political and cultural disasters, for their lack of internationalism as well as for the lack of clearly defined social aims or messages that the monuments of the respective occasions were to convey, proving the claim that cultural programs in Britain were created without accompanying cultural policies (Worpole 2001: 243–244, Ronald R. Thomas 2002: 31). The focus of both enterprises was to sell national identity, though in different terms. While the nineteenth-century Crystal Palace in London could still stand for the center of empire both in spatial and temporal terms, the Millennium Dome in Greenwich only represented time, of which the nation was still master (Ronald R. Thomas 2002: 18–19),[6] and therefore history emerged as the main commodity to sell (Clayton 2003: 11). However, instead of the nineteenth-century ideology of integration, ideas of British devolution were paired with the Millennium Celebrations (Ronald R. Thomas 2002: 27), and the emphasis was less on a display of commodities to assist in defining the nation than on experiencing diverse identities through spectacle, pleasure and leisure, backed up by high-tech products (30). This was part of the process of changing the profiles of museums from purely documentary and educational institutions into theme parks attracting tourists and money. There also seems to be dissimilarity in the location of the buildings: whereas the Crystal Palace was put into the aristocratic green area of London, the Millennium Dome was an urban structure created in the outskirts near the estuary where commercial exchange takes place. Despite their differences, the two monuments are read together as moments of cultural crisis.

3. Post-Victorian Fiction in Its Political and Social Context 89

These changes in the focal points of exhibitions from the eighties to the millennium highlight how twentieth-century heritage industry transforms into twenty-first-century edutainment, since the growth of heritage centers and the sale of nineteenth-century relics have by now become mainstream examples of commodification. A non–post–Victorian but topically relevant and trendsetting fictional example anticipating this transformation is Julian Barnes's *England, England* (1998). This novel satirizes the heritage industry by showing how a business venture of gathering all the national sights and entertainments onto the Isle of Wight leads to neglecting the mainland, which becomes derelict and dangerous. Such a dystopian turn of events unmasks the political narratives of the eighties and nineties that attempted to define national identity based on the appropriation of Victorian discourses of the country's assumed values:

> You — we — England — my client — is — are — a nation of great age, great history, great accumulated wisdom. Social and cultural history — stacks of it, reams of it — eminently marketable, never more so than in the current climate. Shakespeare, Queen Victoria, Industrial Revolution, gardening, that sort of thing. *We are already what others may hope to become.* This isn't self-pity, this is the strength of our position, our glory, our product placement. We are the new pioneers. We must sell our past to other nations as their future! [39–40].

This text proves to be a strong critique of the cultural policy of the eighties and the nineties, as its frequent referencing in critical analyses of the same era shows. With explicit connections to the Millennium Celebrations, the novel is summoned as a warning that the project creators may have taken into consideration, when working on the historical potential of the Millennium Dome (Clayton 2003: 11), as well as a text prognosticating the economic failure of the celebrations (Parrinder 2006: 409). There seems to have been a crisis not only economically, but also on the level of ideas, hilariously narrated in another post–Victorian novelistic example, D. M. Thomas's *Charlotte* (2000), where the person responsible for new ideas in the interior construction of the "giant pin-cushion in Greenwich" invents "a brain-shaped sort of punchbag, in the Body Zone, which would move about and speak jokes in the staccato style of our friend Ben Elton" (D. M. Thomas 2000: 84). This person later suffers a nervous breakdown from a complete lack of ideas, when he has to create something for the Faith Zone.

Claiming that New Labour has continued the cultural rhetoric and policy introduced by the Thatcher administration through maintaining the gap between cultural theory and policy, critics perceive the dome in equally ironic terms: "The Dome is fashioned as a great emblem of what we might call postnational space, the nation as cybermemory of itself. It seemed to be offered as a palimpsestic recollection of the empire upon which the sun never set, of the Great Exhibition, of the Big Ben clock tower, of the prime meridian of the earth, and the place by which the world still sets its clocks" (Ronald R. Thomas 2002: 31). Just as there were of the Crystal Palace, there have been replications of the grand project of the Millennium Dome as well. The planning of the Wales Millennium Centre in Cardiff started in 1996, and the building complex was opened by the Queen in November 2004. The funding of these places was closely related to the cultural policies of incumbent governments. Sections of the Crystal Palace and the Kibble Palace reconstructions were financed from (and the Millennium Dome was also supported by) the National and Heritage Lottery Funds. The example of the Kibble Palace, whose reconstruction planning started in 1990 when Glasgow became the cultural capital of Europe, and which was finished in 2006, proves how the cultural policy of the eighties—making museums part of enterprise culture by the establishment of heritage centers and the introduction of regulations aiming at the conservation of national heritage — has carried on into the new millennium.

The danger of filling exhibition spaces with ideologically determined images and spectacles instead of objects and monuments has already been pointed out in relation to the eighties and appears to equally hold for the nineties and the present. Tangible historical material has been changed into intangible images and storytellings, which echoes Baudrillard's concept of simulation, prognosticating the difficulty of distinguishing between the original and the copy, or the real and the imagined (Baudrillard 1981). The past can be manipulated in a similar way according to predominant ideological interests, which results in the erasure of unwanted individual cultural memories. One example of such an ongoing erasure seems to be the fate of workhouses. As Simon Dentith argues, the fact that workhouses have been transformed into heritage objects or welfare flats for rent "with parking for residents only," slowly diminishes the symbolic legacy their historiography conveys. He proposes to reinsert the workhouse into its historical landscape, striving to free it from neoliberal ideological appropriations that moralize the poor as a model for their own projects (Dentith 2007).

To return to fiction, the readings most likely to provide new interpretive perspectives are those that concentrate on individual narratives and their recovery from, and attempt to process, cultural traumas. According to Clayton, in *Oscar and Lucinda* such effaced memories can be recovered by examining the two protagonists' cultural contexts and their attitude to the glass object to be transported. The author describes how the Crystal Palace, representing London's imperial power in official narratives, meant for Lucinda a number of things from her adoration of engineering instead of high art, through her willpower, to her preferences and desires not fitting for the proper female behavior of the age. These were understood by Oscar, who was motivated by his passion for her, and advanced the idea of transporting the wrong church to the wrong person in the wrong place. The traumatic narratives of their experience of being misfits read on many levels as restorations of effaced cultural memories (Clayton 2003: 18–19). Of course, the reinstatement of such accounts is always power dependent and therefore very complex. Using a more recent novel as her example, Kate Mitchell explains the still ongoing struggles for memory narratives in Australian memory politics. One of the problems she addresses is audience, which also applies to *Oscar and Lucinda*, namely, that if a story is transferred through white consciousness, there is a danger of omitting and thus forgetting aboriginal voices, which seems to be a recurring problem when constructing common narratives of Australian national identity (Mitchell 2010a: 279).

The previously mentioned Chapter 100 of *Oscar and Lucinda* (the only place where natives are accorded narrative space), titled "Glass Cuts," constitutes a novelistic example of providing alternative perspectives on the same object, the glass church inspired by the Crystal Palace. The aesthetic and spiritual qualities of glass highly praised by Lucinda and Oscar are reflected on differently on the receiving end, and remain entirely unnoticed by the indigenous population of Australia that is supposed to admire it. Instead, they respond to the materiality of the object from a practical point of view:

> You know what they saw? It was glass. Up until that time they had not seen glass. There was glass windows down in Kempsey and Port Macquarie, but these fellows had not been to those places. They saw the glass was sharp. This was the first thing they noticed — that it cuts. Cuts trees. Cuts the skin of the tribes [Carey 1997a: 397].

One of the tribe members cuts himself with glass and dies of the injuries soon after. As a result the pieces of glass, originally intended to construct a space for the religious communion with the whites' god, are accorded a rather different fate: "That glass was kept a long time by the elders of the Kumbaingiri, but it was not kept with the sacred things. It was kept somewhere else, where it would not be found" (398).

Such a complexity of stories illustrates variation in cultural memory accounts, as well as the potential and responsibility post–Victorian fiction has in rewriting Victorian events. This diversity of possible responses to history resonates with the term "refraction" in the collection of essays titled *Refracting the Canon in Contemporary British Literature and Film* (2004), which is devoted to interpreting such refashionings. The editors define the term as follows: "We have applied the visual metaphor to literature and film in order to designate a double process involving the ways in which a text exploits and integrates both the *reflections* of a previous text *and* the new light shed on the original work by its rewriting" (7, first emphasis added). Mark Llewellyn uses the same term when referring to the haunting presence of the Victorian past as a "refracted moment of historical fiction" and argues that by researching into the nineteenth century "we are enacting a specifically nineteenth-century preoccupation with the spectral, s(p)ecular and *reflective* possibilities of the historical *mirror*, whether intact or '*crack'd*'" (Llewellyn 2010: 24–25, emphasis added). In his *The Victorians in the Rearview Mirror* (2007), Simon Joyce also works with the metaphor of the mirror, comparing the mediatedness of the Victorian past to looking into the rearview mirror while driving. He underlines "the inevitable *distortion* that accompanies any *mirror* image, whether we see it as resulting from the effects of political ideology, deliberate misreading, exaggeration, or the understandable simplification of a complex past" (Joyce 2007: 4, emphasis added).

The Crystal Palace in its fragile materiality seems a particularly appropriate cultural icon to prompt the reconstruction of various and even contradictory modes in which history corresponds to the present. Similarly to post–Victorian studies, efforts are also made in Victorian studies to deconstruct dominant narratives of the Great Exhibition and the Crystal Palace. The editors of *Victorian Prism: Refractions of the Crystal Palace* (2007) also capitalize on the metaphorical qualities of glass. The main aim of their contribution to Victorian studies is to reexamine the "transparency" (Buzard, Childers and Gillooly 2007: 1) accorded to the cultural memory of this object by revising narratives that "[s]et this ephemeral Exhibition and the removable Crystal Palace in historical stone, *framing* them as distortion-free *windows* upon the past." (5, emphasis added). The title of this collection is likewise saturated with words referential of glass and its diverse effects: "prism" and "refraction" signal many layers and numerous possible views of the same object, emphasizing not their collection into a unified account but their dispersion into many different ones. In her introduction to *Victorian Glassworlds: Glass Culture and the Imagination 1830–1880* (2008), titled "The Poetics of Transparency," Isobel Armstrong establishes a whole discourse of nineteenth-century glass culture, by concentrating on the production as well as the reception of glass, which provides a complex framework of "glassworlds," including social, political, material and aesthetic factors (Armstrong 2008: 1–16). The author calls attention to the problem of mediatedness that glass entails, leading to the reconsideration of the concept of transparency:

> The transparency of glass becomes a third term — something between you and the world. It makes itself *known* as a constitutive element of experience that organizes work on the world as medium and barrier. The transparent medium relates self and other. It grants primacy to the self's perception and to its freedom. The transparent barrier obstructs self and other. It opposes the self as object and reveals it as unfree or subject to limit [90].

This perception of transparency leads her to a similar conclusion as the editors of *Victorian Prism: Refractions of the Crystal Palace*: Armstrong argues that the raised awareness of the mediatedness of experience brings with it anxieties and the unmasking of contradictions, which offers the possibility for change (Armstrong 2008: 361–362). As it emerges from these approaches, contemporary cultural studies concentrating on both the Victorian and the post–Victorian phenomenon define the dissection of cultural material as a crucial methodological tenet whereby historical as well as present narratives are reviewed, thus enriching Victorian as well as post–Victorian studies.

Island Fiction: Caryl Phillips's Cambridge *(1991) and Matthew Kneale's* English Passengers *(2000)*

It clearly surfaces from the previous section that currently the prevalent focus of narratives of identity concerns Britain's colonial legacies and postimperial status. This translates into sensibilities to British colonial vices voiced in post–Victorian fiction, perhaps best denoted by the subgeneric category *island fiction*, which I intend to utilize for the novels in the following analysis. The prototype for this category is Daniel Defoe's *Robinson Crusoe* (1719), characterized from a postcolonial perspective with a specific focus on English expansionism as "a work whose protagonist is the founder of a new world, which he rules and reclaims for Christianity and England" (Said 1994: 70); and this character is, of course, male. In travel narratives of the nineteenth century a similar connection can be observed between the successful management of the colonies and racist conceptualizations of national identity (Gikandi 1996: 192). In the post-Victorian agenda, the strategies of eighteenth-century discovery and nineteenth-century travel narratives are both employed for the description of journeys of ownership within the empire, to assist in recontextualizing postcolonial and postimperial identities. These ventures, based on hope and ignorance, are usually exposed as untenable journeys from one isolation into another and turn into nightmarish failures and clashes with other peoples instead, reinforcing disorientation and detachment. Such plots point towards a specific way of redefining identities, and confirm that adaptations are particularly well suited to provide alternatives for problematic political positions, as also argued by Sanders (Sanders 2006: 98).

Kathleen J. Renk describes how historical discoveries romanticizing new territories as tabula rasa over which imperial control can be claimed are transformed into the colonizing ideology of the nineteenth century. These narratives impose monolithic views on colonized areas—"[t]he ideal, bourgeois family, the political family (the motherland and her children), the notion of England as a garden paradise synonymous with heaven, and the shrines of enlightenment that transmitted English ideology" (Renk 1999: 19)—taming the newly acquired untamed land into an ordered English garden (33). In her *In Praise of New Travellers: Reading Caribbean Migrant Women Writers* (2001), Isabel Hoving also identifies the ethnocentrism in the Western theory of travel and appropriates this discourse to construct identities of ex-colonized writers. As it seems, the trope of travel provides a fruitful tool to (re)interpret (post)colonial and (post)imperial relations, since it engages motion, process and change, involving the simultaneous narrativization of geographical, psychological, social and political spaces. Simon Gikandi identifies the trope of travel as a crucial means of "generat[ing] narratives that are acutely concerned with self-realization in the spaces of the other" (Gikandi 1996: 8), and later extends it into "a mechanism of cultural critique and self-reflexivity" (92). Both definitions bear relevance to my argument, since the formation of identity and its placement into a wider discursive context receive attention in novels employing this trope. As Gikandi explains, in nineteenth-century travel writing, a journey to the other end of the empire was a necessity for the understanding of the meaning of Englishness. These travel narratives were addressed to domestic audiences, therefore they had to prove that the only existing, but nonviable, alternatives to Victorian civilization and progress were "barbarism abroad and decay at home" (117).

What Gikandi considers the main reason for travel in Victorian times, namely, that it was motivated by the crisis and anxieties of changing temporal and geographical boundaries at home (103), resurfaces in today's post–Victorian fiction in travels into the history of empire, inscribing its future in the text together with present-day anxieties similar to those of the Victorians. One of these problems is the loss of the empire and the experience of Britain's, and especially England's, political and economic isolation in the European Union and the European Economic Community. This has enhanced the production of novels emphasizing insularity[7] as a form of existential anxiety of loss of home and history in the face of the reality of the current historical situation, as the following comparison of Matthew Kneale's *English Passengers* (2000) with Julian Barnes's *England, England* (1998) proves. Barnes's novel is not a post–Victorian text, but its status as a seminal work, in the tradition of which later critiques were written of the eighties' and nineties' political redefinition of English national identity footed in Victorian tenets, legitimizes its use as a basis of comparison. Springing from its postimperial status, Britain's isolation proves not only difficult in a European context, but also in a postcolonial one, as argued by scholars pointing out that metropolitan Britain has for a long time been imagined as part of but still separate from the British Empire, portrayed "as an 'island nation' mostly untroubled by its imperial project" (Hall and Rose 2006: 20–21). The ensuing experiences of (mis)-conceptions of home and self are shown through Caryl Phillips's *Cambridge* (1991). The third area of political conflicts consists of the ongoing devolution of power, eventually leading to the unmasking of what Susan Bassnett calls one of the most misleading British myths, the idea of a single island whose island people form a collective against the rest of the world, an idea that has long served as a convenient cover-up for internal difficulties (Bassnett 2001: 500). The novelistic illustration of this aspect is presented in the detailed analysis of *The Eyre Affair* in the last chapter. Insularity and isolation emerge as common characteristics of the mentioned anxieties addressed in the post–Victorian novels whose analysis is to follow, all of which feature interinsular travels and interactions, hence the categorization *island fiction*.

Written in the tradition of Barnes's seminal *England, England*, debunking Englishness, the characters of Kneale's *English Passengers* are on the lookout for a new home to replace England. Both titles denote the strong national referentiality of the novels, the former doubling the place, the latter indicating travel from it. Curiously, these journeys do not lead to another mainland but to another island, with the respective aims of building another England on the Isle of Wight to serve tourists' stereotypical knowledge of the country, and to discover the Garden of Eden in addition to carrying out some trade transactions in Tasmania led by a captain from the Isle of Man. The imperial practice of transporting criminals to the colonies in order to keep England morally clean becomes unmasked by the initiators of such an exchange who turn into criminals themselves: the heads of the business venture in *England, England* thrive in corruption that accompanies the heritage industry, and the dubious crew of *English Passengers* engages in a range of crimes from smuggling to murder. Colonial functions are also reversed in both novels: being full of convicts, sick and demoralized people, the Old England, that is, the original home of the colonizers of the Barnes text, begins to look like its colonies in the nineteenth century, whereas the Isle of Wight, suggestively echoing the idea of tabula rasa when pronounced, features as an Atlantis-like new England. However, soon corruption thrives on this island as well, revealing a dystopian society, possibly without a monarch, since the royal family may also just be a Madame Tussaud's imitation, owned and governed by a multinational company. Hence, the Barnes text reads as a clever debunking of the idea of national memory and identity (Bényei 2008: 24), which holds for *English Passengers* as well.

Similarly to Barnes's entrepreneurs, Kneale's seafarer opportunists also assist in destroying their supposed paradise in Tasmania, by partaking in ethnic cleansing and attempting to fulfill the usual nineteenth-century colonial mission. "The novel is based on the need to find religious, moral and scientific justification for the Atlantic slave trade, colonization and the wholesale slaughter of millions of natives in the 'new world'" ("Novel Approach to the Roots of Racism" 2001). What motivates the legitimization of their enterprise is the "epistemological context of the evolutionary theory" (Letissier 2010: 87), which marks the crisis of knowledge and faith in the mid–nineteenth century. However, this venture fails on many levels, yielding contrary results to the ones the ship's crew has expected. For example, the scientist figure, Dr. Thomas Potter, treats the aboriginals as mere objects of a case study. Later, he himself becomes a curiosity exhibit, demonstrating the colonizers' loss of their power position. This way Potter's racist project to prove the superiority of the English is exposed, just like the similarly amateurish theory of his antagonist, the Rev. Geoffrey Wilson, advancing that the Garden of Eden actually exists and is located in Tasmania. Both accounts are narrated in a self-important, respectively quasi-scientific and quasi-religious language, making the two characters ridiculous. The escalation in rendering these extreme versions of nineteenth-century eugenics and Christian fanaticism is in accordance with these characters' distance from their own country: "As the ship moves farther from British waters, the perspective of its passengers seems to shrink, as if in losing sight of their homeland, they lose all capacity for reason" (Friedman "Humor, Horror in the Voyage of Sincerity" 2000). If geographical dislocation from home increases the production of British theories of cultural difference which are irrational, then the identities formulated and actions initiated on their basis must necessarily misuse colonial power.

Disillusioned by the negative turn of events, the failed mission returns home. The reverend does not confront the irony and vanity of his quest, namely, that before their arrival "Tasmania might indeed have been that Garden of Eden" he was seeking. "Yet when he finds it, he fails to recognise it; and irony of ironies, he and his companions become the very serpent who caused man to be banished" ("Novel Approach to the Roots of Racism" 2001). The aboriginals reject the idea of Eden and its assumed creator, God, on an ideological basis, since these are part of the colonizing mission they try to combat. Peevay's mother thinks Eden is a person, and in Peevay's explanation the place sounds more like a garden of disenchantment and the creator as a vicious ruler: "Eden Garden was made by white men's God long ago, to put two white men inside, till he got hateful and made them eat special fruit and go away" (Kneale 2000: 324–325). Rejecting this definition in terms of her own concept of time, the mother pragmatically addresses the reverend: "But this cannot be. You say God made Eden Garden long ago? Well, everybody knows God never came here till you white men brought him in your boats" (325). Experiencing the failure of his pursuit, Wilson gives up his earlier aim to find paradise in Tasmania, which, considering what actually happens in the place, "seems a sick joke" ("Looking for Eden" 2000: 107). Instead, he starts constructing an alternative ideal, this time at the point of their departure: "Was Eden here, in England, all along? Is this the answer? Has all of this great venture merely been some kind of grand test? *But then why didst thou send me all that way?*" (Kneale 2000: 426). This zealous search for an ideal immediately becomes a farce in the next paragraph, as Wilson continues his musings:

"Lord my Father who art in heaven, at least couldst thou not ease this hunger that I feel? Surely that is not so much to ask? I have such a strong longing for apples, and see them often in my dreams. Even the miracle of an *onion* would be greatly welcome, or perhaps a raw potato" (ibid.).

The scientist's failure and fate are more dramatic, as he does not survive the journey. Once he starts interacting with the indigenous population, Potter also modifies his perception of aboriginals and updates his journal of racist theories. First he advances a very clear scheme of racial hierarchies in order to prove the superiority of the Anglo-Saxons: "This=of greatest importance. Here=potent evidence that separate races *cannot* and *will not intermix* (...). Weaker nations (e.g., black, Indian, Oriental, Norman etc., etc.) will be swept away. New era will begin. May occur *imminently*" (205). This grows into a tract he titles "The Destiny of Nations," in which he constructs the "Black Type" as an uncivilized savage destined to die out and therefore pitiable. Once he senses the danger he faces from the Tasmanian natives, he rewrites this entry into a long, vehement justification for their extinction, where the dominant moment is fear rather than pity: "Do not underestimate the savage, for though he lacks any faculty of reasoned thought, he is possessed of a brutish cunning" (406). After many battles, he finally becomes victim to the indigenous peoples. As a complete mockery of his racist ideas, his physical remains are exhibited for other theorists to speculate on under the following label:

> UNKNOWN MALE PRESUMED TASMANIAN ABORIGINE
> POSSIBLE VICTIM OF HUMAN SACRIFICE [454].

Such reversal of positions in parallel with cultural dislocation has various implications. For instance, the questioning of the existence of an original home island may raise the anxiety that today's Britain is already a replica only, an anxiety emphasized by Barnes and especially relevant in the framework of the flourishing heritage industry, analyzed earlier. The fear of a nonexistent original, making everything we perceive a mere copy, reverberates with Baudrillard's concept of simulation, which is especially applicable to the theme parks of the heritage enterprise of the eighties and the nineties:

> Disneyland is presented as imaginary in order to make us believe that the rest is real, whereas all of Los Angeles and the America that surrounds it are no longer real, but belong to the hyperreal order and to the order of simulation. It is no longer a question of a false representation of reality (ideology) but of concealing the fact that the real is no longer real, and thus of saving the reality principle [Baudrillard 1994].

This depiction of Disneyland in its relation to the U.S. is also true for England, England compared to England, in Barnes's text, and the Garden of Eden projected onto either Tasmania or England, in Kneale's novel. Theorized on the basis of Baudrillard's concept introduced above as "a perfect copy of a history that never existed" (Hewison 1991: 174), such an image-making of possible homes and their (hi)stories radically destabilizes fixed national and cultural identities. In the ventures depicted in the fictional worlds of these two novels, characters strive for a new start in an imaginary home, an "England" which does not exist and, once constructed, turns out to be utterly dysfunctional. An enterprise similar to these fictional ones actually took place in real life as well. As part of the Dubai project of rebuilding the earth in the Persian Gulf, two Irish businessmen bought the island reproduced in the shape of Ireland, where they set to rebuild the "original" island of Ireland. Just like the short-lived Millennium Dome, this investment proved equally to be temporary: the company managing the project went bankrupt at the end of 2009, the owner of the Ireland property committed suicide, the man who bought Britain has been serving seven years in jail for bouncing checks, and, not able to withstand the forces of nature, the island complex is sinking (Spencer "The World Is Sinking: Dubai Islands 'Falling into the Sea'" 2011). This phenomenon has been epitomized as the possible fate of the earth as well, as the following title shows: "'The World' Islands in Dubai Sinking, Does It Signal Earth's Future?" (Sinha 2011).

In addition to this anxiety about physical dislocation, the other concern raised by the reversal of authority positions with the locals of Tasmania in *English Passengers* is that of developing new political and cultural identities. Western societies' imperialistic behavior towards island cultures in the nineteenth century may in the long run be reversed, as the fictional accounts of the British Isles, and especially England, exchanging positions with its ex-colonies, both in geographic and political terms, indicate. Such reversals of power have become especially threatening in the framework of ongoing devolution within Britain and the country's increasing isolation from the surrounding political and cultural contexts. This fear comes across convincingly from the narrative tension produced by the juxtaposition of multifarious voices in Kneale's text. The tragic rapes and murders on the island are mainly related by the young aboriginal Peevay and the opportunistic projects happening on the ship are accounted for by their initiators: Captain Kewley's repeated attempts to close the best deal of his life, the Rev. Geoffrey Wilson's zeal to prove that the Garden of Eden does exist and Dr. Thomas Potter's aim to confirm his racist theories by pseudo-scientific research yield a comic mix. As critics also claim, *English Passengers* is at the same time "horrifying as it is funny" (Friedman "Humor, Horror in the Voyage of Sincerity" 2000), making the stories within the text often feel like separate novels "because one stream of its action is essentially foreordained and tragic, the other unpredictable and comic" (Hochschild 2000: 26); and they meet only towards the end of the novel, when the reversal of powers and actual cultural dislocation also take place. Georges Letissier, who reads this novel within the framework of trauma studies, considers it to oscillate between parody and fictionalized testimony. In his interpretation, Kneale's technique of employing multiple narrative voices is the only way to represent genocide, as in the case of such events it is impossible to acquire testimonies: "Through the extermination of the aboriginals, Kneale grapples with extreme historical situations, of the Holocaust type, setting a challenge to discursive representation" (Letissier 2010: 92). Similarly to the tension of conflicting narrative voices, acts of naming and renaming also indicate the opposition of cultures and cultural anxieties. Both Peevay and his mother, Walyeric, were modeled on and named after Tasmanian aboriginals who protected their home against the British in the first half of the nineteenth century. During the invasion, both were given English names, the former renamed Cromwell and the latter Mary. This recontextualization not only deprived them of their singularity (Letissier 2010: 93), but also foreshadowed their behavior and tragic fate. This means that with the powerful act of renaming, the colonizers inserted the existence as well as the extinction of the aborigines into their narratives.

Both Renk and Hoving, introduced above, focus their analyses of travel narratives and displacement on Caribbean writers. As postcolonial criticism maintains, in order to write about their home space and create the conceptual category of Caribbean literature, local authors had to leave the West Indies, many of them settling in Britain (Su 2005: 54).[8] Similarly, the English may have to do the same, that is, leave their country for another island, in order to create their own identity again. This way, as it is also the case in post–Victorian island fiction, all participants can experience what scholars regard as long ago due: "both the utopian and the dystopian sides of imperial relations" (Kaplan 2006: 192). The range of these relations is well illustrated in Caryl Phillips's *Cambridge*, a novel addressing personal and cultural displacement, by activating both imperial travel accounts and slave narratives. The main narrative space is given to an Englishwoman,

Emily Cartwright, who makes a journey to her father's plantations in the West Indies. During her sea voyage, she learns and records new nautical expressions in a similar fashion to characters in *English Passengers*, and keeps this scientific interest once she arrives at her destination to also record local terms, concepts and events. Thus we learn about the narratives of the empire concerning local races, creolization and various social and cultural processes. Her initial imperial perspective — making statements like, "This first part of my journey was over and I was breaking the last remaining link with a past that I understood. From this moment I would be entering a dark tropical unknown" (Phillips 1991: 22) — gradually changes into realizing the great variety in local existences, from the Obeah woman Christiania, through the black slave Cambridge speaking perfect English, to her servant, the Creole Stella. She develops a sensibility to some of them and understands their loss of identity, "the rootlessness of these people who have been torn from their native soil and thrust into the busy commerce of our civilized world. It is much to be doubted that they will ever reclaim a true sense of self. The evidence before my eyes suggests that such a process will unfold only after the passage of many decades, perhaps many centuries" (70–71).

In parallel to this, her own sense of place becomes unstable as she travels around the island. Again starting out from an imperial perspective, utilizing the terminology of travel narratives, she confirms that sugar industry is inefficient, so "[s]oon the English must abandon this seeming paradise" (86). England, identified as her home, is later perceived in more questionable terms, as she thinks of her status in it from afar just before going to sleep: "And to dream of what? England, of course. And a life sacrificed to the prejudices which despise my sex. Of loneliness. Of romance and adventure. Of freedom" (113). The referent of the last sentences may meanwhile have shifted to the West Indies, as right after waking up she realizes that she has adjusted and taken a liking to local circumstances, so she begins to reconcile herself to the idea of remaining there. She becomes infatuated with a local person, Mr. Brown, gives birth to a dead child, and contracts tropical fever, but, contrary to other nineteenth-century characters, she survives all these. By the end of her stay, she acquires a different identity concerning both herself and her location, as it emerges from her reply to the question of her English doctor:

> "And when will you be returning to our country?"
> "Our country?"
> "England, of course."

England. Emily smiled to herself. The doctor delivered the phrase as though this England was a dependable garment that one simply slipped into or out of according to one's whim. Did he not understand that people grow and change? Did he not understand that one day a discovery might be made that this country-garb is no longer of a correct measure? And what then? [177].

The black servant Cambridge similarly experiences various adjustments to his identity that are also determined by his location. As a child he is taken away from his parents and transported from his home, Guinea, to England first. His vision of his white capturers counters the imperial narrative constructing the black as savages: "I wondered constantly if these men of no colour, with their loose hair and decayed teeth, were not truly intent upon cooking and eating us, for they seemed overly fond of flesh" (135). This perception of the white as greedy and corrupt human flesh merchants equates cannibalism with slave trading for profit. As in other postcolonial post–Victorian novels, the issue of naming also emerges in the case of this text, in particular concerning the marginalized figure of the black slave: the Guinean Olumide is christened Thomas on the boat to England, where he also learns English. His religious spiritual leader in London makes him into a Christian person named David Henderson, and that act changes his self-perception too: "Truly I was now an Englishman, albeit a little smudgy of complexion! Africa spoke to me only of a history I had cast aside" (147). Then he marries a white Christian woman, Anna, and they start traveling around England as missionaries with this new identity, campaigning for abolition. His wife and newborn baby die in childbirth, so he leaves for a mission to Guinea on his own with an inheritance he gets from his benefactors. However, as his money is stolen on the boat and he is made into a slave again, he has to readjust his identity once more:

> That I, a virtual Englishman, was to be treated as base African cargo, caused me such hurtful pain as I was barely able to endure. To lose my dear wife, fair England and now liberty in such rapid succession! ... yet another passage of loss. The horrors of this second illegal journey I have chosen to forget, although this unnatural and painful murdering of the memory has caused me distress at least as great as that suffered whilst enduring the voyage [156].

Compared to the examined narratives of heritage culture, in the case of which the dominant ideologies annihilated unwanted (hi)stories, this act of David Henderson murdering his own memory gives an interesting twist to the effacement of cultural memories. Extending this concept, here it seems that the acquisition of a new self-identity provokes similar reactions on an individual level. David Henderson is finally bought by his present owner; he is renamed Cambridge and remarries, this time to the black woman, Christiania, feared for her obeah powers.

It seems, then, that in this novel the attitude of both characters is determined by their location: Emily and her antislavery approach in England become imperialistic in the Caribbean, as long as she is dominated by her fears of her new surroundings and rather identifies with her far-off home; once she immerses in the life on the colony, she cannot fully relate to her previous home any more. Cambridge becomes an abolitionist missionary in England but rids himself of his African identity; while back in the Caribbean, he is closer to the civilizing operation of the English and looks down upon Africans. As critics also note, "In Caryl Phillips's work, people are rarely home" (Kurnick "Middle Passages" 1993). Hence, the post–Victorian rethinking of imperial relations is a process of destabilizing personal, national and cultural identities, in order to construct them anew in different terms. These different terms could emerge through the urge to form new identities, which are complex, individual, multiple and relational. Following the footsteps of Butler, Levinas and Bhabha, in her *Reclaiming Difference: Caribbean Women Rewrite Postcolonialism* (2005), Carine M. Mardorossian challenges categorical definitions of identity. The author adds a third phase to the perceived history of postcolonial literature: the sixties' anticolonial national narratives were followed by texts of delegitimation, exposing the concept of the nation as a Western construction, and at present, as she suggests, rewritings engage in transforming identity from a fixed root into a fluid and multiple category. The reason for the necessity of such a transformation is that differences of all kind have by now become a marketable category, so they are used for purposes of appropriation and commodification. This way heterogeneity becomes a narrative that supports the dominant ideology or subject. Therefore, instead of static categories depicting difference, she suggests dynamic ones that underline relations, thus the "other" becomes something to which one is not opposed but related, and difference is not a concept but a process. She claims that readings conscious of these transformations can be produced by activating contemporary relational paradigms, focusing on the global interconnectedness in the mappings of identity, instead of fixed variables such as gender, race or cultural difference. In this context, the term "relation" seems an adequate replacement of the term "identity." This change creates a new theoretical framework of transgenerational, transracial, translinguistic and translocal analytical territory, with the help of which the postcolonial approach itself can be reinterpreted as well. (Mardorossian 2005: 1–9). Indeed, as the above analyses demonstrate, the protagonists of the discussed post–Victorian novels exist in relation to various national and cultural narratives. Similarly, the reading of these fictional texts together with other cultural narratives makes a critic undergo the same integrative process. This relationality theory proves a productive tool for reading accounts of displaced characters in post–Victorian fiction, and my interpretations of such figures in the following chapters align with this view.

In the present argument, the category of the translocal is especially relevant, as by its application the conception of place, in particular the characters' home, can be revised into a more fluid variable. Contextualizing the concept of home in the discussion of the trope of travel within the theoretical framework of the translocal, the reading of the travel-home contrast could be changed into an understanding of travel *as* home. If this happens, dislocation becomes the norm and not the exception, acquiring the function of a constructive interpretive tool. The trope of travel thus activated in the reading process shows conceptual similarities with the act of (re)writing itself, especially if perceived in Linda Hutcheon's terms. She regards adaptations as traveling stories that undergo "*transculturation* and *indigenisation* across cultures, languages, and history" during their accommodation process, which radically change their implications (Hutcheon 2006: xvi). As it emerges from this explanation as well, as a subtype of historical fiction, post–Victorian novels constitute a category of double displacement, not only a temporal but also a spatial one, adding new perspectives to the understanding of changing narratives of identification.

Emily and Cambridge's accounts in Phillips's text can be read as possible reconstructions of effaced individual cultural memories, similarly to the stories of the outcast protagonists in *Oscar and Lucinda*, discussed earlier. Just as in the case of the accounts of *English Passengers*, critics also underline in this novel that Emily and Cambridge's narratives run in parallel but do not join (Chavanelle "Caryl Phillips's *Cambridge*" 1998, Kuurola 2007: 144). In addition, these accounts, countering reader expectations, are not diametrically opposed either, framed by the colonizer versus colonized dichotomy, but unravel in their own complexity, exhibiting a more complicated web of sympathies (Kurnick "Middle Passages" 1993), as shown above in the illustrations of the ambiguity of the two characters' attitudes. Even if both accounts are produced by marginalized characters, Cambridge's status as an oppressed black slave does not prompt his identification with Emily's feminist pleas but keeps him in the role of the dominant male in his own marriage (Kuurola 2007: 142). Though the ending of the novel is saturated by losses and deaths, as results of mishaps and misunderstandings caused by communication difficulties, critics look beyond the pessimistic solution and rather see the effort of mediation as a possibly productive means of raising awareness of present frictions by calling attention to the disjunctive nature of past cultural memories (Kurnick "Middle Passages" 1993, Kuurola 2007: 144). The choice of title may be a good example of this. Even if the bulk of the narrative is given to Emily, the representative of the dominant culture, Cambridge's short account has a similarly powerful effect, which is further emphasized by the title's exclusive focus on him. Besides, as Chavanelle notes, the extension of the semantic field of Cambridge denoting a prominent English center for learning to naming a black slave in the West Indies also endows him with the authority of the center (Chavanelle "Caryl Phillips's *Cambridge*" 1998), to which I would add that, in the same sense, Cambridge also provides a site of symbolic education for the reader concerning imperial legacies.

On the basis of this section's readings of *English Passengers* and *Cambridge*, the following definition of *island fiction* emerges: novels belonging to this category have in common the trope of travel, from one island (usually the British one) to another (mostly an ex-colony), involving controversial adventures connected to the colonial experience, offering the possibility to face British colonial follies as well as to create new narratives of identification in postimperial Britain. Hence, the novelistic category of *island fiction* serves the purpose of an additional reading tool for elaborating these possibilities.

Apart from the post–Victorian novels discussed so far, island fiction could incorporate other contemporary texts in English as well. J. M. Coetzee's *Foe* (1986), a postmodern rewrite of *Robinson Crusoe* with postcolonial and feminist foci, provides one such example, the cunning title of which implies a paradoxical relationship to the author, the plot and the main character of the earlier text. The novel mainly concentrates on its characters' life after Susan Barton, the heroine, arrives on the island of "Cruso" and the tongueless Friday. Jeanette Winterson offers another such instance in her comic refashioning of the Bible, *Boating for Beginners* (1985), which focuses on preparations prior to leaving on Noah's Ark to survive the approaching flood, adopting the form of a utopistic romance and a dystopia of capitalism at the same time. These texts reverberate with similar novels in the post–Victorian context, which not only emphasize the exchange between the travelers and the colonized but a wider range of island-based activities, serving as additional means to imagine various new relations. Viewed in a wider context, these novels could also contribute to redefining how "Western postmodern poetics of travel are connected to the construction of the shifting, mobile identity of (post)modernity" (Hoving 2001: 16), providing new interrelations of self and home in today's postcolonial and postimperial context.

4

Jane Eyre Tailor-Made: A Case Study of the *Jane Eyre, Wide Sargasso Sea, Charlotte* Adaptive Chain of Novels[1]

> *"The experience of employing a plot, even though it was the invention of some other writer, had liberated her imagination; and, from that time forward, all her novels were her own work."*— Peter Ackroyd, *Chatterton* (1987)

The fact that Charlotte Brontë's *Jane Eyre* (1847) has, ever since its publication, maintained the status of a cult text in the English literary canon is confirmed, not only by its continuous republication, the ongoing critical interest and the filmic interpretations it has generated, but also by the large number of novelistic adaptations born from this text. In this chapter, I devote close attention to two of these rewritings, Jean Rhys's *Wide Sargasso Sea* (1966) and D. M. Thomas's *Charlotte* (2000). In terms of post–Victorian fiction, *Wide Sargasso Sea* is mostly regarded as the first canonized revision of the Victorian novel, and it is usually read in the critical framework of the eighties as a significant feminist and postcolonial addition to the literary canon. Due to its long creation process it conforms to both the modernist and the postmodernist literary conventions, employed in depicting a solely nineteenth-century plot, mostly functioning as a prequel to the original text, *Jane Eyre*. *Charlotte* also appears a particularly relevant work in several respects. Firstly, it provides a creative and critical context for the nineties, anticipating changes in the twenty-first-century production and reception of post–Victorian fiction. Secondly, through its double plot and references to both earlier novels, it revises *Jane Eyre* as well as *Wide Sargasso Sea*, thus creating an adaptive chain of literary texts and assuming a synthetic function across three centuries. In what follows, I closely read the two adapted texts, in particular the newest and least well known one, *Charlotte*, together with critical analyses of all three novels. Since *Jane Eyre* and *Wide Sargasso Sea* have received ample scholarly attention, the employed critical material here does not include related classics of literary criticism. It rather consists of recent analyses that indicate possibly new directions of thought and have not (yet) been canonized. Moreover, I also read post–Victorian novelistic revisions of *Jane Eyre* as items of literary criticism, not only because they critically engage with their Victorian source text, but also because their revelations often precede those of scholarly works.

I begin the subsequent comparison by examining circumstances and anxieties of authorship, looking at how reception has unintentionally or purposefully blurred the notions of author, narrator, character, and the reader functions in and of the three novels. The investigation involves the survey of the respective literary scenes, for which I utilize the framework of celebrity culture and its effects on the market, analyzed in Chapter 2, outlining how the critical perception of authors has changed in the last two centuries. After that, I analyze various narratives of identification in the three texts, including self, national, and cultural-identities, on the basis of their theorization in Chapter 3. My critical perspective for tracing aspects of identification, such as female *Bildung* and trauma, sexuality, slavery and the concept of home, integrates feminist, postcolonial and postimperial discourses. In addition to applying critical material, I closely read the two twentieth-century adaptations in terms of their characters' relationship to place and cultural objects. Linda Hutcheon raises a methodological constraint concerning the application of the case-study model, namely, that such a comparison of texts necessarily prioritizes an original or a source text (Hutcheon 2006: xiii). Since I examine how adaptive trends have changed historically, my analysis is conducted chronologically. Therefore, its starting point is a source text. Yet, three factors all aim to complement the possible shortcomings of conducting a case study. Firstly, rewriting happens on a large scale not only concerning plots but also topoi; secondly, variations of the original novel materialize on many levels often including more than one source text; and thirdly, readers cannot necessarily reconstruct the initial order of the publication of the texts in question.

"Reader, I Married Him": Authors (Narrators), Readers, Criticism and the Market

Charlotte Brontë's critical evaluation has changed from that of a minor popular novelist not present in the Great Tradition to that of a major canonical figure of Victorian fiction (Langland 2005: 395). In her *The Brontë Myth* (2002), Lucasta Miller traces the author's reception history as a cult figure from the nineteenth century to the present. The critic claims that Elisabeth Gaskell's famous biography *The Life of Charlotte Brontë* (1857) established Brontë as a victimized Victorian woman perfected by human suffering, which changed into her modernist perception of a sexually frustrated, thus masochistic and neurotic, Victorian spinster, to branch off into various postmodern conceptualizations of her, ranging from one extreme to the other: she is both idealized as an icon of artistic creativity and female courage, and demythologized and further pathologized as an aggressive author corrupting real-life portraits in a wicked manner.[2] Miller also underlines how consciously Charlotte Brontë aimed at becoming popular (Miller 2002: 19) and speculates on the Victorian author's role in creating her own public figure (40). She considers Brontë a chameleon character, as far as the author's relations to the literary scene are concerned, providing a contradictory example of her communications about *Jane Eyre*: to G. H. Lewes she presented the pleasing of the market as her major aim, whereas to Gaskell she communicated that she would never write for money (44). The scholar's assumption of these two points of view as opposites seems to rest on some kind of moral preconception romanticizing the authorial genius, the acclaim of which necessarily lacks financial compensation. However, in the case of contemporary writers like J. K. Rowling or Jasper Fforde, the satisfaction of readerly desires is accompanied by earning a high income, not to mention that the market has become a complex web of relationships, entailing more aspects than just representing the audience's affective recognition. It seems, then, that both authorship and the market require theorization anew if utilized for interpretive purposes, in order to adjust to their changing meaning in today's literary and cultural context.

Subtitled *An Autobiography*, in *Jane Eyre*, Brontë's authorial persona has always been closely associated with her first-person narrator: "Jane is Charlotte Brontë speaking of the mesmerizing experience of writing *Jane Eyre*" (Oates 2006: 198). Examined through various theoretical approaches, researchers follow how Jane slowly acquires authority through her narrative, constructing her in this empowerment at all levels of the creative process: as a narrator growing into an author-in-print, as a writer and even as a reader. From an autoethnographic perspective,[3] Jane's ability to distinguish between the space of the story and the discursive space in her narration provides her the "authority to author her own life" (Buzard 2005: 199). Therefore, the novel is read as a process of authentication by the end of which Jane gains "the freedom to speak-in-print" (207). Interpreting the novel from a Marxist-psychoanalytic framework, a similar claim is made. Jane is perceived to be in economic competition with other, more privileged characters for narrative authority, which she wins by converting her dreams of self-authorship into text (Ronald R. Thomas 2006: 49–54). Both critiques draw attention to the textualization of authorship, and they not only understand this conventionally as a struggle against social inequalities but, just like Miller, they also connect it to authorial self-perception and self-advertisement. This approach indicates that the examination of authorship related to writers' behavior on the literary market merits increasing awareness in readings of nineteenth-century texts.

Centering Jane as a reader and writer, recent analyses also survey how readership establishes a connection with the text and how this relationship is encoded in the narrative itself, determining the authority of the narrator, author and text alike. Reading *Jane Eyre* with J. Hillis Miller's deconstructive classic, "The Critic as Host," Valentine Cunningham identifies women readers in the novel to be parasitical upon the texts of their male host, meaning that Jane and other female characters decipher and thereby exercise their authority on male writing, such as the inscription of Lowood School or the holy script. Due to Rochester's blindness, by the end of the story Jane reads and writes all his texts, so she even takes over authorship and readership from him (Cunningham 1994: 343). Of course, she also submits to male texts, especially the Bible, which gets the final word in the novel (356), but all this is put to paper in Jane's own writing — in India ink, which provides her identity as a writer.[4] Thus the ending is left open and she can carry on writing (359), which she does in many of the adaptations of the novel. As Joyce Carol Oates points out, Jane's authority and autonomy (which she reads in parallel to the author's, as quoted above) receive special emphasis if the sentence "Reader, I married him" is read closely. The agent in this account is neither Rochester nor the two of them together but Jane alone (Oates 2006: 202). The same utterance can also be read as an emblematic sentence of the collaborative motivation of narrator and reader, showing that reader-experience is troped from within the text (Garrett 1996: 23). Stewart Garrett regards both the reader *in* the novel as well as the reader *of* the novel as an audience, and while Cunningham and Oates survey the growing power of the former, he examines the influence of the latter. The author's argument is based on Walter J. Ong's observation that since the nineteenth century was still a transition phase from oral to print culture, such a direct address of the audience could signal the nervousness of the author about the role of the reader, warning the narratees that they are not listeners but individual, invisible readers. Accordingly, Garrett analyzes *Jane Eyre* as a novel where reading is a topos, underlining the importance of including the reader as character with the accorded role to assist in constructing the text (Garrett 1996: 14).

This reader function becomes more explicit in some later adaptations. For example, in Clare Boylan's *Emma Brown*, the reader invocation is used as a call for collaborative authorship. At the end of the novel Emma, the protagonist, and her young companion visit a grave which Emma claims to be that of the man of her destiny. However, the secret is never unveiled; instead the text finishes with the following number of questions waiting to be answered: "What epithet is etched into that timeless granite? Whose grave do I keep fresh with my tears? I pull back the brambles that in summer will be bright with roses. The clever little creature [her young companion] makes laborious sense of the graven symbols (for I have been teaching her to read) and deciphers the name of my designated mate. Which name? Reader, you must decide" (Boylan 2004: 437). The above critical analyses and the novelistic example show how the reader(function) is gaining increasing importance in contemporary literary criticism. The appearance of the reader in the literary text is not only due to historical reasons, that is, the switch from oral to print culture, but also to the acknowledgment of the crucial role of readership in partaking in the production as well as the reception of fiction. Through its textualization, the function of the reader has clearly emerged in the writing process already, which ensures its continuity, from collaborating in creating and deciphering novels, to participating in the celebrity culture that is responsible for the cult status of authors and their work. This way the reception side of reader contribution to the literary market is amended by the production side, possibly paving the way for readdressing existing conceptualizations of reader functions in critical thought.

The importance of acquiring the reader's sympathies in the context of the competition of narrative voices for authority, authenticity and autonomy also appeared in other fictional responses to the nineteenth century, already in the early nineties, preceding critical reactions. One such example is Alasdair Gray's *Poor Things* (1992). Chronologically, the character-narration starts with Archibald's diary, from which one version of Bella's story emerges: she is created as a medical experiment, by putting a child's brain into the body of a young woman who has committed suicide. She develops quickly, starts traveling, uses and abuses men both sexually and financially, meets her ex-husband, General Blessington, who tells her about her past and, finally, becomes a doctor and a promoter of female suffrage. The happy ending of Archibald's diary, giving an account of their marriage and the grounding of a family and career, echoes the closing chapter of *Jane Eyre*, emphasized by the remark "Reader, she married me and I have little more to tell" (Gray 2002: 240). Here the function of addressing the reader and requiring her/his involvement and sympathy resembles that of the Victorian novel. Bella/Victoria revises this ending, and asks for the reader's sympathy challenging her/his credulity (again in a very *Jane Eyre*-like fashion): "You, dear reader, have now two accounts to choose between and there can be no doubt which is more probable" (272). She claims that she is a plain woman (just like Jane Eyre), that the crack in her head is not because of any kind of medical experiment but because she was hit too heavily by her father for being impertinent, and that the reason she got married to Archibald was that Godwin Baxter (the would-be performer of the experiment, with whom she was in love) did not want her children. This chronologically and historically later account completely shatters the credibility of the first narrator. What complicates the matter further is that these character-narratives are enclosed in the framework of the author's introductory and closing remarks. In the introduction, the implied author brings the dichotomies of fact and fiction as well as originality and copyright into play, desperately trying to both prove and disprove the authenticity of the documents on which the novel is allegedly based. Additionally, he makes value judgments of the ensuing character-narratives, which become even more explicit in his conclusion. His basic argument is that Archie's version is correct and Bella/Victoria is a liar, and that he has placed the woman's narrative after the man's to demonstrate this.

Still, even if her narrative is enclosed between the two men's, Bella/Victoria's account appears to overwrite both her husband's boring diary and the implied author's similarly tedious notes; she successfully demonstrates how she develops an identity by slowly acquiring a voice. The depiction of her development can be paralleled to that of Jane: while Jane has a wiser, retrospective and an inexperienced, younger narrative self catching up, Bella/Victoria has the body of a woman and the brain of a child, the difference of which needs to be evened out — if the male version of her story is trusted — or a split identity, also present in her double name, connected to her sexual identity and marriage (judged as madness by some characters in the text, thus relating her to *Jane Eyre*'s Bertha), requiring a cure — if her version is accepted. Whichever version is privileged as plausible, a common trait between the two heroines seems to be their acquisition of a self and a narrative-identity through the process of writing. To sum up, the competition for narrative authenticity, autonomy and thus authority appears to settle in Bella/Victoria's favor. Though his text takes up the bulk of the novel, Archibald gets dismissed, both by his wife and by the author, for the reason of lacking the imagination and talent to write well. The author-editor figure of Alasdair Gray, who comes second after Archibald in terms of independent textual contribution to the novel,[5] attacks Bella/Victoria's narrative, nevertheless only on content points, and seems to be rather jealous of her authority as a writer: "I print the letter by the lady who calls herself 'Victoria' McCandless as an epilogue to the book. Michael would prefer it as an introduction, but if read before the main text it will prejudice readers against that. If read afterward we easily see it is the letter of a disturbed woman who wants to hide the truth about her start in life. Furthermore, no book needs two introductions and I am writing this one" (xiii). This comment proves the implied author figure's authorial anxiety of the autonomy of one of his characters (having an exceptional talent at storytelling), which can loosely be associated with anxieties concerning one's literary predecessors, an example of which is presented in what follows.

In the process of adapting *Jane Eyre*, Jean Rhys felt a need to legitimize the project and accordingly voiced her concerns about moral issues, the anxiety of authorship and distortions to the original text. In her correspondence, she pays homage to and criticizes Charlotte Brontë at the same time, conscious of falling prey to similar accusations by her own critics: "I have a very great and deep admiration for the Brontë sisters (Though Charlotte did preachify sometimes). (And all the rest). And often boring perhaps. (Me too!)" (Wyndham and Melly 1984: 271). More than once she expresses her dissatisfaction with the character of Bertha/Antoinette in the Victorian novel, whose missing story she then supplies, struggling to separate her own venture from that of Brontë's: "I think there are several Antoinettes and Mr Rochesters. Indeed I am sure. Mine is *not* Miss

Brontë's, though much suggested by *Jane Eyre*" (263). This statement is followed by a description of differences between the characters in the two texts to prove the distinction. At the same time, Rhys is afraid of distancing herself from the original novel, even though she keeps reminding herself of her very good reason to do so: "I realise what I lose by cutting loose from Jane Eyre and Mr Rochester — Only too well. (Indeed *can* I?) Names? Dates? But I believe firmly too that there was more than one Antoinette. [...] How then can *I* of all people, say she was wrong? Or that her Bertha is impossible. *Which she is.* Or to get cheap publicity from her (often) splendid book?" (271). This last remark also summons the questions of plagiarism and creativity, and the author's concern that she may embark on the dubious project of making her name by feeding off someone else's intellectual property that has already become a cultural commodity. Rhys's anxiety of authorship confirms that Robert Macfarlane's argument presented earlier, namely that, compared to the primacy of writing in romanticism, rewriting became privileged over writing by the twentieth century, may not be a unanimously accepted claim, and even if it were, it does not necessarily have a direct impact on writerly behavior. The author still fears to interfere with the texts of her cultic literary predecessor without being accused of capitalizing on Brontë, and thus becoming infamous for being the Victorian writer's cheap imitator.

    Critical responses to Rhys's text as a novel written out of Chapter Twenty-Seven of *Jane Eyre*, supplying Bertha's life story (Sanders 2006: 102), position *Wide Sargasso Sea* straightaway as an adaptation. Considering the ensuing proliferation of refashionings of the Victorian novel from the perspective of various characters' untold stories, it also functions as an important initiator of this tradition. The adaptation affects the perception of *Jane Eyre* as well, reinforcing its central status in the canon, on the one hand, and triggering a rethinking of its critical reception, on the other. However, as time has shown, *Wide Sargasso Sea* acquired a valid place on its own in the literary canon. This may be due to various factors, for example, that Rhys supplied a missing storyline which mostly precedes that of the original text, or that she wrote back from the doubly oppressed position of a woman of the colonies, which constituted the main subject area of the then-forming feminist and postcolonial critical schools. Her authorship is mostly reflected on in this context with a focus on the autobiographical references in her texts, probably incited by the correspondences of her subject position and the employed referential theoretical perspectives of interpretation. Rhys's biography is read as one of fractured identities situated between high modernism and postmodernism, West Indian and European authorship and that of woman in the age of the disintegrating empire, which all find expression in her texts (Shaffer 2006: 108); the criticism of Caribbean fiction focuses on the author's outsider status in a European context, which is a struggle that features in her heroines' lives as well (Mardorossian 2005: 5). Accordingly, filtered through these data of Rhys's life, *Wide Sargasso Sea* summons analyses that stress its counter-discursive quality, being a narrative of resistance to dominant discourses (Shaffer 2006: 109–110, Sanders 2006: 106). This critical approach to Rhys's texts has by now become canonized; what seems interesting, however, is that the figure of the author is acquiring a more emphatic position in the process, which is likely to have resulted from the recentralization of authorship.

The evolving title of the novel from such working titles as *The Ghost* or *The First Mrs. Rochester* to *Wide Sargasso Sea* indicates how the author slowly managed to dissociate herself from her Victorian predecessor. If examined in terms of narrative authority, the title *Jane Eyre* serves as a proof of its presence, while *Wide Sargasso Sea* as a proof of its absence. This is also how other scholars analyze the difference between the two titles, claiming that the title of the Rhys text could not have been *Antoinette Cosway* (or, for that matter, *The First Mrs. Rochester*) because, though the heroine narrates the bulk of the text, she is neither in control of her narrative nor of her life as much as Jane is in *Jane Eyre* (Oates 2006: 203). Jane gains her narrative authority by the end of the novel, whereas Antoinette does not; she sees herself as a ghost in the mirror and inflicts her own death (Stoneman 1996: 183–184). Thus, instead of reflecting the privileged perspective of the main character as the Victorian title *Jane Eyre* does, *Wide Sargasso Sea* focuses more on location or space. It is also reminiscent of Virginia Woolf's *The Waves*, which may point toward modernist readings of the novel that are concerned with characters' psychological state. For example, Brian W. Shaffer associates the title *Wide Sargasso Sea* with the inner life of characters, especially since the sea is mainly offstage and the islands feature instead, and the seaweed Sargassum is surrounded by a myth of unknowability just like the psyche. The author deduces that the novel can thus be grouped as a psychological one (Shaffer 2006: 119).

This focus on inner space also materializes in terms of the authorial decision of whether or not to accord a voice to various speakers. Rhys's first important move is that of reversing Jane's priority in the competing narratives of the Victorian novel. Here the English white middle-class woman's perspective is simply omitted, by completely denying her a voice and foregrounding narratives of hybrid identities instead. Opposing the straightforwardness of *Jane Eyre*'s one-narrator concept, in *Wide Sargasso Sea* there are three narrators. Antoinette, Edward Rochester's first wife, gets the most narrative space, as it is her story that Rhys has aimed to correct, while Rochester, complementing her story, remains an unnamed speaker, since his relationship to the heroine seems to matter more than his identity. Unlike Jane's in *Jane Eyre*, Antoinette's child and adult voices are not harmonized, and Rochester does not appear coherent either. This way the immediacy of their experience emerges more strongly. The third narrative instance constitutes a short but curious intermezzo: it begins as a third-person account about Grace Poole's job, then grows into a second-person address of the servant Leah, to finally become Grace's own first-person musings about her situation and the state of Antoinette, all this in one and a half pages (Rhys 1968: 141–142). Perhaps it is due to its brevity that Grace's narrative has been largely neglected by criticism, and as there is no reader invocation in this novel probably her status is the closest to a reader's. I think that her function as (reader-)character-narrator is important since, as the connection between Jane, Antoinette/Bertha and Rochester, she has access to crucial pieces of information which she could keep to herself or use otherwise for manipulative purposes; her position resembles a little that of Nelly Dean's in *Wuthering Heights*. Fictional responses to *Jane Eyre* have realized this, and, although there is no novel yet which focalizes Grace's narrative perspective, she assumes a more pronounced role in *Charlotte* as well as *Adèle*.

Wide Sargasso Sea, then, emerges both as an adaptation, developing from a single response to Brontë's Bertha figure to an independently acknowledged text in the literary canon, and as an icon of in-betweenness, depicting the dislocation of its author, narrator(s) and literary categorization. This last issue, whether to regard the novel as a modernist or a postmodernist text, is worth a brief look, as it may also influence the relevance of various terms used for rewritings of Victorian material. The difficulty of grouping *Wide Sargasso Sea* in a literary historical era emerges from the fact that Rhys started working on her novel quite early; in fact, she finished its first version before 1940, whereas the final product was published in 1966. This divides critical opinion as to whether modernist or postmodernist characteristics dominate in the text (Mardorossian 2005: 73, Shaffer 2006: 106, 112). The dilemma receives a resolution by underlining the work's interim status, claiming that *Wide Sargasso Sea* commemorates the move from the modern towards the postmodern (Shaffer 2006: 106), or that it anticipates postmodern practices (Waugh 1995: 203–204). Rather than engaging in this both aesthetically and chronologically dubious debate, attempting to distinguish between modernist and postmodernist features and determine the beginning of a literary historical era, I would just like to emphasize that Rhys's novel rewrites the nineteenth century in the spirit of *post–Victorian* twentieth-century literary and theoretical movements. The strangely ambivalent opinion that, on the one hand, *Wide Sargasso Sea* started the whole tradition of post–Victorian fiction, on the other hand, it still does not serve as a perfect example of this genre, since it deals not with the Victorian tradition but with gender and ethnic issues instead (Gutleben 2001: 111) raises the question why the social position of women, colonialism and Englishness would not count as part of the Victorian tradition, even if the articulation of these features became more pronounced in the framework of (post)modern counter-discourses only. I think that the term *post–Victorian* becomes especially relevant in this context, since it could provide a means to bridge concerns of grouping *Wide Sargasso Sea* under different literary periods. As argued earlier, read with regard to the integrative nature of the postmodern, *post–Victorian* offers itself as a category to include texts springing from and emerging after Victorian conventions, in the same way Brian McHale defines the relationship between modernism and postmodernism. In the case of the Rhys novel, the best solution is neither to try and squeeze it into either modernism or postmodernism, nor to call it *neo–* or *retro–Victorian*, thereby ignoring its modernist connections, but to group it as a *post–Victorian* novel incorporating Victorian, modernist and postmodernist correspondences alike.

After this short detour concerning the complexities of categorizing *Wide Sargasso Sea*, let us return to the notion of authorship and examine its functioning in the context of the late–twentieth-century adaptation of *Jane Eyre*, D. M. Thomas's *Charlotte*. As mentioned earlier, nineteenth-century authorship is regarded as a site of projection of hopes and anxieties of Victorian society (Deane 2003: xi). This statement also seems to apply in the case of the two post–Victorian writers discussed here, underlining their subversive potential, although in very different ways. While Rhys could be construed as an early agent of hope, anticipating and promoting social changes to be brought about by feminist and postcolonial thinking, D. M. Thomas appears to embody the anxiety part, being constantly accused of plagiarism, distasteful pornography and abuse of historical events in his writing. Standing on the positive side of the sharp division of critical opinion about the author, his biographer, Bran Nicol, outlines the controversial points in Thomas's career. The suspicion of his incorrect use of sources first appeared in connection with his almost Booker Prize-winning *White Hotel* (1981) then provoking a symposium about plagiarism and keeping his readers alert ever since. His pathological approach to sexuality and its vivid, often sadomasochistic portrayals in his writing constitute the other site of critical attack, especially if this erotic strain is juxtaposed with such sensitive historical events as the Holocaust in a contested way (Nicol 2004: 2–4). Thus the authorial anxiety characterizing Rhys's attitude to adapting Brontë becomes transferred onto the readers in the case of Thomas: instead of the author, the readers are the ones who are critically engaged in discussions of invention and plagiarism.

In his defense of Thomas, Nicol raises issues that are important in current critical discourse. Refuting the accusation of misusing sources, the author, on the one hand, constructs plagiarism as a legal category rather than a literary one (Nicol 2004: 6), on the other hand, he argues that postmodern authorship differs from the romantic by legitimizing the literary ventriloquism Thomas engages in (7–11). To support this latter point of allowing writers to mimic their predecessors, Nicol conducts a survey for appropriate terminology to characterize this way of literary composition. He arrives at *intertextuality* and *translation* as the two most adequate terms depicting the author's working method and concluding that "authorship is always a matter of masquerade and collaboration" (11). This discussion well illustrates the originality debate concerning post–Victorian adaptations, evoking critical reactions related to authorship and plagiarism while triggering terminological queries for an accurate designation of both the process of rewriting and the relationship between source texts and their adaptations. In my view, both the questions of plagiarism versus adaptation and the (mis)representation or corruption of historical events underline the importance of ethical concerns, which seem prevalent in discussions of post–Victorian fiction. In contrast to deconstruction, where it was only the textual that mattered, in the case of these two issues, it is the premise of an assumed empirical reality that appears to cause the controversies: in the first one, a subject, the person of the author, fulfills this extra-textual reference (not to mention his reading public), and in the second one, some kind of "true" or "real" version of historical events summons this control function.

What emerges from all this is that D. M. Thomas has gained his celebrity status by shocking his audience. Although he wrote twelve novels, rigorous scholarly attention has been devoted only to *The White Hotel* (Nicol 2004: 2). While the previously discussed two authors feature in most university syllabi, Thomas's works are largely neglected. Nevertheless, by way of the controversies thriving around his 1981 novel, he seems to have entered the domain of popular culture and, as attacks continue mainly through literary journalism, he has maintained this status. The event of becoming an (in)famous public figure was accompanied by an ironic twist in Thomas's private life: he resigned from a job in academia to escape becoming a celebrity, which he nevertheless ended up being. Nicol traces how the author's getaway route directly led into follow-up articles, scandals and eventually into television appearances, despite his great fears of becoming a "media monster" (ibid.). This way, the "meet the author culture," introduced earlier, assumes the curious form of detective journalism and moral accusations in the case of Thomas's career.

As far as *Charlotte* is concerned, Thomas lives up to all the above critical accusations in connection with this novel as well. He plagiarizes *Jane Eyre* at the beginning of the text, which is followed by a detailed account of Jane and Rochester's sexual intercourse with special attention to Jane's worries about the normal functioning of the male member, and in the remainder of the text various sexual perversities are outlined on both plot levels, making specific connections between these and postcolonialism. Unlike in the case of Rhys's fear of producing a cheap imitation of her Victorian predecessor's cult text, there are no similar anxieties voiced by Thomas outside the framework of his novel, while questions of originality, copyright and plagiarism emerge as crucial topics within the novelistic text. One of the two female narrators appropriates the voice of Jane of *Jane Eyre*, but as the novel progresses, she diverges from her original; whereas the other speaker, Miranda, who narrates the twentieth-century plotline, engages in ghostwriting the Victorian novel *Jane Eyre* and relates the whole process of literary ventriloquizing that Thomas was accused of earlier. Accordingly, the text has a double plot, a nineteenth-century one continuing the original story of the Brontë novel, narrated by Jane and authored by Miranda, and Miranda's contemporary narrative in which she, first by mistake then for fun, assumes the name Charlotte Brontë in the West Indies. Male characters have little say in this text; Robert Rochester, Edward's son and Jane's later lover in Martinique, and Miranda's father earn narrative space only at the end of the novel where their letter and diary, respectively, amend the text.

These different accounts are sometimes contradictory, especially concerning issues of authorship and rewriting, which can be read as a metacommentary on the process of adapting a literary classic, fictionalizing what Thomas has experienced in connection with *The White Hotel*, and anticipating what criticism he may receive for *Charlotte*. Miranda confesses in her twentieth-century narrative that she faked an alternative ending of *Jane Eyre* in the name of Charlotte Brontë for her father's sixtieth birthday and created a hoax around how she had acquired the missing manuscript. In her father's diary, this story appears in quite a different light: he is certain that the Victorian writer is the author of the manuscript and the manuscript itself is an authentic piece of writing. He also reports on engaging in a dialogue with his daughter about how she should proceed with the adaptation, addressing the copyright problem, which they decide to disregard, based on the assumption that it must be outdated, as the person the money should be paid to has most likely been dead for a while. Finally, they tackle the issue of plagiarism and its relationship to the supposedly existing original manuscript (a dilemma that reappears in the analysis of Fforde's *The Eyre Affair* as well): "'But that leaves the problem, if I declare Charlotte's part-authorship, everyone's going to think me dotty, and the vultures will come after the manuscript. But if I don't declare it, it's a kind of theft.' 'An innocent theft. And you'll change some of it?' 'Of course; I want to take up where she left off; but also, naturally, make some changes in what she wrote'" (D. M. Thomas 2000: 151). If these exchanges are juxtaposed, what emerges is a playful fraud, discrediting the father as naïve, the daughter as deceptive and, through their dialogue, the concept of the original as implausible or outdated and the whole hassle around copyright and plagiarism as a theatrical farce which no one believes in any more. If one wants to, this can also be read as Thomas's reply to his critics.

By engaging historical and fictional authors as well as their fictional character(-narrator)s in a dialogue, the writer exploits the multiple authorship he constructs, refocusing authorial intention, a concern seemingly legitimate again in today's academia, leading to both fictional and critical reactions to the original (con)text of *Jane Eyre*. For example, Jane's reflection on the situation of female authorship—"I have observed that such histories as this conclude at the matrimonial altar: and it is because we writers are rightly fearful. In particular, every female writer, I believe, is a girl writing painstakingly, in a silent room, in a bleak, silent house, striving with a sense of desperation to be pleasing to her master" (D. M. Thomas 2000: 20)—echoes critical reactions to both Jane's eventually gained authority in the Victorian novel as one that is located in a male drawing room (Tsomondo 2007: 96), as well as Brontë's authorial success as one that is due to her succumbing to conventions of male authorship (Sue Thomas 2007: 105). However, both Jane and Brontë's situation appear a bit more complex than these critics perceive. Jane is not only subordinated to Rochester because she is a woman, but also due to her social status, so it is no wonder she does not have access to the drawing room: As Nóra Séllei argues, she has a very narrow space from which to communicate, due to the ambivalence of her status as a governess, which means that she is neither a servant nor a mistress owning Thornfield Hall (Séllei 1999: 168–169). In Brontë's case, there was a dominant tradition, the qualities of which she had to adjust to first if she wanted to get published, for example, by assuming a possibly male identity through taking up the pseudonym Currer Bell, and only once her work had reached the audience could she start changing the existing tradition.

The beginning of the above quote from *Charlotte* also merits some attention, as the problem of resolving stories at the point of a happy wedding leads to Jane's dissatisfaction with authors of novels with similar endings: "It is well known that in novels — for example, the novels of Miss Austen — the pen falters just at the point where, perhaps, the most interesting narrative begins: *after* the wedding ceremony. With the consequence that not only are the rituals of the marriage-chamber avoided but the ordinary, humdrum details of the start of a married life" (D. M. Thomas 2000: 17). This becomes more emphatic as the narrative progresses and culminates in her attack of her own author: "No novel, whether a virile, rumbustious concoction by Mr Fielding, an urbane social comedy by Miss Austen or — dare I say it? — a gloomy, muffled romance by one of the Miss Brontës, can be more than a feeble echo of what actually occurs to all of us" (37). These comments picture the Victorian writer and her historical predecessors as weak writers in terms of the realist novel they should have been producing. Though for another reason, a similarly daring twentieth-century reaction to Brontë is produced by Miranda, in her lecture, constituting the author as a murderer of her characters: "But Grace had the saving grace of getting drunk now and then; so allowing the 'madwoman in the attic' to escape for a while — allowing Charlotte, more importantly, to slash men, rip up wedding apparel, and set fire to beds!" (120).[6] Viewed from the perspective of rewriting, D. M. Thomas liberates Jane by allowing her to produce the narrative "*after* the wedding ceremony" that she was missing from most novels, while Brontë's recognition as a romancer and murderer of her characters appears to be confirmed through her fictionalized emplotment of an affair between Jane and Robert Rochester, but only by killing Edward Rochester before, and Jane shortly after, the liaison begins. The above observations on authorial intentions tend to conflate the author, the character(-narrator) and sometimes even her double, all earning the status of an angry young woman.

Such a purposeful mixture of the notions of author, narrator and character appears in the full title of the novel as well. *Charlotte: The Final Journey of Jane Eyre* can be interpreted on many levels. Related to authorial power, even without knowing the plotline, the colon can be understood as a separation between author and title, thus it reads as Charlotte Brontë's sequel to her own novel; if one is acquainted with the story, it can be understood as Miranda ventriloquizing the Victorian author, bringing her novel to an end. On the narrative level, it may be read as Brontë narrating the events of the novel she could not include in the Victorian times or Miranda narrating her life as an impersonation of the historical author. As characters, both Brontë and Miranda could assume the role of Jane for their autobiographical accounts. Christian Gutleben construes the title in the context of market demands, claiming that it may be misleading on purpose. Without an awareness of the plot, the title only provides potential readers with Victorian references, which are further strengthened by the blurb, promising a continuation of the Victorian plotline. The author argues that even the choice of Jane Eyre as a protagonist is suspect of being a commercial move, since Thomas's aims would have been served by any anonymous Victorian figure as well (Gutleben 2001: 182–183). This argument fits in the above paradigm of accusing Thomas with the exploitation of historical material for sensationalist purposes. Even if this is the case, I do not see it as a problem, as increased readership may mean, not just financial gain for the author, but also a prevailing interest in canonized texts and their rewriting, often enhancing the revisitation of historical narratives and the facilitation of long-term social changes.

Similarly to *Jane Eyre*, the reader is also appealed to in *Charlotte*. The nature and function of this plea, however, change as the text progresses. The initial "Reader, I married him" (D. M. Thomas 2000: 7) is lifted straight from the original text and likewise calls for the reader's sympathy and inclusion. Later, the same address emerges as a warning that readerly expectations might be upset by an anticipated change in the narrative: "Reader, you will expect me to draw a veil over the intimacies which transpire between a man and his wife. I am sorry to disappoint and offend you"

(14). This narrative sequence culminates in an outright contrasting of the Victorian story and its refashioning in progress, clarifying the kind of story to follow:

> Reader, this is a very different picture of my marriage from that which you were presented with in what I would call my "romantic" version. *Reality*, however, does not often coincide with *romance*. I will remind you: "When his first-born was put into his arms, he could see that the boy had inherited his own eyes, as they once were — large, brilliant and black...." Well, events did not quite happen like that [44, emphasis added].

The reader-phrase features in the twentieth-century narrative as well, yet its function seems to change in parallel with the altering contents in the process of rewriting. In sentences like "There you have it, dear reader" (109) and "Reader, I told him to piss off" (136) readers assume the role of mere receptors of Miranda's frustrations, whereby the formula, though mimicking some past sense of inclusion, appears void of its original function. The context of the latter remark is that of a marriage offer to Miranda by one of her lovers, which is "outside her scenario" (Sue Thomas 2007: 109), so she refuses, by making the whole situation as well as the original affective content of the sentence ridiculous.

The fact that the famous "Reader, I married him" utterance is reinvigorated in D. M. Thomas's adaptation proves that, in addition to the numerous reactions of critical and readerly dissatisfaction, a disbelief concerning the happy ending of Jane's marriage gets voiced in the realm of fiction as well. Similarly to the above quote from *Charlotte* indicating the realistic turn Jane's story is to take (as italicized), other post–Victorian texts also comment on this major problem constituted by the romance-realism dichotomy in the resolution of *Jane Eyre*, mainly in emotional terms. The characters in Gail Jones's *Sixty Lights* (2004), for example, pass the novel on from generation to generation as a cult text of self-identification and cherish its romantic qualities, even though they are aware of its implausible aspects as well: "In the novel *Jane Eyre* a tree is cleft by lightning. The goddess Nature is so responsive to the movements of lovers that she sends prophesying icons to confirm the progress of their romance. 'I know it's preposterous,' Honoria said. 'But isn't it also wonderful?'" (Jones 2004: 47). Though acknowledging it, the narrator in Michel Faber's *The Crimson Petal and the White* is more critical of *Jane Eyre*: "In terms of sum total of pages she [Sugar, the novel's heroine] seems to have read almost as much as he [William Rackham, Sugar's lover, master and employer] (although some of it, inevitably, is the sort of piffle written for and by her own sex —

novels about timid governesses and so forth)" (Faber 2003: 111). When thinking about the fictional plots she constructs aspiring to become a novelist, Sugar explicitly expresses anger with Brontë's romantic solutions of fortune and marriage, protecting her own text of such a mistake: "Otherwise this novel, conceived as a cry of unappeasable anger, risks becoming one of those 'Reader, I married him' romances she so detests" (246). In sum, in the case of *Sixty Lights* we can see a clear distinction of romance and realism, while in *The Crimson Petal and the White* the romance quality is specifically characterized by the reader invocation analyzed above. The affective feature of addressing the reader in *The Crimson Petal and the White* is put into perspective just like in *Charlotte*, but while the invocation is ridiculed in D. M. Thomas's text, in Faber's novel it gets angrily discarded as some kind of superfluous nuance.

"Who Am I?" "Where Am I?" "Is This Home?": Narratives of Identity

Self-identity presents itself as a central question in all three novels. Its foremost component is the matter of finding one's voice both in the course of growing up and among possible competing narratives. At first sight, both of these processes appear to be easily decipherable in the case of *Jane Eyre*. Jane's account is usually read as a typical Victorian bildungsroman in which the heroine's child narrative catches up with that of her wiser adult self as she writes herself into an authentic character. On her way, she encounters various alternative scripts which she learns to assimilate or discard, and once her status is clarified by her inheritance and marriage, she lawfully enters an integrative position of authority. This reading of the novel as a feminist ur-text[7] has by now undergone a series of revisions. After the integration of feminist criticism with postcolonial, postimperial, Marxist and psychoanalytical readings, Jane's coherent identity has been further refracted, highlighting its creation at the expense of omitting important sites of identification. This process was strongly inspired by Bertha/Antoinette's fictional account, supplied in *Wide Sargasso Sea*, which also incited modifications in the critiques of Jane's self-perception, topicalizing the issues of slavery, racism, (re)patriation, economic dependency and madness. In what follows, postcolonial and postimperial accents are scrutinized in Jane's identification process to see how the Victorian novel has been reread in these current theoretical frameworks, which enhances a better understanding of its two adaptations as well as the critical frameworks themselves.

In line with Sandra M. Gilbert and Susan Gubar's perception of Bertha as Jane's angry double, Valentine Cunningham reads *Jane Eyre* as a narrative proving that marriage in Britain in the nineteenth century is comparable to being enslaved in the East. In this framework, Bertha's Gothic appearances are interpreted as manifestations of post-abolitionist anxieties of the 1840s, questioning the empire's self-enrichment at the expense of its colonies, which in the case of the Brontë novel makes both Rochester's house and Jane's fortune suspect, since these originate in the West Indies. (Cunningham 1994: 351–353). Although Jane defines herself against her potential male partners and their stories, missions and texts, she finally submits to marriage and colonial wealth (359), including the India ink with which she writes her story. Hence, even if in a slightly modified version (she marries a Rochester dependent on her and shares her fortune with her relatives), she accommodates to and bases her adult identity on existing imperial ideologies. Cora Kaplan argues that such ideologies are necessary as a basis for the explanation of differences and inequalities between people, and in the British Empire, after the abolition of slavery in 1833, political, social and economic discrepancies were explained through racism. Like Cunningham, she identifies *Jane Eyre* as a novel representing this post-abolitionist ideological turn in British culture, but with a much stronger emphasis on the complicity of Jane's narrative with creating racist identities: in Brontë's text everything in the plot depends on the empire, which nevertheless gets a poor press, and Jane's narrative functions as a slave-narrative with a slave imagery "conditioned by post-abolitionist racial thinking" (Kaplan 2006: 205–206). The author explains how reading Jane's account as a slave narrative becomes increasingly problematic, considering the novel's solution whereby Jane and Rochester retreat into provincial England escaping (from) the legacies of slavery. From this postcolonial perspective projected upon a post-abolitionist period, Kaplan concludes that today's engagement with *Jane Eyre* can contribute to raising awareness of the metropolis's failure to solve "the Pandora's box of problems let loose after the abolition of slavery," and of the unsuccessful strategy of naïve idealism and escapism that was employed instead (207).

Such an answer of repatriation and restoration in an English landscape to Jane's quest for the right alliance in the right location is also viewed as a definitely negative choice by critics, assessing the novel from the (post)imperial perspective of English history and identity. They claim that she ends up as a social outcast, her marriage to both country and husband constituting an alienated enjoyment (Parrinder 2006: 202–208). Reading *Jane Eyre* together with Carlyle's *Occasional Discourse on the Nigger Question*, David Deirdre not only underlines the implicit imperial discourse present in the novel but also concludes that Jane participates in creating an English national identity by acting as an idealist purifier of Rochester's alliance with another race, whom, though maimed and blinded but cleansed, she finally marries (Deirdre 2005: 91–93). In the case of both arguments, the assumption from an imperial perspective would be that Jane's inheritance, marriage and purifier role established her as a fully accepted member of English society and the British Empire, yet she stays an outsider. Such an interpretation would be an interesting challenge to the common perception of the ending of *Jane Eyre* as a romance one. Despite the fact that Jane comes into the possession of the above assets, alliances and roles enabling her integration, she is not allowed into the social milieu of the Ingrams or into the empire. Consequently, there must be something wrong with both of these environments; this, in turn, makes the ending of the novel into a realistic one.

Still using the framework of national identity but juxtaposed with the self, Jane's narrative appears in a more optimistic light from an autoethnographic point of view, wherein it is regarded as an English national tale, "a quest for a positive national identity that will supplement and transcend other identities but not obliterate them, that will sustain the condition of being other than one thing," with Englishness understood as a restricted heterogeneity "that has to turn aside from engagement with forms of otherness deemed unmanageable or threatening to the integrity of the system of differences constituting the national culture" (Buzard 2005: 197). The utopistic nature of the ending also counts as a disturbing factor in this analysis, yet Jane's pilgrim's progress is seen as one leading from a series of antihomes or homelessness to (an idealized) home, from anticulture towards culture in which she can retain both "a protestant, protofeminist individualism and a condition of intersubjective integration" (200). The solution of Jane's narrative quest is perceived in a similarly productive way by some feminist scholars: "The stories made up independently of Jane's subjectivity and exclusion are, thus, in a cause-effect relationship and have further implications inasmuch as finding a voice means not only controlling her story and life, but also means that constant exclusion can be replaced by inclusion, by belonging somewhere, to someone" (Séllei 2002: 10). Séllei traces Jane's narrative development from her early childhood and points out that her first authorized attempt at relating her story not only makes her realize how storytelling influences one's future, but also how this growth through narrative power enables her to access the secret of her origin (15), which can be read as her first step towards finding her roots and home. It seems, then, that as soon as national identity is separated from postimperial and postcolonial narratives and paired with self-identity formation, it loses its explicitly negative overtones and focuses on the concept of home in more individual terms. Probably, the most fruitful reading of Jane's identification quest emerges from the consideration of current national and cultural discourses as well as accounts of (recuperating) outcasts, similarly to the case of *Oscar and Lucinda*, discussed earlier.

In the text and interpretations of *Wide Sargasso Sea*, feminist, postcolonial and postimperial aspects are already combined. In contrast to Jane's, Antoinette's narrative reads as weak and problematic because her childhood and adulthood accounts intertwine, and she does not acquire authority before she dies at the end of the story. As Stoneman observes, the first analyses constituted Antoinette/Bertha as Jane's "other," who is repressed in terms of rationality, sexuality and race in the context of women's liberation from roles of servitude (Stoneman 1996: 6). This interpretive framework has already been criticized above, in the case of *Jane Eyre*, as far as the understanding of Jane's account as a slave narrative is concerned, and proves similarly controversial for Antoinette's narrative in *Wide Sargasso Sea*, as Benita Parry and Chakravorty Spivak's seminal debate on the subject confirms. Parry's claim that the historically repressed subject and her knowledge reveal themselves if put into a speaker position is refuted by Spivak, who points out that this position functions as a mediated one, since it is constructed according to Western worldviews; therefore, this way of accessing silenced knowledge remains impossible. Not even Christophine, who could be a plausible colonial subject, receives enough narrative power in the novel, because *Wide Sargasso Sea* is written in the interest of a white Creole, in the European tradition, rewriting a canonical English text. Thus, Spivak concludes, instead of challenging the ethos of *Jane Eyre*, *Wide Sargasso Sea* reinforces it (Stoneman, 1996: 185–186, Mardorossian 2005: 61–64). Laura Ciolkowski refines this argument by pointing out racist and sexual reasons behind the sacrificing of the colonial subject, Antoinette, for Jane's feminist individualist career. She claims that the sacrifice of Antoinette as a sexualized "other" is necessitated by the imperial perception of the English as a pure race. In this framework, sexually overproductive subjects not fitting into the patriarchal family traditions due to the biological boundaries of Englishness are criminalized, therefore, Antoinette/Bertha constitutes an unchaste Creole woman who must be controlled by state legislation, as the empire is disinterested in mixing races. Thus *Wide Sargasso Sea* reads as a rewriting of the imperial aspect of *Jane Eyre* in the form of a battle for imperial control (Ciolkowski "Navigating the Wide Sargasso Sea" 1997).

This battle raises a number of issues constituting the contents of Kaplan's "Pandora's box," from people's mental and cultural (mis)conceptions of one another, through frustrated ventures of transforming colonial plantations into English patriarchal homes,[8] to post-abolition slave economy threatening the purity of the English race with contamination. Using the relationality paradigm for identity formation introduced in the previous chapter, Carine M. Mardorossian considers the reason for characters' failing attempts at identification to be in the lack of stable identity categories. The concept of race becomes undermined because its definition depends on characters' shifting relationship to other categories of identity: the often contradictory classification of these categories is based on the individual perspectives from which the figures view one another. Hence Mardorossian's conclusion that *Wide Sargasso Sea* "dramatises the possibility of a mutual and creative 'interculturation' between white and black Creoles, hints at ways in which this interaction could have been propitiously sustained, and foregrounds the reasons why it was stopped" (Mardorossian 2005: 71). John Su arrives at a surprisingly similar conclusion, approaching the topic from a very different angle. He constitutes nostalgia as a dynamic historical concept which comprises a critical tool to examine responses to different crises. This way, nostalgia becomes a symptom of aspects of social dissatisfaction and assumes an ethical dimension: "The ethical value of nostalgia resides in its potential to open up epistemological investigations foreclosed by dominant cultural narratives" (Su 2005: 87). Utilized as a constructive tool, nostalgia aids in the identification of persisting political, social and cultural ailments. Su argues that Antoinette's stubborn nostalgia, her longing for her childhood's would-be relationships and circumstances, serves as a "means for Rhys to explore and ultimately articulate a vision of community prohibited by colonial ideologies of racial difference" (9). The knowledge thus mediated is that her internalization of colonial narratives prevents Antoinette from forming certain relationships, such as a genuine friendship with Tia, and immerse in certain communities, such as that of the natives (89). These two newer lines of critical inquiry modify the classic postcolonial and postimperial paradigm. Mardorossian does this by dissolving identity, a conventional category of reading in this framework, and replacing it by the more diverse category of fluidity, while Su achieves the same by introducing a new interpretive tool, nostalgia, that has so far mostly been used in a conservative context, to be utilized in the discursive space of cultural criticism with a more liberal agenda.[9] These innovations also influence the following close reading of *Wide Sargasso Sea*, where I examine how Antoinette engages in the process of interculturation in various contexts.

Initially, Antoinette tries to accommodate to their new English-Jamaican context: "We ate English food now, beef and mutton, pies and puddings. I was glad to be an English girl but I missed the taste of Christophine's cooking." "So I looked away from her [Myra, one of the new servants] at my favorite picture, *The Miller's Daughter*, a lovely English girl with brown curls and blue eyes and a dress slipping off her shoulders" (Rhys 1968: 19). The cultural object of the painting provides a source of identification for Antoinette. After glancing at it, she attempts to place the people surrounding her in the imaginary context of the picture and envisions "Mr Mason, so sure of himself, so without a doubt English" and her mother "so without a doubt not English, but no white nigger either" (ibid.). The identity of Antoinette's mother is described in the binary negative only, so besides narrating what she is not, it also becomes clear what the dominant discourse is against which she appears a nonentity. Later, Antoinette busies herself with idealizing England as a place of escape where she can more successfully construct her identity: "I will be a different person when I live in England and different things will happen to me ... England, rosy pink in the geography book map" (84), which image, based on an even more abstract visual representation than the painting, is countered by Christophine, who says it may be "cold to freeze your bones and they thief your money"; she even goes as far as doubting its existence altogether: "'England,' said Christophine, who was watching me. 'You think there is such a place?'" (ibid.).

The ambivalence Homi K. Bhabha depicts in describing the relationship between the colonized and the colonizer (Bhabha 1994: 86) can be extended to the geographically displaced character-narrators' perception of each other's territory, illustrated in Antoinette and Rochester's exchange in trying to understand each other's concept of home:

> "Is it true," she [Antoinette] said, "that England is like a dream? Because one of my friends who married an Englishman wrote and told me so. She said this place London is like a cold dark dream sometimes. I want to wake up."

"Well," I [the unnamed Rochester] answered annoyed, "that is precisely how your beautiful island seems to me, quite unreal and like a dream."
"But how can rivers and mountains and the sea be unreal?"
"And how can millions of people, their houses and their streets be unreal?"
"More easily," she said, "much more easily. Yes a big city must be like a dream."
"No, this is unreal and like a dream," I thought [Rhys 1968: 58].

As a consequence of Rhys's revision of *Jane Eyre*, most of *Wide Sargasso Sea*'s plot takes place in the tropical West Indies, foregrounding a colonized female narrative voice. Antoinette's marriage and sexual explorations take place here in her home and not in the English country house where she is later locked up. Nevertheless, England retains its curiously idealistic role in her narrative. Once they arrive there, the place does not provide her a new source of identification, neither does it assume the role of the safe haven of escape the English countryside setting means for Jane and Rochester in the Victorian text. Though admitting her disappointment, Antoinette still keeps the image of the country void of criticism and simply refuses to recognize the place as "England":

> It is, as I always knew, made of cardboard. I have seen it before somewhere, this cardboard world where everything is coloured brown or dark red or yellow that has no light in it. As I walk along the passages I wish I could see what is behind the cardboard. They tell me I am in England but I don't believe them. We lost our way to England. When? Where? I don't remember, but we lost it [144].

As Antoinette cannot find another way but to stick to her dreams, discrepancies between perceived and experienced "England" appear, resulting in an ambiguous image of the country unable to emerge as a stable entity in her narrative, legitimizing its perception as a blank space filled by the hearsay and imagination of Jamaican natives who have never been to the place. The same question reappears in Beryl Bainbridge's *Master Georgie*, a post–Victorian text retelling the Crimean War. When one of the characters, an archaeologist, is asked why he lives away from England, he treats the question similarly: "'What is England?' he retorted. 'Where is England?'" (Bainbridge 1999: 97). From this statement it similarly surfaces that even if "England" exists, its semantic field is uncertain, and if it is treated as a territorial entity, there is no central space against which characters are displaced, thus both the definition and the location of "England" remain open. In V. S. Naipaul's *Guerrillas* (1975), a postcolonial novel using motifs of *Jane Eyre* and *Wuthering Heights* alike, the guerrilla leader, Jimmy, in his dialogue with Roche — the postmodern version of Rochester — denies the country a realistic or practical existence: "'England isn't real' [...]. 'The problems aren't going to be solved there. You know what happens in England. Everybody goes to the demo and the meeting and then they leave you and go home to tea" (Naipaul 1976: 26).[10] From a postcolonial perspective, England as a home does not assist in framing characters' national or cultural identity in these texts.

Finally, Antoinette does not survive her stay in England and dies as a social outcast. Considering the generic consequence of her narrative account, if *Jane Eyre* is read as a bildungsroman, *Wide Sargasso Sea* could be read as an anti- or a negative bildungsroman. In contrast to Jane's progress, Antoinette rather seems to stagnate or even regress according to the generic conventions of the bildungsroman. Also, the Rhys text does not include longer sequences describing the development of any character but concentrates on their identification process as a sequence of repeated attempts changing their behavior depending on the surrounding forces instead. While in Jane's identification process, in *Jane Eyre*, the Gothic elements appear to move her towards gaining narrative authority, in *Wide Sargasso Sea*, the traumatic scenes Antoinette repeatedly faces, for example, her confrontation with Tia, do not heal or assist her in her recuperation but indicate her further disintegration. For instance, in the Victorian text, after Jane has experienced the vision of Bertha in the mirror or has had nightmares, she relates these to Rochester, who encourages her to discard them as unnecessary obstacles in her life. Thus capitalizing on her ignorance and lack of information on her surroundings, Rochester hinders Jane from further, possibly more complex diversions in her identification process. In Rhys's rewriting, Antoinette is deprived of her mirror once they relocate to England, so she does not get a chance to face her other selves this way. Her renaming by her English husband deprives her of her identity even more: "Names matter, like when he wouldn't call me Antoinette, and I saw Antoinette drifting out of the window with her scents, her pretty clothes and her looking-glass. There is no looking-glass here and I don't know what I am like now [...]. Now they have taken everything away. What am I doing in this place and who am I?" (Rhys 1968: 143–144). Losing England, she also loses contact with her own imagined self that she has projected into her new place of residence, and due to her circumstances, she cannot access her old, Caribbean self either.

The event of (re)naming intertwined with (the loss of) identity is very similarly reiterated in another post–Victorian text, Clare Boylan's *Emma Brown*. Just as in *Wide Sargasso Sea*, in this text, allegedly based on a Charlotte Brontë fragment, a young woman's entry into marriage also involves her being re-christened by her husband: "I even forfeited my given name, for Albert declined to call me Isabel or Isa. In his household I was Belle. Belle Chalfont! It was a name for a plump, youngish but settled matron. This was not the reflection my mirror threw back at me" (Boylan 2004: 100). The reverse happens to the protagonist, who is called Mathilda Fitzgibbon by those who surround her. Whenever she comes across a mirror, she keeps asking "Who am I?" in a similarly hopeless, lost and wrecked state as Antoinette does in the Rhys text; however, the outcome appears more constructive, as, slowly leaving her traumatic amnesia behind, she painfully identifies herself as Emma, and thus begins to reconstruct and narrate her story as a member of society with a known origin.

Antoinette's refracted narrative is usually read in terms of resistance. Su, for example, interprets it as a postcolonial revision of Jane's colonial narrative of linearity, progress and consolation, since it lacks all these qualities. He argues that the linear time of the colonial narrative gets distorted by Antoinette's regretful reiteration of past events and experiences, as well as her contrasting the negative present in England with a longing for her past in the West Indies of her youth, which was not undisturbed either. The author concludes that such an alternative temporality, prioritizing past loss over a terrible present, summons an alternative (in this case, postcolonial) interpretation of experience as well (Su 2005: 56–64). Also juxtaposing the aspects of development and linearity, Mardorossian claims that, unlike in *Jane Eyre*, due to the often indistinguishable blending of the experiencing child and the older narrating Antoinette, the convention of the nineteenth-century first-person narrative grows disrupted in *Wide Sargasso Sea*. Since the child narrator is not subordinated to the adult one, this narrator does not develop a transparent central ideological position based on her acquired knowledge, thus the conflicting narrative representations obliterate the "real" or any possibility of reliability, a basic convention of nineteenth-century narratives (Mardorossian 2005: 67–69). These critical associations of narrative inconsistencies and temporality within the respective frameworks of nostalgia and relationality inspire further engagement with the concept of time. Such an engagement appears a fruitful path of future analysis of how the intermingling of the Gothic and the bildungsroman may be determined by trauma and repetition, for example.

The achievement of D. M. Thomas's *Charlotte* is that, juxtaposing the Victorian novel and its first canonized postcolonial rewriting, it utilizes both the narrative of the novel of development of *Jane Eyre* and the negative bildungsroman in *Wide Sargasso Sea*, which return in the narrative voices of Jane and Miranda, respectively. In Thomas's novel, Jane's first-person narrative continues from the first sentence of the last chapter in Charlotte Brontë's text: "Reader, I married him" (Brontë 1999: 397). Her narrative assumes a less authoritative quality, not discarding all disturbing factors in her life but facing and learning from them, though her white middle-class imperial bias mostly stays intact. This is the line of storytelling into which Miranda, ghostwriting Jane's account, seems to channel her more collected self, whereas her other narrative, relating her own life, emerges as a much more disoriented confession, where her adult experiences intermingle with her childhood traumas. The connection between the two accounts becomes clear for the first time when the storyline of Jane's life is followed by Miranda's where she takes responsibility for ghostwriting Brontë. She admits that in the first version of her adaptation, characters stand for her nuclear family members, her mother featuring as Bertha, her father impersonated by Rochester and herself identifying with Jane. Miranda and Jane, the two narrators, are often read together by critics, too, Miranda regarded as a parallel character or even as a re-embodiment of Jane (Gutleben 2002: 16). Miranda's appropriation of Charlotte Brontë's name complicates her identity further, as she also fictionalizes herself as the Victorian author. She even envisions a twentieth-century career for Brontë, very similar to her own: she would have studied English, got a Ph.D., taught at university, "which might have interfered with her creativity,"[11] got married or divorced or been a single mother: "In other words, she'd be a much less interesting person!" (D. M. Thomas 2000: 121). This last comment on the hopelessness and unexciting nature of present times acknowledges opinions of the Victorian age as complex and colorful, in contrast to perceptions that attribute such qualities only to the twentieth century, as well as signaling Miranda's identity crisis for whom an alternative life of a nonconformist creative writer would seem more appealing than her present one, even if it was in the nineteenth century. When she explains to her roommate in Martinique that she has by mistake been identified as Charlotte Brontë instead of Miranda Stevenson, she comments: "Well, I feel I know her better than I know myself — though that's not saying a lot" (77).

In addition to her accidental renaming to Charlotte Brontë, which she passes on to Juan, one of her lovers, Miranda also has other names: her mother used to call her Mandy, while her husband, David, called her Andy to disguise their relationship from his then wife. When her father,

Ben, puts her in the role of her mother, Miranda is called Emma, which was her mother's first name. Besides, she assumes the pen name Jennifer Trefusis, Trefusis being her mother's maiden name. The fact that *Charlotte* functions as an adaptation of both *Jane Eyre* and *Wide Sargasso Sea*,[12] the latter text being "paid graceful tribute to" by Miranda in her conference presentation "as a brilliant exploration of Bertha" (D. M. Thomas 2000: 119), further multiplies the identities she owns and the resulting legacies thereof. Her tasks are to integrate her childhood self and the memory of her dead mother, her role as a lover of the married David, her function as a sexual substitute for her mother trying to please her father, and her writerly self assuming the identity of her mother. The missing mother, often pointed out in readings of the Brontë sisters' texts, seems to feature equally strongly in *Charlotte*: juxtaposing Antoinette's mother, Annette, from *Wide Sargasso Sea* and Jane's mother of the Victorian novel, Emma's assumed madness and early death are both emphasized. The fact that Miranda fictionalizes her mother as Bertha and makes her thus jump off a cliff, and that she steps in for Emma to please Ben imply either that her sympathies lie with patriarchal readings or that she demonstrates how women become victims of patriarchal power. The exciting quality of the novel is exactly that we are offered both possibilities of interpretation, and the two may even work together. Miranda's relationship to her husband can best be compared to that of Jane's with St. John, as the Victorian characters' relationship is usually read as a desexualized one, and Miranda is given a male name, which underlines the complicity or friendship between her and her husband rather than a sexualized bonding. The couple does have children, yet Miranda rather looks for sexual satisfaction elsewhere, and both she and her father seem to look down on David as a weakling and the marriage as a failure. The dead mother has many substitutes among the father's lovers: in the ghostwritten Brontë novel, there is Grace, and in Ben's case, that is a re-enactment of Rochester's story, a possible affair between Miranda's father and the historical author, Jean Rhys, surfaces in addition to numerous other lovers. This is how Rhys's biography, as well as Brontë's, also gets fictionalized.

D. M. Thomas is often criticized for his problematic portrayal of women (Nicol 2004: 12, Sue Thomas 2007: 108). His accomplishment in *Charlotte* is summarized as a "cross generational proliferation of pathologised Bertha Mason figures" (Sue Thomas 2007: 101). Most of these female characters, who, as argued by Sue Thomas, can be read as versions of one figure, suffer ample mental or physical pain or both: Jane wants to commit suicide and dies of tropical fever; Grace loses her son to the pond where Jane attempts her suicide, and later Grace also contracts tropical fever; Emma is depressed and commits suicide; and Miranda is traumatized by her mother's death as well as her father's sexual harassment, in addition to being depressed by her marriage and life in general. These tragic female fates echo some scholars' view on Charlotte Brontë's treatment of her characters, except that the Victorian author is charged with handling most of her male characters in such a negative way. If, however, one surveys the male figures in *Charlotte*, the picture does not look that different either: Rochester falls off his horse and dies very early on in the novel; Miranda's husband gets a nervous breakdown; her father is playing with the idea of committing suicide; and her roommate's boyfriend dies in a plane crash. Although the identity quests are analyzed from the points of view of the main narrators, who are both female, it is visible that the situation of the male characters is just as bad. However, in my view, the emphasis is not on "proliferating pathologies" per se, signaling the author's perversities, but rather on the construction of white middle-class identities (both male and female) as outcasts in a society where they are not marginalized or oppressed. To sum up, what emerges in terms of Miranda's identification process is that she has to account for so many identities that she has acquired through her role playing games and has created through her ghostwriting, some of them quite traumatic, that she cannot develop a coherent self.

Accordingly, *Charlotte* does not show constructive signs of narrative authority and *Bildung*. First, Jane's development is quickly terminated by her death, a prototypical fate still provoking fictional mention in twentieth-century plotlines of post–Victorian fiction: "Those pathetic, semi-arranged marriages involving a shipped-out bride and ending in tropical fever" (Swift 1992: 34). Second, Miranda's disconcerting account rather resembles Antoinette's Gothic finishing of her story. Christian Gutleben and Julian Wolfreys interpret Miranda's narrative as one that shows no development and so denies any kind of faith in progress (Gutleben and Wolfreys 2010: 48). Miranda is pregnant, not knowing whose child she is carrying, but she tells her father it is his, not being quite clear whether she means it literally or metaphorically, and she splits up with her husband, David, who breaks down and refuses to move out of their flat. Her father suggests that she find a Grace Poole to mind David in the attic room he is finally accorded. This turn of events appears to reverse the first marriage attempt in the Victorian text with Bertha still alive, making David, the husband, a prisoner and Miranda, the wife, the master of the house. This interweaving of fiction with the empirical reality of Miranda's existence admittedly results from her complete dissatisfaction with her life as it is:

> I'd gone to university, got into sex and drugs, failed my first exams, had my first breakdown, then went to a third-rate poly where I scraped a pass (almost impossible not to) and met David, Art and Design Tutor with Wife and Toddler [...]. Then marriage, kids, Valium, a flat in Sidcup, a maisonette in Blackheath, a lectureship in Women's Studies in the same third-rate poly, now laughingly described as a university, a minor reputation as a narrowly-based academic, Prozac, an increasing urge to escape from reality into fiction as that eighteen-year-old gym-slipped girl did. There you have it, dear reader [D. M. Thomas 2000: 109].

Compared to Jane's anxious call to her "Dear Reader" asking for understanding and acknowledgment, Miranda's reader inclusion of the last sentence indicates a disillusioned pilgrimage, admitting a number of problems inherent in white middle-class (women's) life. As the quote shows, the concerns range from the twentieth-century refashioning of the Victorian madness topos by transforming the nineteenth-century social epidemic, hysteria, into today's *Prozac Nation*,[13] through questioning the validity of available white middle-class identities of married women and academics, to the escapism into fictional identities, eventually leading into (re)reading and (re)writing that could pave the way for the reconsideration of available social models.

In the sense of channeling her dissatisfaction with her status into (re)writing and thus attempting to break out of social conventions, Miranda's narrative resembles Jane's in *Jane Eyre*. In parallel to allowing Jane a second marriage and an alternative fate in the West Indies, in the ghostwritten version, Miranda herself explores the ex-colony in her escape from her own dysfunctional marriage in the twentieth-century plotline. Already in Martinique, she remembers having met Jean Rhys in her childhood and equates the author with her most famous novel, which Miranda rereads for her story. This is how *Wide Sargasso Sea* becomes contextualized and underlines a historical continuity[14] in rewriting *Jane Eyre*. If Miranda is read as a twentieth-century version of Jane or, for that matter, Charlotte Brontë, then the rewriting happens doubly, that is, in both plotlines, not to mention the other female figures that, as described above, could all prefigure alternative fates for the female narrator. Finally, through divorcing David and being pregnant with her third child, Miranda seems to follow the line she has mapped out for the Victorian author, Brontë: "She'd have married ... I'm rather unusual in that I've only married once and I've stayed married ... she might by now be on her second marriage, or be divorced and bringing up a couple of children on her own! Who can tell?" (D. M. Thomas 2000: 121). Having escaped "with Jane" to the West Indies and repeatedly attempting to remedy her own traumas by constructing narratives similar to both Jane's and Antoinette's, Miranda returns to England to live the life she has imagined for Charlotte Brontë in the twentieth century. Thus, (re)writing gains the important function of substituting, sometimes even foreshadowing life.[15]

"Jane Eyre's daydreaming stems from an unsatisfying life, and she was not alone," comments Stoneman on the sensitivity of creating parallel worlds in *Jane Eyre* and its adaptations (Stoneman 2006: 182). Not only imaginary characters regard reading and writing as an escape from life, but also authors of fiction, as the example of Anita Brookner proves, whose novels also reverberate with various motifs of *Jane Eyre* (Jones 2008), not to mention readers of literary works. Ironically, the *Oxford World's Classics Complete List* (2008), addressed to potential readers, advertises *Jane Eyre*, together with some other novels, under the heading *Escape* with the following introduction: "This is a collection of books to provide an escape for anyone who needs to get away, whatever it is they're fleeing from. Take them on holiday, read them on the bus, snuggle into bed with them at night, give them to someone who needs to break out" (*Oxford World's Classics Complete List* 2008: 48). Jane, the self-conscious narrator of *Charlotte*, openly admits that her writing is a flight from life, which can also be read as a twentieth-century comment on both the Victorian author and her novel *Jane Eyre*: "Do we not read and write novels in order to escape from the sheer terror of real life?" (D. M. Thomas 2000: 37). Concerning the authorship of post–Victorian fiction, Miranda's status of a mediocre lecturer producing such dubious texts may read as Thomas's devaluation of Victorian pastiche (Gutleben 2001: 180), which would then function as a metacommentary, having the author criticize his own work. This way, similarly to the fictionalizing of the originality versus plagiarism debate his *White Hotel* triggered, Thomas has also already encoded into *Charlotte* the critique of the suspect phenomenon of professors of English adapting nineteenth-century fiction. It emerges, then, that the role of rewriting mainly consists of providing a way of escape and a source of remedy, so it has both the nostalgic function of searching for an imaginary home and a remedial one of easing or possibly curing traumas.[16]

The process of rewriting yields multiple products in *Charlotte*: a faked manuscript with an alternative ending to the novel *Jane Eyre*, the entire novel itself as a post–Victorian adaptation of the Victorian text and *Wide Sargasso Sea*, and two extra-textual visuals thematizing the adaptations. The fake Brontë manuscript is an explicitly cherished cultural object by its intended audience, Miranda's father. In the two other post–Victorian novels considered here for comparison, the authorship of the respective nineteenth-century novels is unquestionable, whereas in *Charlotte*, the father and his graphologist expert's belief in the authenticity of the forged manuscript puts such blind insistence on the originality of historical texts into question. *Jane Eyre* and *Wide Sargasso Sea* also feature as acknowledged source texts, cultural objects which, together with their authors, assume the roles of being central determinants of Miranda's life and narrative. There are two visual objects in the novel, which are extra-textual in the sense that they are not reflected on by either narrator. Still, they provide a commentary on the themes of colonization, its legacies and sexuality prevalently featuring in both accounts, thus influencing emerging narratives of identity. One of these is a nineteenth-century map extract titled *Martinique, French West Indies 1847* (D. M. Thomas 2000: 6) and the other is a photograph of two almost naked headless characters, a man and a woman, facing each other at the seaside, titled *Martinique, French West Indies 1999* (D. M. Thomas 2000: 68). The first image immediately precedes Jane's narrative, so this is the first thing we see right after the title, which provides the reader with some hints as to where the journey might lead in the Victorian plotline. The puzzle gets resolved by the end of Jane's narrative, once she decides to travel to Martinique to find Bertha and Rochester's son, Robert. The twentieth-century plotline is introduced by the second image, the photograph of the two half-nude figures, and accordingly the whole of Miranda's account that follows takes place in Martinique and is full of sexual encounters.

Critical reactions to this second image are mostly negative. D. M. Thomas is either accused of a similarly sensationalist bias for the insertion of this photograph as in his use of a title that only includes references to a celebrity Victorian author and her character (Gutleben 2001: 183), or of turning his audience into resistant readers disgusted by the picture's shocking focus on sexual organs (Sue Thomas 2007: 109–110). I think that the reason for inserting this photograph into the book may have less to do with popularistic aims than with the subversive aspect of the novel. Looking at it in terms of space, time and plot, this is where Jane and, a century later, also Miranda is going. The sexuality of both female characters receives emphasis in the tropical location: Jane becomes a lover and happily married though short-lived wife to Robert Rochester in the West Indies, after the death of her impotent husband back in England, and Miranda gets involved in various similarly fleeting sexual affairs with the locals of Martinique, helping her to temporally forget her frustrating marriage back home. The two plotlines are usually read as complementary, Miranda authoring Jane's relationship as a romantic and recuperative contrast to her own disconcerting experiences (Gutleben 2001: 202–203, Sue Thomas 2007: 103). Accepting this reading, the image on the cover page featuring a woman in full travel outfit, emphasizing her face and upper body,[17] can be countered to the photo corresponding more to Miranda's experiences of impersonal promiscuity. The impersonality of promiscuity is emphasized, on the one hand, by the fact that the photo, probably taken around sunset, is black and white, which makes it difficult to establish the color of the two half nude figures. The most likely version is that the male model is black and the female one is white, but other hybridized identities are also possible. On the other hand, the fact that the original title of the photo—*Brazil, Rio de Janeiro, Partially Clothed Man and Woman on Beach (B&W)* (Pillitz 1993)—refers to a different location from the one in the title accorded to it by D. M. Thomas—*Martinique, French West Indies 1999*—also seems to suggest that it does not really matter where such encounters take place; the image of one can be plagiarized for that of another.

The shocking nature of the picture following the account of Rochester's impotence can be interpreted differently again if viewed from the subversive perspective, in which case the end of Jane's narrative detailing the sexual failure with her husband foreshadows the kind of rewriting that is to be expected. Also, related to the first image of the map, which neither critic accounts for, the photo has an additional contrastive function, especially since the only difference between the titles of the two images inserted into the novel is their time reference. Hence, if one follows the order of the images, from the Victorian woman in travel outfit on the cover page, through the nineteenth-century map of Martinique, to the photo of the two half-nude figures on the "West Indian" seaside, the transition is more subtle than it emerges at first sight. This sequence of images depicts the Englishwoman's journey announced in the title (all three women, Jane, Charlotte Brontë and Miranda assuming the Victorian author's name, included) to the Caribbean, indicated by the visuals (and thus referring to the Rhys text), where she has sexual encounters with the locals.

The photo summons further readings, if examined in close connection with Jane's story and all accounts that follow the insertion of the picture.

The storylines thus juxtaposed invite an analysis of the connections between sexuality and (post)colonialism, the dominant narratives of which the text subverts in both centuries. Clearing the ignorance Victorian women were left in concerning their sexuality, through her unsuccessful liaison with Rochester, Jane is paired up with Rochester and Bertha's child, Robert. This move, according to Gutleben, makes her a parallel character to Bertha, due to the foregrounding of the repressed sexuality of the Victorian woman locked away in the attic (Gutleben 2001: 96). However, opposed to Bertha, Jane experiences a sexual-sensual pilgrimage, which ends in a quasi-incestuous relationship with her stepson. Her liberated state does not last long, since she soon dies of tropical fever, a prototypical ending suggesting that metropolitans cannot accommodate to the climate of the colonies, or more dramatically, that the colony takes its revenge on the body of the colonizer.

Acting as sexual enlighteners and knowers of secrets, Miss Temple and Grace get accorded a more complex role here than in the previous two texts. Miss Temple, as a friend, helps Jane realize that something is wrong with Rochester, since their sexual encounters do not provide the heroine with either satisfaction or children. The role of Grace is rewritten so that she is not only Rochester's confidante but also one of Rochester's secret affairs, a possibility that could be speculated on in connection with the Victorian text. Hence, in *Charlotte*, Grace has the knowledge she has had in *Jane Eyre*, the connective function between Jane, Rochester and Bertha emphasized by her additional narrative instance in *Wide Sargasso Sea*, which is completed by her access to Robert, and a temporary membership in the family once she bears the child from the affair until it later drowns. By becoming one of Rochester's lovers, she impersonates one possible script for Jane, as do all the similarly unwritten narratives of the other women from Rochester's past: the French Céline Varens, the Italian Giacinta and the German Clara. Finally, Grace assumes the role of the psychological prison warden of the Victorian author as well; in her conference presentation Miranda analyzes her as a discipliner of "Charlotte's unruly id" (D. M. Thomas 2000: 119). All this knowledge and her ability to become a discipliner, not only of the desires of characters but also of those of authors, make her, also in this novel, reminiscent of Nelly Dean in *Wuthering Heights*, who may be read as a possible manipulator of events as well as an agent and representative of patriarchy, aiding in the repression of the female subconscious.

Miranda also appears to revisit Charlotte's oppressed sexuality, by adopting the nineteenth-century writer's name for her various affairs in the West Indies. However, the assumed identity of the dead Victorian author, though entertaining Miranda, also has a ghastly and depressing quality. She experiences these sexual encounters in a similarly dead state: "From somewhere near the ceiling I looked down at our entwined bodies, distantly, with amusement. It's said that newly-dead people do this—look down at their corpses. The difference was, I wasn't newly dead; I died a long time ago. I have drowned. I am underwater" (D. M. Thomas 2000: 71–72). This statement, underlining her ghostwriter status, not only reflects her negative judgment of her own life but also provides further possibilities of identification with her mother, who jumped off the cliff into the water in Miranda's first version of ending *Jane Eyre*, as well as with Grace's child who drowned in a pond.[18] These two identities become one in her father's diary, when the father relates how Miranda accuses him of having ruined her life: "how I'd drowned her, as I drowned her mother; how she existed underwater, like a submarine; how all those years alone with me made it impossible for her to find a different life" (153).[19] This motif of death-in-life also occurs when Miranda characterizes her husband to one of her West Indian lovers. First, she lies that she has lost him due to a heart attack, then she admits that she does not like her married life, describing her husband as she has described herself earlier: "My husband's alive; but dead—you know?" (92). Miranda fantasizes about her husband's death to Juan, a local teacher, who becomes her lover and later turns out to be a gay-hater gay man, who adopts the name Charlotte out of his reverence for Miranda. Miranda's sexual affairs include numerous locals; she seems to pick her partners randomly and enjoy interracial sex, which she sees as her longing for color. These affairs raise various issues, including sexuality, oppression, interracial exploitation and promiscuity, that point back to nineteenth-century practices as well.

Robert Young construes Victorian cultural interaction between races as copulation: "Nineteenth-century theories of race were not about differentiations between self and other: they were about people having sex" (Young 1994: 34). The way he compares forms of sexual exchange incited by colonialism to modes of economic exchange as "commerce," blends in with what Ciolkowski claims about a slaveholder, in her analysis of *Wide Sargasso Sea*, "producing 'half-caste' bastards almost as quickly as he produces profits" (Ciolkowski "Navigating the Wide Sargasso Sea" 1997). Rochester's rejection of sex with Antoinette/Bertha in the Rhys text is also perceived as his rejection of cultural and racial mixing. In *Charlotte*, this imperial narrative returns when Robert Rochester attributes the failure of his father's marriage to the fact that he was born a black child, which sometimes happens in genetics, but Rochester straightaway understood it as his wife's unfaithfulness and the burden of color as a proof thereof. The union of Jane and Robert is thus understood as a revision of imperialist English identity, since the Creole and mixed identities change from the status of constituting a threat to that of a fruitful hybridity; and all that is repressed in Victorian narratives appears remedial here (Gutleben 2001: 179). To qualify the statement could appear remedial if Miranda's twentieth-century reflections, voiced in the similarly interwoven context of sexuality and postcolonialism, did not indicate that not only does the nineteenth-century exploitative context remain still unresolved, but its ideology continues to affect twentieth-century identities as well:

> He was fucking me, seeing me as French, probably a *métropolitaine*, in my hired car — and he was also fucking France and Europe, that had given him good roads and unemployment benefit, and in return demanded that he give up only his proud independence and become a slave. And the tragedy was [...] that he couldn't see any way of *not* being a slave; trapped by the state's benevolence, and the petrol stations and the shopping malls, and the car in almost every family (so my guidebook informed me). The plantation slaves of the last century could rebel, or try to escape, because life was toil and suffering; but there was no escaping from the soft life [D. M. Thomas 2000: 80].

As Miranda reports, eighteenth and nineteenth-century slavery is transformed into modern-day slavery, where sexual and political exploitation continue in the framework of consumer society and commodity culture. She is aware of the harmful effect of this process on the locals, yet she is part of it, assuming the status of a member of the dominant culture, seeing herself as a metropolitan, coming from the center of the historical empire to the periphery of the ex-colony. Sex and colonization are closely intertwined in her narrative; for example, when she asks one of the natives to go home with her, this is how she describes his reaction: "I could see desire and decorum fighting in his anguished face, like the English and the French over the Antilles" (104–105). Though both are acknowledged in the English Miranda's account, as critics also claim, the English and the French colonizers are not given equal commemoration: it is mostly French colonialism that receives criticism in the novel, and little is said about the English one. While Rhys offers a revision of English abolition in *Wide Sargasso Sea*, D. M. Thomas advances a protective attitude towards it in *Charlotte* by leaving its legacies unexamined (Sue Thomas 2007: 111).[20] In the above block quote, Miranda twice refers to France specifically and Europe as a global colonizer, but does not mention England, and items of French vocabulary are constantly mixed into her English account whenever colonization becomes the focus of attention: "The black islanders had been liberated by being absorbed, as a goose is liberated from its nature by being stuffed with food and turned into *foie gras* (D. M. Thomas 2000: 87).

The profane reference to sexual intercourse keeps appearing in a postcolonial context, amongst others, when Miranda is having sex with Caribbean men for their color and is fantasizing about butterfly-intercourse, "wanting to know how does it feel to be weightless and fucking! [...] me so white yearning for blackness" (D. M. Thomas 2000: 83), and also when she inquires about her father's relationship to the author, Jean Rhys: "Did you fuck her, Daddy?" (152) — which, as Gutleben also notes, metaphorically implies the rape of her text as well (Gutleben 2001: 181), though "fuck" and "rape" may not mean the same thing. Rochester's death once he gets confronted with his impotence, Miranda's access to her father's sexual perversities preserved in journals for after his death and the numerous sex scenes verging on violent pornography while reflecting on historical injustices would probably summon similar critical voices as D. M. Thomas's *White Hotel* did, attacking his frequent connections of sex and death while appropriating important historical events as distasteful, with a minority claiming that it is precisely by the boundary-breaking juxtaposition of such extremes that he effectively shows the violence of historical events (Nicol 2004: 12). Whichever group one agrees with, what *Charlotte* achieves is connecting the prevalent discourses of colonialism and sexuality with those of producing and reproducing literature, thus linking the political and the erotic to the aesthetic. This linkage, overtly fictionalized by interweaving and topicalizing the act of writing with sexual and (post) colonial accounts, is much more apparent than in other postcolonial novels like Rushdie's *Midnight's Children*, for example.

Connecting sexuality to spaces of identification, *Charlotte* presents a very similar rewriting to *Wide Sargasso Sea*: in neither of the plotlines of D. M. Thomas's text do sexual experiences in England yield pleasant memories, whereas such explorations in the West Indies appear more liberating. Jane's futile attempts at sexual intercourse with the impotent Rochester take place at Thornfield Hall, which she leaves and never returns to after Rochester's death. Miranda's sexually frustrating marriage is located in London, and the traumatic sexual abuse she has been experiencing since her childhood takes place in Cornwall, where her father still resides. Jane's nineteenth-century pilgrimage then leads to the West Indies in search of

Antoinette and Rochester's son, a journey which Miranda repeats, giving a conference paper on Charlotte Brontë there in the twentieth-century part. Robert Rochester's letter is also addressed from Martinique, thus it is the postcolonial location where the bulk of the narratives is set. Here Jane has the space to explore her sexuality and get pregnant by Robert, and Miranda also engages in numerous affairs with the locals and similarly expects a baby as a result, later confessing to her father that she has planned this in advance. Jane dies during her pregnancy but Miranda "takes" the fetus back to England and decides to settle with it in Cornwall. If Miranda is read as a twentieth-century Jane, then she completes her predecessor's pilgrimage by both reinstating the dominant narrative, since she "imports" an embryo to England to exert her ownership, and deconstructing it, as she purposely acts in favor of hybridization. This double interpretive potential makes the novel so intriguing: both Jane and Miranda essentially produce colonial accounts in the West Indies, yet their life choices and narrative comments partially constitute postcolonial critiques of these. Jane, though full of patriotic feelings and national pride for England, marries the black Robert and opens up to the perspective of the colonized,[21] and Miranda, despite her sexual exploitation of the locals, is equally open to understanding them, not to mention her bitter or ironic comments on the still ongoing Western colonization.

In terms of characters' finding their own space or home, the nineteenth-century plotline seems more radical than the twentieth-century one. Jane does not return to England, as she realizes that her love for Robert is stronger than her homesickness, especially that all that still connects her to England, such as language or literature, is cultural, which she can share with Robert. Robert's position is very clear all along; in contrast to Antoinette, who idealizes England, he shows no interest in going there: "I was and am a child of the sun, of the tropics; and I had no wish to take possession of a mansion where my mother had been made to suffer so much" (D. M. Thomas 2000: 166). Thus, Jane gives up her home for the West Indies, with the awareness that she is resettling in an English colony; however, her author, Miranda, does not allow her to maintain this decision and kills her, thereby joining the line of historical authors accused of disposing of their characters the same way: Charlotte Brontë and D. M. Thomas. In the twentieth-century plotline Miranda herself establishes a connection between her own lineage and that of her literary predecessors, which makes Cornwall, the place she moves back to from the West Indies and eventually identifies as her home, a site of cultural heritage. In parallel to Charlotte Brontë's mother, Miranda also grew up in Cornwall, and like the Brontë sisters, she also had a Cornish mother. She might have met Jean Rhys while the author lived in Cornwall, and Miranda's father might have had an affair with the postcolonial writer at the same time. Sue Thomas also speculates on Cornwall as a site of internal British imperialism, constructing the unsuccessful English/Celtic marriage of Miranda's parents in the light of repeated failures of attempts at acquiring Cornish autonomy based on their Celtic heritage put down by the English (Sue Thomas 2007: 112). The discovery and romanticization of Cornwall that emerged in the 1870s (Samuel 1999: 59) and led to later revivals seems to take a different direction in the post–Victorian *Charlotte*. In this novel, Cornwall assumes a paradoxical function of a site for the search for lineage and a place of disturbing memories to which Miranda is driven at the same time as she strives to get away from them. That is why her eventual return to Cornwall and her father seems rather ambivalent. On the one hand, it may be claimed that after various detours, she again finds her roots integrating literary lineage as well as colonial legacies, by choosing a place she associates with Brontë and Rhys, both of whose texts she rewrites, and expecting a child from a black West Indian man, respectively. On the other hand, this decision can also be read as Miranda's succumbing to her father's abuse by assuming her mother's role in the nuclear-family-to-be, thereby exposing herself to the repetition of the sexual perversities she experienced as a child and to being further traumatized rather than healed.

Both Jane and Miranda perceive the West Indies in their own national and cultural terms, which means that experiences of Martinique are reported contrastively, best observed through their commentary concerning local cultural memory. One such place of commemoration is Diamond Rock of Martinique, which was occupied by the English during the Napoleonic Wars. Jane expresses her pride in the English navy for its victory over nature and the French (D. M. Thomas 2000: 114), while Miranda is not proud of English colonialism, yet she makes an imperial association, which again is embedded into a sexual comparison: "The surf is restless, angry, white-crested here [at Diamond Rock], because it's the Atlantic; and it strikes me that there is no land between here and Land's End in Cornwall where I grew up. It's a kind of close connection, and at the same time far distant, like sex" (D. M. Thomas 2000: 102). Apart from some small groups of islands, it is only the Atlantic Ocean that separates Britain from its ex-colony, bringing the memory of Diamond Rock being in British colonial possession dangerously close. The description of Diamond Rock, "[c]ut into many facets, it did seem to glitter like a diamond" (ibid.) echoes the qualities of glass objects that similarly refract light, discussed in the previous chapter. Similarly to those of the glass church in *Oscar and Lucinda* or the Crystal Palace, cultural memories related to Diamond Rock are also diverse. As it emerges from the quotation, Diamond Rock not only provides various possible readings through its multifacetedness, but also incites promises of wealth, like the perception of the Crystal Palace from within, in *Emma Brown*: "We are inside the largest diamond in the world" (Boylan 2004: 395).

The other West Indian cultural memento offering equally versatile readings is a place called *tombeau des caraibes*, introduced as an important site of cultural memory for the locals: "He [Juan] said it was where the last surviving Carib chiefs jumped off the cliff to their death, after drinking poison, rather than be killed by the white men. 'And as they leapt into the sea, they called on the sacred mountain to avenge them'" (D. M. Thomas 2000: 94). Miranda keeps searching for a memorial, some material sight commemorating this important historical event, but her local companion reminds her that there is nothing to see; they only remember. Her behavior is understandable from her cultural context, where everything of relevance requires monumental architecture and huge media coverage, as illustrated by the example of the building of the Millennium Dome, which her husband, David, engages in constructing. Read contrastively to the Caribbean locals' belief in their sacred place for which they do not need an object, it seems ironic that David gets a nervous breakdown trying to model the Dome's Faith Zone, for which he is desperately trying to find a material representation but fails to do so, possibly due to his lack of faith. He illustrates the problem with a black joke, which, apart from providing his opinion about institutionalized religion, involves massacre just like the case of the *tombeau des caraibes*: "he had to come up with ideas for what to put in the Faith Zone. No one wanted it except the Church. There would be endless opportunity for causing offence to people. David said, with a black chuckle he thought they should just have giant TV screens showing the Christian Serbs killing innocent Moslem Albanians" (D. M. Thomas 2000: 100). This ironic view of the whole venture of the Millennium Dome pushing up housing prices, ruining the economy and characterized by a complete lack of ideas, as described earlier, is maintained in the entire novel. As we have seen, D. M. Thomas's *Charlotte* facilitates a complex reading of (post)colonial and (post)imperial spaces related to national and cultural identities.

5

The Way We Adapt Now: Endings, Novel Series and Adaptive Maps

> *"Chatterton knew that original genius consists in forming new and happy combinations, rather than in searching after thoughts and ideas which had never occurred before."*
> *"True,"* murmured Philip gloomily.
> *"And this,"* Charles went on, *"was the foundation of his everlasting fame."*
> With a grimace he flung the pamphlet at Philip; then he tore another strip from a page of Great Expectations, rolled it into a ball and popped it into his mouth. He settled back into his warm seat and murmured to himself, with increasing cheerfulness, *"New and happy combinations. New and happy combinations. Does that mean,"* he asked as he chewed, *"that we just need to switch around the words?"* — Peter Ackroyd, Chatterton (1987)

As the case study of the consecutive rewritings of *Jane Eyre* in the previous chapter also illustrates, adaptation has inspired a popular trend in post–Victorian fiction: the reintroduction of the novel sequel. Paul Budra and Betty A. Schellenberg contextualize the *sequel* as a site of intriguing connections among author, narrative and audience. They contend that sequelization is repetition-with-variation, whereby authors respond to readerly desire concerning an earlier text, which "is particularly acute at certain historical junctures, or, to put it another way, that the sequel is possible only under certain (repeating) cultural conditions" (Budra and Schellenberg 1998: 17). Although the authors survey the eighteenth century, I think that this remark proves equally useful in establishing a connection between nineteenth-century texts and their contemporary rewritings. "The literary scene" appears an appropriate umbrella term to characterize the field of "historical junctures" between the two eras. On the one hand, today's literary scene displays an enormous development in publication technologies and forums, comparable to the fast evolution of print culture in the nineteenth century (Kucich and Sadoff 2000: xxii). On the other hand, it focalizes authorship, author-reader interaction and ensuing marketing strategies, similarly to Victorian times. Hence, it stands to reason that all these overlaps result in the increasing popularity of the sequel.

In the Victorian era, the novel sequel was perceived as a series of plots produced by the same author, involving the same characters, sometimes even the same setting, produced more or less in a chronological order, like Anthony Trollope's *Chronicles of Barsetshire* (six novels published between 1855 and 1867). Contemporary adaptive series expand the nineteenth-century understanding of this generic mode, by purposefully distorting the timeline, fragmenting the narrative through reporting the same events from more perspectives and being independently produced by different writers. But post–Victorian adaptations seem to aim for precisely such distortions: they disrupt chronologies as well as deconstruct the concepts of authorship and originality, thus affecting the literary canon. This subversive potential of adaptations shifting power relations is identified both as a reason for their popularity (Hutcheon 2006: 174) and as a decisive feature assisting in promoting their academic study (Sanders 2006: 98). I also think that such power shifts take place on the interpretive level. Critical analyses simultaneously focus on more adaptations, instead of just tackling one text: discussions of Charlotte Brontë's *Jane Eyre* rarely occur without a mention of Jean Rhys's *Wide Sargasso Sea*, for example. In addition, adaptive texts themselves tend to include intertextual references to more than one "original": as we have seen, D. M. Thomas's *Charlotte* comprises an adaptation of both *Jane Eyre* and *Wide Sargasso Sea*. Some post–Victorian adaptations completely disrupt the chronological, narrative and plot references to nineteenth-century texts, in which cases the terms *adaptive chain* or *adaptive series* seem insufficient to incorporate relationships between adaptations and their source texts, hence the term *adaptive map*.

In contrast to the focus of the last chapter largely following the diachronic principle of the historical temporality of revision, in the following readings of reworkings, current thematic, critical and adaptive trends of the last decades receive attention in a more synchronic manner. First, I scrutinize the main drifts according to which the ending of *Jane Eyre* gets (re)interpreted in post–Victorian refashionings of the Victorian original. I analyze Jasper Fforde's *The Eyre Affair* (2001) in more detail, which features on the adaptive map of *Jane Eyre* at the same time as belonging to another novel series on the adventures of a literary detective. I examine this adaptation as an absorbing example of the contemporary novel sequel that interrogates the connections of literary production and reception, addressing issues from authorship and celebrity culture and their relations with literary value and originality, to social, political and cultural concerns Britain faces today. Second, I further demonstrate how diversified adaptation can be, by studying various refashionings of Dickens's life and work. Starting out from the theme park Dickens World and post–Victorian fiction called Dickensiana, I look at two independent rewritings of Dickens's *Great Expectations* (1861) that closely interconnect authorship, identity and imperial legacies: Peter Carey's *Jack Maggs* (1997) and Lloyd Jones's *Mister Pip* (2006). In both of these novels, which can also be read sequentially, different reading techniques get problematized, of which I pay in-depth attention to the reintroduction of serializing installments, as yet another way of generating and digesting post–Victorian fiction.

It All Begins Where It Ends: Finishing Jane Eyre *and Jasper Fforde's* The Eyre Affair *(2001)*

Perceived as "the motor force behind literary evolution" (Lefevere 1992: 2), rewriting is becoming a popular scholarly topic, resulting in attempts at finding the suitable terminology to denote the body of texts in question. *Fluidity* is one of these terms, mostly used to mark the disruptive postmodernist text in contrast to the fixity of homogeneous forms (Waugh 1995: 157). As John Bryant defines it, "a fluid text is any literary work that exists in more than one version. It is 'fluid' because the versions flow from one to another" (Bryant 2002: 1). Hence, fluidity is understood in a wide sense, including different stages of the rewriting process from creation through publication to adaptation — in other words, incorporating steps of authorial, editorial and cultural revisions (Bryant 2002: 101). Working with the theoretical background of intertextuality, Patsy Stoneman adopts Christopher Richard's term *incremental literature*, which denotes all pieces based on previously existing texts without specifying the nature of this relationship (Stoneman 1996: 239). She remains true to her flexible use of terminology in her later works as well, by employing the term *literary continuum* to describe predecessors' influences on adapted literary texts (Knight and Stoneman 2004: 2). These choices prove vital to establishing a connection between literary texts avoiding value judgments which, as Linda Hutcheon also points out, affect adaptations as well, since they are often rated as "secondary and inferior" (Hutcheon 2006: xii, 31). Even if only for heuristic purposes, it is helpful to determine terminological categories as exactly as possible, since they may point to more specific conclusions. For example, delimiting sequels as a specific group of texts prompts the connection of writing in installments and changing reading habits. Scrutinizing the nature of rewriting and sequelization in more detail, especially concerning the anxiety related to the temporality and authenticity of adaptations or appropriations, further terms, such as *prequel, sequel* or *aftering*, emerge.

There have been attempts to organize *Jane Eyre* adaptations in order to establish some kind of relationship among the ever-growing number of texts that engage with the novel. Patsy Stoneman's *Brontë Transformations: The Cultural Dissemination of "Jane Eyre" and "Wuthering Heights"* (1996) has proved a seminal work in this respect, exhaustively documenting and summarizing reactions to the Victorian text from within a few years of its publication until the mid–1990s. Apart from some classic refashionings also addressed by Stoneman, a more recent collection titled *A Breath of Fresh Eyre: Intertextual and Intermedial Reworkings of "Jane Eyre"* (2007) additionally includes twenty-first-century responses to the nineteenth-century novel. Stoneman's survey is organized chronologically, within which she separates thematic entities as well that contextualize the adaptations according to the critical and theoretical trends and movements of the past two centuries. The survey is appended by a chronological list of *Jane Eyre* (and *Wuthering Heights*) reproductions which are grouped according to adaptive genres with short comments indicating their relationship to the Victorian text(s). The editors of the 2007 anthology, Margarete Rubik and Elke Mettinger-Schartmann, organize the essays according to representational media, with individual sections for fiction, films and paintings, and stage adaptations. Within each subdivision incidental thematic sections emerge as well, which in the case of the novels means some chronology (*Wide Sargasso Sea* analyses precede *The Eyre Affair* ones) and that papers concerning particular texts are published consecutively. The two collections complement each other. Stoneman's is a useful diachronic account, highlighting historical tendencies in responding to *Jane Eyre*, with the practicality of the appendix providing an encyclopedic source. Rubik and Mettinger-Schartmann's assists both in drawing attention to rewritings that have become important in the past ten years, and in perceiving the forums and range of products appearing simultaneously at present. Neither of the books undertakes to argue a specific genealogy or organizing principle among the refashionings. Being a pioneer in this endeavor, the first survey naturally assumes a more descriptive function, while the second assortment appears as a demonstration of the importance and popularity of the phenomenon rather than a scholarly account of any theoretical or methodological concern.

One such concern is precisely the problem of terminology, which influences the scope and conclusion such critical works may draw. Rubik and Mettinger-Schartmann remark in a footnote that although they are aware of the abundance of terms denoting and differentiating among responses to the Victorian text, due to the wide variety of interpretations they introduce, they have not synthesized the terminology (Rubik and Mettinger-Schartmann 2007: 11). Stoneman reflects on the difficulty of finding the appropriate term for her project, which is not only influenced by its historicity but also by the diversity of texts she includes:

> Multiplied across genres and discourses, and across the one hundred and fifty years since the publication of the Brontë texts, the potential field becomes vast. Dissemination, moreover, is an unsystematic process which may take the form of almost exact reproductions (editions), versions in other media (stage plays, films), selective reproductions or versions (dramatised scenes, visual illustrations), parodies, allusions, structural parallels (which may not even mention the original text) and what Christopher Richards calls "incremental" writings (sequels, prequels, etc.) (Richards, C. 1989) [Stoneman 1996: 3–4].

The author maintains this terminological variety in her survey, using the most appropriate one for individual sections and texts, and apparently opting for *derivatives* as the common denominator, which she also employs to denote the list of rewritings in the appendix. This abundance of terms used by scholars indicates that the research area concerned with post-Victorian fiction is still in the making.

When reiterating the ending of *Jane Eyre*, most readers and adaptors remember Jane's renowned sentence "Reader, I married him" (Brontë 1999: 397), whereas it is only the first sentence of the last chapter of the Brontë text. The novel actually ends with St. John's words, "Amen, even so come, Lord Jesus!" (Brontë 1999: 401). A common feature of these two utterances is that they both constitute difficulties in interpreting the resolution of the plot and the narrative, discrediting attempts at comprehensive teleological readings. Critics mostly blame Brontë for her inconsistencies. One such accusation points towards the author's illogical confusion of genres, by allowing a romantic solution of a realistic plot, letting Jane inherit a fortune and enter a marriage, even though her fate points in a very different direction (Levine 1981: 182). This view results in categorizing the text as romance fiction. Other critics regard the novel as an instance of sensation fiction characterized by a generic mix of Gothic and romance fiction, related to the detective novel, the novel of mystery and fashionable life, all in all, a genre symptomatic of the decline in nineteenth-century literary taste (Marsh 1995: 100–101), which sounds rather prescriptive in its apparent distinction of high and low genres. In addition to such devaluations of its literary merits, the feminist achievements of *Jane Eyre* are also attacked, not only disapproving of the heroine's marriage and inheritance, but also objecting to the fact that her account ignores important feminist and postcolonial narrative aspects, as described earlier.

Juxtaposing these concerns of plot resolution and narrative authority/authorship, Carolyn Williams argues that the ending of the novel recreates exactly the same ambivalence of voice in the text which Charlotte Brontë had to confront as a female author in the nineteenth century. This way, St. John not only represents the other male, the life-option Jane rejects, but also a powerful narrative that determines literary history "which like apostolic succession, has been structured as a chain of inherited authority" (Williams 1997: 246). Consequently, finishing her narrative by the Bible quote through the mouthpiece of the rejected character, St. John, Jane acknowledges that she writes herself into the male tradition at the same time as distancing herself from it: "In closing her book, Jane closes with the other Book" (ibid.). This juxtaposition seems fruitful in more respects. On the one hand, it synthesizes contradictive opinions about the text's feminism, amalgamating attacks on Brontë's bias in letting Jane disregard other marginalized voices and praises on how through Jane's narrative her author established herself in the literary tradition: we cannot expect Brontë to have written a post–Victorian novel in the nineteenth-century literary environment, especially considering that in order to acquire a reading public, she had to succumb to the reigning male literary tradition first. On the other hand, it sheds light on the current status of *Jane Eyre* adaptations. Most adaptors engage with the last major plot move, Jane's marriage to Rochester, introduced by the first sentence of the final chapter, and work on rewriting it into a more plausible story, producing so many versions that scholars have already started grouping them (Detmers 2007:

81–97). The very last passages of the novel usually feature in these texts to signal the impossibility of Jane's opting for St. John[1] and not, as Williams reads them, in terms of narrative and authorial power.

One major trend *Jane Eyre* adaptations follow is the rewriting of the Victorian ending, with the aim to correct the implausible happiness of Jane and Rochester's marriage. A representative contemporary example of this is Clare Boylan's "*Jane Eyre* Revisited: An Alternative Ending" (1990), which was commissioned by the women's magazine *Good Housekeeping*. This version starts with Jane returning to Thornfield Hall and marrying the maimed Rochester. They move to Ferndean, where Rochester entertains Jane with the stories about women of his earlier travels, and Jane describes her daily exquisite clothing that she fantasizes for her blind husband. One day it turns out that Rochester is not blind at all — he just plays tricks on Jane, as he has done earlier when he cross-dressed as a fortune teller, for example. The appalled Jane confirms this with their staff and is further shocked: "Reader, I cannot fully express the dismay I encountered when the servants met my gaze. 'You knew!' I exclaimed. 'You have all been party to my deception'" (Boylan 1990: 139). When she confronts Rochester, he admits that he has tricked her into the marriage because he did not want to lose her. Even his mysterious telepathic call to Jane, which critics have difficulty finding an explanation for, has been part of this cheat because, as Rochester relates, he followed Jane, crouched below her window and produced it himself. Jane hits her husband in return and reveals her knowledge of how Rochester has tricked all previous women into bigamous marriages so that he can keep on playing his secret games in various liaisons. Rochester's reply is "You are mad" (140), and thus Jane gets put into the role of Bertha and locked into the attic, while her husband roams about in Europe. However, this state of affairs is again reversed when Jane receives a telegram with the news of her husband's death in a Paris shooting incident, so she is freed from her prison and travels to India to care for the ailing St. John. "What is to follow I do not know" (ibid.) is the last sentence of the story, leaving it open to further sequels.

This intriguing revision is followed by another advertisement renewing the competition titled *Can You Beat Brontë?* (Boylan 1990: 141), featuring Boylan as one of the judges, this time asking for revisions of the Victorian novel from the point where Jane leaves Thornfield Hall after the unsuccessful marriage attempt with Rochester. This choice is probably not coincidental, as until this point the plot seems coherent, lacking the later impeding telepathic cry, inherited fortune, and unlikely marriage.

Ironically, the forum announcing the competition is a regular women's magazine that includes household, cooking, and beauty tips as well as literature, as its name, *Good Housekeeping*, also betrays. In this context, Boylan's angry ending is doubly framed, also inviting a twentieth-century reading. The fact that it is a women's magazine that announces such a competition reinforces traditional stereotypes that the audience of romance novels are necessarily women, especially housewives who, after finding the recipe of the day and the newest fashion tips, have the time to read such works. If we go along with this assumption, *Good Housekeeping* could be perceived as a forum for married women who grew up on romances and live in realistic marriages to vent their experiences mismatching their earlier readings. In this sense, the call for twentieth-century women to change romantic endings of canonical novels in the framework of a traditional women's magazine recalling Victorian manuals of good female behavior, resembles Brontë's ambivalent situation in writing herself into the nineteenth-century literary tradition. The other cultural significance of the competition is that, just like reading clubs, such events not only creatively engage readership in collaborative authoring, but also enhance the (re)reading of canonized fiction and, as the prizes to be won are further books, of reading per se.

Seven years after Boylan created her ending, John Sutherland published *Can Jane Eyre Be Happy?*, where he speculates on the possibility of the same closing, activating the Bluebeard parallel as a legitimate source text for the novel: "But what if, like Edward Rochester, after ten years of marriage, his sight were to return and — barring the minor blemish of a missing hand (common enough, end even rather glamorous in these postwar years) — Bluebeard still cut a handsome figure. Could one be entirely confident that his wife-killing ways would not return?" (Sutherland 1997: 80). Just like Rochester himself in Boylan's revision, Sutherland also stresses the character's fear of losing Jane as the only possible subject to marry in his maimed state. The author claims that Rochester would not have asked Jane (a person who is unimportant enough not to attract too much public attention) to marry him if his marriage to Bertha had not been detected, and neither would he have approached her for a second time, had he not been too maimed to be suitable for anyone else (79–80). These two reactions, again, prove that fictional revision often precedes critical analyses of the same kind so, as underlined earlier, it is essential that fiction is also read as criticism. Fascinated with Brontë, Boylan has finally made her name by writing an ending to another one of the Victorian author's stories, a fragment titled *Emma*, which became the novel *Emma Brown* (2003). As she says in an interview published after the novel, proudly bearing the same initials as her literary predecessor, Clare Boylan wanted to be true to the nineteenth-century writer's supposed intentions and wrote this story after some research as a great London novel. This novel also endeavored to echo *Jane Eyre*, which Boylan essentially regards as: "sexual excitement generated through intellectual debate" (Boylan 2004: 440), as her finishing touches to the text, reviewed above, also prove. The novels Ines Detmers analyzes under the title "'The Second Mrs Rochesters': Telling Untold Stories of Jane Eyre's (Im)Possible Married Lives" also concentrate on the aspect of sexuality and unmask the happy ending of the Victorian text as a marriage haunted by Rochester's past (Detmers 2007: 89–94).[2] The same happens in *Charlotte*, with the difference that Rochester is quickly disposed of, and Jane receives a second chance to re-enact the marriage scene with Rochester's son in the West Indies. However, this option is also short-lived, as she soon dies of tropical fever.

The other important trend in adapting *Jane Eyre* is the confirmation of the original ending, complemented by an abundant supply of alternative stories to amend the plot. Strangely, however revolutionary it is otherwise, *Wide Sargasso Sea* is such a text, leaving the plot of Brontë's work largely untouched. Since it constitutes a prequel to the Victorian novel, it excludes Jane's perspective and provides Antoinette/Bertha's story instead. Likewise, in Emma Tennant's *Adèle*, which refashions *Jane Eyre* in three slightly different versions, Jane and Rochester's happy marriage is retained and subordinated to the story of the latter's ward, the little French girl Adèle. In her preface, the author makes sure that her audience identifies the heroine by explaining Adèle's function and story in *Jane Eyre* as well as by quoting the passage which last addresses her fate in the Victorian novel, promising a more complex depiction of her full story than Jane has done in *Jane Eyre*. Similarly to *Wide Sargasso Sea*, the novel has a more complicated narrative structure than their nineteenth-century source text. Five narrators are employed, out of which Adèle features the most, Edward Rochester the second, and Grace, Mrs. Fairfax and an impersonal third-person narrator get accorded minor roles. This adaptation clearly shows the influence of previous refashionings and critical analyses. Neither Jane nor Antoinette/Bertha have their own narrative voice, but Jane's story is maintained and Antoinette's identity as a "normal bride" is consistently distinguished from Bertha, the "madwoman's," which is surely related to the author's knowledge of *Wide Sargasso Sea* as well as Sandra M. Gilbert and Susan Gubar's famous reading of *Jane Eyre*. Rochester is in love with Céline Varens in Paris, and thinks to have killed his rival, the *vicomte*, in a duel, but he turns out to be wrong, as the *vicomte* survives.[3] In *Adèle* it is Mrs. Fairfax who stands behind all the follies, which is also a conclusion Sutherland comes to in his article five years before the novel's publication. According to him, it is Mrs. Fairfax who twice gives away Rochester's marriage plans to Mr. Mason in Brontë's *Jane Eyre* (Sutherland 1997: 78–79). She also does so in *Adèle*, where her character gets further demonized as a serial killer of Antoinette, Grace and almost Jane as well.

As it also concerns a minor character and is set in her home as well as in England, *Adèle* is comparable to *Wide Sargasso Sea*. Although not followed by a detailed analysis, the claim that this centering of the "other" "serves to remedy *Jane Eyre*'s inherent xenophobia" (Schaff 2007: 30) not only describes the Rhys text but also appears to stand for the Tennant novel in many ways. Firstly, by way of reversing English prejudices against the French, as addressed by Adèle, for example, after the furious Rochester has ruined their furniture: "This shocking display of emotion — smashed conservatory and all — must warn my mother finally of the unsuitability of allowing an Englishman into her home" (Tennant 2003: 25). Secondly, by way of Adèle's reaction to her dislocation that echoes Antoinette's concerns with her identity and home in *Wide Sargasso Sea*. Not knowing where her mother is and unacknowledged as his child by her father, standing on the trapeze of a Paris circus, she ponders: "Who was I now? When I began to fly, would I realise I had no identity I could call my own?" (Tennant 2003: 174).Once she learns about her mother's death and is urged by her helpers to go home, Adèle becomes clueless and disoriented: "So ... 'Where should I go back to?' I shouted like the angry child I still knew myself to be. 'Where is my home?'" (193), but contrary to Antoinette, she finally finds her home at their old lodgings, where she both discovers her mother's grave and makes peace with her father, Rochester.

Despite the happy ending for both Adèle and Jane, Thornfield Hall seems to be full of neglected, abandoned or imprisoned women: Bertha the locked-in wife, Adèle the rejected bastard, Mrs. Fairfax the cousin servant, Jane the orphaned governess, and other oppressed servants like Grace. The fate of these women, similarly to those of Helen Burns, Miss Temple, St. John and Jane's other cousins in *Jane Eyre*, is waiting to be written up. So far, as I discussed in the analyses above, Grace, Miss Temple and Mrs. Fairfax have been touched upon in *Wide Sargasso Sea*, *Charlotte* and *Adèle*. The same process of fictionalizing each character's perspective is already happening in the case of Jane Austen's novels: author Amanda Grange, for example, plans to devote individual diary novels to the figures in *Pride and Prejudice* ("Enduring Love" 2007: 14–15), by which she will probably secure a steady income and career as a best-selling novelist for the coming decades. Likewise, Tennant has become famous as a literary adaptor, revising classic texts by Robert Louis Stevenson, Jane Austen and Emily Brontë. These engagements appear to spring as much from critical dissatisfaction with the historical works as from a readerly desire to keep the encountered protagonists and their narrative worlds alive (Budra and Schellenberg 1998: 8). As it emerges from this description, a proliferating adaptation industry is being built on supplying versions or endings of *Jane Eyre* that are coded in Jane's narrative and are based on the close connection of academic criticism and popular readership that, as argued earlier, post–Victorian fiction is prognosticated to incite.

Jasper Fforde's *The Eyre Affair*, analyzed later in this section, constitutes a curious in-between as far as the ending of the Victorian novel is concerned: it rewrites and confirms it at the same time. Like *Charlotte*, this novel has a strong twentieth-century plotline, which in this case dominates the plot and constitutes the perspective from where the *Jane Eyre* commentary emerges as well. As it slowly turns out, the original ending of the Brontë text was that, as phrased by a dissatisfied American tourist at Haworth museum, "She agrees to go with this drippy St. John Rivers guy but not to marry him, they depart for India and that's the end of the book? [...] I get the feeling from what she wrote that she just kinda pooped out" (Fforde 2003a: 65). Thus Fforde offers the St. John choice as closure but immediately rejects it as well, reasoning that this plot resolution would have been just as disillusioning as the romance one for causing a similar feeling about the writer's cheap solution, in this case, of losing patience and opting out. Instead, as it gets voiced in *The Eyre Affair* many times, the audience of the Brontë novel yearns for a romance ending and since they have not got it, they feel cheated. Rochester also dislikes this ending and asks the protagonist, a female detective of the 1980s called Thursday Next, who is able to contact the hero through time travel, to adjust it to one where he and Jane are happily married. She does this by numerous interferences with the historical text, which also serve as explanations for various supernatural scenes: Jane and Rochester's first meeting, caused by the strange behavior of the latter's horse, is provoked by Thursday, and she is also responsible for producing the telepathic call that lures Jane back to Thornfield. To sum up, in *The Eyre Affair*, another ending is temporarily toyed with, disapproved of, and then discarded to reassert the actual ending of the Victorian text, paradoxically as a secondhand one.

The endings of the two other main texts in the chain of adaptations, discussed in the previous chapter, are also worth a brief survey, to see how their plot resolutions diverge from that of the Brontë text. Interpreting the ending of *Wide Sargasso Sea* is a controversial process. Firstly, any adaptation invites a double reading, especially those which do not distort the plotline of their source text but inform it from alternative perspectives. In the case of the Rhys novel, we need to add the ending of *Jane Eyre*, in which Bertha's death is reported, to be able to decipher *Wide Sargasso Sea* as well, otherwise the Antoinette/Bertha story is left unfinished. Secondly, even if we do so, the evaluation of the revengeful and suicidal nature of this last act of putting Thornfield on fire remains hotly debated. Aided by one of its working titles, *The Ghost*, some critics, reading the novel as an experiment in evoking an authentic experience of madness (Oates 2006: 195), an exploration of hereditary tendencies of madness researched in Victorian psychology (Vrettos 2005: 77), or even paranoia (Shaffer 2006: 118), regard Antoinette/Bertha's final move as an act of madness. The writer herself seems to support this view in an autobiographical remark, in one of her letters to Francis Wyndham, claiming that such an ending is quite possible since she, Jean Rhys, also living England can easily imagine becoming mad (Wyndham and Melly 1984: 277). Other scholars mostly distance themselves from associating the heroine with the concept of madness, either by slackening the verdict or by strongly refusing it. Carine M. Mardorossian provides an overview of their various readings: Antoinette's suicide can be seen as a reinforcement of the impossibility of transcending racial boundaries; as her assertive gesture of identification towards the black Creole community; or, on the contrary, as a logical outcome of her passivity and defeat, lacking any positive gesture of self-assertivity (Mardorossian 2005: 156–158). John Su appears to combine these approaches, claiming that, on the one hand, Antoinette's nostalgic reflection does not provide an alternative to her fate in *Jane Eyre* but helps to show that that fate is inescapable (Su 2005: 62); on the other hand, this escapist approach guides her to recast the past and utopistically reunite with Tia through a suicide leap in her dream, which leads to the recognition of herself and her location, triggering this act of resistance to colonial narratives when she wakes up (88–89, 190–191). This interpretation, describing the ending of *Wide Sargasso Sea* as logical, utopistic and reactionary at the same time, indicates its complex and contradictory nature.

To complicate the matter further, even if Jean Rhys makes it clear in her correspondence that her heroine kills herself after burning the house (Wyndham and Melly 1984: 297) — and most critics are in accord with this view (Stoneman 1996: 184, Sanders 2006: 103) — some, quite correctly, underline that the novel has a life of its own too. It is pointed out that, since the sentence "Now at last I know why I was brought here and what I have to do" (Rhys 1968: 152) is in the present tense with no definite indication of Antoinette's next step, thus also including the possibility of her escape, the ending can also be read as an open one (Sanders 2006: 104, Su 2005: 191). Therefore, even if most critiques and adaptations generally assume the heroine's death, on the basis of the narrative, the story may still be continued. Similarly to the reactions to the ending of *Jane Eyre*, the questionable ending of *Wide Sargasso Sea* has also provoked fictional revisions, in addition to these critical reflections. In one of these, *Charlotte*, rewriting both *Jane Eyre* and *Wide Sargasso Sea*, the aspect of madness gets emphasized. In Miranda's first revision of the Victorian text, Bertha is a manic-depressive who commits suicide by jumping off a cliff, and in her second version, the same character seems to reappear as a ghost when Grace's face, while making love to Rochester, becomes Bertha's. In contrast, in *Adèle*, Bertha features as a more harmless figure onto which other characters readily project their problems: Grace perceives herself imprisoned and little Adèle rejected like Bertha. The real cause of Bertha's death slowly emerges towards the end of the novel, as a result of juxtaposing various narratives: Adèle blames herself for having assisted in Bertha's suicide, because she did not let Bertha inside when she found her on the rooftop before the fire broke out; according to the official story of the villagers, Bertha jumped out of the window during the fire (which is the closest to the solutions offered by *Jane Eyre* and *Wide Sargasso Sea*); finally, Mrs. Fairfax reveals that she murdered Bertha much earlier than the fire incident, and during the fire she dressed up the drunken Grace in Bertha's clothes and pushed her out of the window.

If *Wide Sargasso Sea* requires a double reading, *Charlotte* invites a multiple one, since it integrates aspects of the Brontë and the Rhys texts, as well as possessing a double plot with a strong twentieth-century storyline, which also functions as a rephrasing of the earlier novels. In this sense, Thomas's work proves to be a perfect example of retrospective novelistic refraction, at the same time rewriting and reconstructing canonical texts, in the process of which it is not only old texts that are renovating the new ones but vice versa as well. Onega and Gutleben argue that eventually D. M.

Thomas's novel, with all its closures and definite answers, presents itself as more Victorian than its nineteenth-century predecessor (as well as its early-twentieth-century one, we may add), which, in turn, with all its ambiguities and uncertainties, appear(s) more postmodern (Onega and Gutleben 2004: 11). Indeed, in *Charlotte*, all major Victorian characters die, except for Bertha and Rochester's son, the newly invented Robert Rochester in the West Indies, whose letter closes the book. It is from this correspondence that the identity of Rochester's ward is revealed: Adèle turns out to be Bertha and Rochester's second child who, since her father did not want her, had to be removed to France and was pronounced his love child with a French actress. Besides indicating the possibilities Charlotte Brontë did not write, all these unwanted and hidden children also echo Miranda's traumatic abortion as well as her new pregnancy after her visit to Martinique, not knowing who the father of her child is. The result of letting these characters survive marks, on the one hand, the author's aggressiveness of tying up loose ends and closing possibilities for continuing the major nineteenth-century plotline, on the other hand, his opening the potential for a sequelized recounting of the stories of the new generation.

As *Charlotte* has a complex subplot continuing the Victorian story, it is worth looking into the exploitation of nineteenth-century characters from a twentieth-century perspective, especially concerning their fate. Though more realistic in terms of her marriage with Rochester and occasionally funny revealing her ignorance concerning sexuality, Jane's narrative and life remain mostly uninteresting. She experiences her sexual liberation with Robert, instructs him in English ways, tries to learn his colonial ways and finally dies of tropical fever without learning crucial facts about Edward Rochester's past or accommodating to life on the colonies. Except for Boylan's ending, where her self-narrated fate is more intriguing and uncertain, Jane remains marginal in the three other texts discussed here. She does not get a voice in any of them: *Wide Sargasso Sea* and *Adèle* focus on other characters while keeping her in the background, and in *The Eyre Affair* she simply gets abducted from the novel. Rochester, on the other hand, seems to have activated the imagination of most adaptors. He receives the most sympathetic treatment in *Wide Sargasso Sea* and *Adèle*, in both of which he is accorded a narrative voice. This way he gets an opportunity to provide his perspective of the events, at the end of which he most probably finds his destiny in the promise of a happy marriage with Jane, conforming to the closing of *Jane Eyre*. However, his potential as a womanizer becomes revealed even in these texts, not to mention the others where he falls victim to his male pride: in Boylan's he is killed in a duel, while in *Charlotte* he falls off a horse. These two texts also unmask his psychosexual games, followed by the abandonment of the exploited women as well as their children. The most powerful figure Rochester cuts materializes in *The Eyre Affair*, where he is capable of altering the nineteenth-century narrative through contacting the twentieth-century plotline, and even though he comes from the previous century, he knows things in advance, is able to retain Thursday in the historical setting, or influence her life in the future, as well as entertain tourists at Thornfield to keep it economically adrift. This way, not only are his ventriloquizing qualities magnified, but he also assumes the identity of a financially self-conscious entrepreneur.

Jasper Fforde's *The Eyre Affair* (2001), which I examine more closely now, takes up a peculiar position in the literary canon, as it is part of more adaptive series at the same time: it functions as a first book of the heroine's serialized experiences as a literary detective as well as a sequel on the adaptive map of *Jane Eyre*.[4] In contrast to the *Jane Eyre* chain introduced in last chapter's case study, writing back to the nineteenth-century original, this novel rather makes use of the Victorian story for the purposes of its own plot, exploring potentials in appropriating and reproducing literature. In addition to showing a theoretical awareness of issues related to authorship, adaptation and originality, the novel also concerns itself with postcolonial, postimperial and (post)feminist identities. All these receive attention in a predominantly entertaining mode, through utilizing the tools of comedy, utopia, dystopia, and with considerable metafictional input, yielding an exciting generic mixture of detective and science fiction. This text convincingly exemplifies, therefore, how the listed interests interact in current post–Victorian fiction with genre-specific solutions that also differ from the previously analyzed adaptations.

The novel maintains two parallel realms of action: one part of the plot takes place in an Orwellian England in the 1980s and the other occurs in the fictional world of *Jane Eyre*. The ending of the Victorian novel interweaves the two settings. The story finishes by Jane going to India to work with St. John Rivers, an ending late–twentieth-century readers dislike. Rochester also refuses to accept such a conclusion, and once the twentieth-century literary detective called Thursday Next enters the novel through the futuristic Prose Portal, he uses her as his assistant[5] for changing it to Jane and Rochester marrying instead, which supplies the contested ending we know now. "The Brontë Society" and other authorities oppose

Thursday's intervention, but the "Brontë for the People" popular organization overrules objections, realizing how much more the readers admire the novel after this interference. In return for the detective's kindness, Rochester also interferes with the twentieth-century plotline by sending the same lawyer to save Landen, Thursday's lover, from a disastrous marriage to another woman who thwarted his first attempt to marry Jane. Once that relationship gets rectified as well, the literary detective receives another important task, which is the point where the novel ends.

This plot, centered on the fate of literary texts in both the phase of their production and reception, raises a number of controversial issues. Firstly, how much power do publishers and readers have in shaping the final version of a literary text? This appears a legitimate question for an author who has entered the domain of literature through the doors of the film industry. Fforde concedes that he chose *Jane Eyre* as the central intertextual reference for his novel because he assumed that readers would be familiar with its plot (Fforde "Beginnings"), which already carries the grains of the ensuing interactive novelistic production both within and outside the text. The conflict between academic and popular institutions interested in the Brontë novel echoes the dichotomy between texts of aesthetic value and bestsellers that I pointed out earlier in the discussion of the Henry James novels. Here, it finds an integrative solution whereby elitist and non-elitist aspects of reading become juxtaposed.[6] The readers' agency, prompted by the open ending of *The Eyre Affair* and the address of the website on the back cover of the book, materializes in their comments and adaptations online, which have by now evolved into a whole fictional universe. Some fans even reproduce, in real life, the fictional act of Jane and Rochester naming their second child Helen Thursday Rochester in Fforde's novel, by naming their children after characters in the book (Fforde "Thursday"). They also organize special commercial events, such as the Fforde Ffiesta (Fforde "Ffiesta"), where relics are bought and sold that relate to the novel series the detective's adventures have since grown into.[7] This course of events shows the range of receptive responses the concept of sequelization inspires. Endings also acquire an additional quality to being open or controversial, namely, that they are corruptible as well: out of a character or author's dislike and for the sake of the market, endings can be changed in a way that even novelistic characters profit from, as in *The Eyre Affair*. In this sense, the debated ending of *Jane Eyre* gets lifted out of its realism-romance dichotomy and is transferred back into the economic territory of commodity fiction.

The chronology of both the fictional events and our reading of different rewritings of the same text lead to some difficulty in determining the "original" among adaptations. Some scholars react to this problem by orienting the reader through refining terminology: thus among the main *Jane Eyre* adaptations discussed in the previous chapter, *Wide Sargasso Sea* reads as a prequel to *Jane Eyre*, while *Charlotte* constitutes its sequel. Following the same logic, narratives retelling the same story from other characters' perspectives, such as Emma Tennant's *Adèle*, could then be termed "midquels"[8] or "paraquels," which sound rather strange, yet readers obtain some assistance in interrelating texts by the consistent use of morphemes. Even if the same author, Tennant, wrote all editions in the case of this last text, a confusion of titles further complicates the originality debate, as different publications bear different titles and earlier versions get revised for various audiences. Thus on the basis of Bryant's argument, namely, that due to their meaning-changing quality, different editions also count as rewriting (Bryant 2002: 66), the titles *Adèle: Jane Eyre's Hidden Story*, *The French Dancer's Bastard: The Story of Adèle from Jane Eyre* and *Thornfield Hall: Jane Eyre's Hidden Story* constitute different versions of the same midquel.

For understanding the status of *The Eyre Affair*, the term "parallelquel" was coined to depict fiction with a storyline that runs parallel to a canonical novel, thus "break[ing] the rules of continuity by proposing an alternative text that interrogates the workings of the original" (Berninger and Thomas 2007: 186). This interrogation develops into a complete confusion, as *The Eyre Affair* seems to provide us with the genuine ending of *Jane Eyre*, making the version believed so far to be the original into an alternative one (Berninger and Thomas 2007: 188). With such a distortion of our chronological reading process, the reconstruction of an "original" plot, that is, our understanding of the plot on the basis of the historically first text, becomes problematic, consequently testing any text's claim of owning the status of the "original." This also finds a parodic echo within the novel by the paradox of obviously questioning the existence of a detectable genuine script, yet making characters literally kill each other for the *Jane Eyre* manuscript, insisting that "[a]ll copies anywhere on the planet, in whatever form, originate from that first act of creation. When the original changes, all the others have to change too" (Fforde 2003a: 208), which is an attitude echoing the divine romantic concept of authorship and creation. Thus in this novel, the mid–nineteenth-century primacy of originality and the prevalence of invention that have reigned since the late nineteenth are juxtaposed and paradoxically coexist. This fictionalizing of chasing the original and the pinning down of its rewritings by applying terms like *midquel* or *parallelquel* that particularize their relationship are symptomatic of the originality debate that they mock at the same time.

To ensure the consistency of the Victorian text, Fforde abducts Jane from the novel, thereby making any interference with the story told in her first person narrative impossible. As the author confesses, it took him a three-year writer's block to arrive at this solution because he did not want to commit "literary heresy" by putting too many extra words in Jane's mouth (Fforde "Beginnings"), a remark which resembles the preservative argument in the fidelity debate in film studies concerning text-film correspondences in heritage film. A similar imprinting also appears at the textual level, when twentieth-century readers protest about changes to their favorite Victorian novel caused by the abduction. Critics argue that Fforde's implied readers would probably have done the same, had the original canonized version not been maintained with the only addition of a parallel ironic perspective to it by recontextualizing some of the plot moves (Rubik 2007: 175–179). Fforde not only paid homage to the original storyline but also to characters: Thursday Next shows remarkable similarities to Jane, and Landen resembles Rochester in various respects as well (Wells 2007: 200–203). In addition, the two endings, both attributable to Charlotte Brontë due to the twists in the plot, function as a kind of homage, raising the profile of the historical author and providing even more space for speculation related to authorial creativity and intention. Hence, *The Eyre Affair* is mostly read as an entertaining tribute to *Jane Eyre* which reinforces the canon (Berninger and Thomas 2007: 184, Wells 2007: 205–206). I think it could also be read as an allegory of the writing process, implying through the case of *Jane Eyre* how novels come into being or are continuously in the making, thus bringing the productive and receptive ends of the process closer, which indeed may affect long-term canon formation. Besides illustrating writing, Fforde's text can also be read as a satirical comment on the whole enterprise of rewriting: when the readership and the authorities notice that the ending has been revised, they regard the pastiche as "pure Charlotte Brontë but it *definitely* wasn't there before!" (Fforde 2003a: 346). This remark sounds at least ambivalent, partly confirming characters, readers and critics' keenness on Brontë's original ending, but partly also emphasizing that in the metafictional game of rewriting the "revision" to get the "original," these concepts lose their points of reference.

By addressing the pressing contemporary issue of (re)imagining English identity, *The Eyre Affair* confirms Sanders's claim that adaptations are prone to supply alternatives for difficult political situations (Sanders 2006: 98). The novel responds to this concern by contextualizing postcolonial and postimperial anxieties, such as Britain's relationship to its historical empire and the consequences of the devolution of power. The political situation in which the plot is set emerges as strongly dystopian: England is a state constantly involved in wars and conflicts with its neighbors as well as other countries, and London is a city of criminals and detectives where nothing is sacred or safe, governed by dubious corporations similar to the ones in Barnes's *England, England* (1998). The Crimean War gets fictionalized as one that has lasted for the past 130 years, involving the testing of the cold war–like weapons of the corporation and dividing public opinion: agreeing with the industrial entrepreneurs, war veterans argue for its continuation until their final victory, otherwise they feel that all the loss of lives was wasted; while others think that "[w]hat we began as an excuse to curb Russia's expansionism in 1854 [...] has collapsed over the years into nothing more than an exercise to maintain the nation's pride" (Fforde 2003a: 8). This exposes Britain's desperate clinging to its historical empire, further emphasized by the interventions of agents like Thursday's father, whose task involves the adjustment of historical events in favor of the British.

Colonial and postimperial conflicts feature together: immediately after the television broadcast of the Crimean War, a report on the English-Welsh atrocities follows. Wales, a socialist republic since 1854, remains independent from, but constantly threatened and mistreated by, England:

> The next news item was about a border skirmish with the People's Republic of Wales; no one hurt, just a few shots exchanged across the River Wye near Hay.[9] Typically rambunctious, the youthful president-for-life Owain Glyndwr VII had blamed England's imperialist yearnings for a unified Britain; equally typically, Parliament had not so much as even made a statement about the incident [Fforde 2003a: 9].

This kind of fictional relationship between the currently two most connected countries in postimperial Britain points towards the difficulties in working out new identities and forms of governance among entities left over from the empire, unmasking what Susan Bassnett labels one of the most misleading British myths, of a single island whose inhabitants unite against the rest of the world, an image that has long provided a convenient escape from internal difficulties (Bassnett 2001: 500). In his *Island Stories:*

Unravelling Britain, Raphael Samuel describes some instances of a four nations-history that is to replace the Anglocentric one promoted so far, as a necessary consequence of the devolution of power that radically reconceptualizes perceptions of history: "Anglo-Saxon England, which [...] was a precocious unity — the starting-point of 'our island story' and the foundation of representative government — is now seen as more of a hybrid, politically unstable, racially indeterminate, linguistically pluralist" (Samuel 1999: 23). Jasper Fforde has constructed such a history in *The Eyre Affair*. In addition to fictionalizing the present fitting Samuel's description, he has also invented Victorian events as they could have been and gives a detailed account of these on his webpage titled *The Socialist Republic of Wales* (Fforde "Sovietreppage"), which provides a good example of Cora Kaplan's argument about the functioning of literary sources: "In the fantasmatic register in which literature operates an alternative history opens up, with a complicated narrative of its own, but one that is at the same time constitutive of the social real, representing most eloquently and sometimes scarily its affective dimensions" (Kaplan 2006: 211). Fforde supports his choice of Wales and the project of creating its alternative history as follows: "In common with most English schoolchildren, I wasn't taught any Welsh history in school — nor Irish, either — I wonder why that was? The birth of trade unionism bad reading for schoolchildren?" (Fforde "Sovietreppage").

Thus the (post)colonial and (post)imperial conflicts featuring in *The Eyre Affair* also substantiate the concept of isolation introduced earlier, though in a somewhat more abstract way both in temporal and spatial terms. Colonial struggles on the Crimean Peninsula appear in the surreal framework of time travel, and journeys into the space of fictional texts, such as *Jane Eyre*, also take place, which is called book travel (Berninger and Thomas 2007: 186). These latter journeys result in literary tourism not only to famous places connected to canonical works, but also into the works themselves, enabled by the so-called Prose Portal exclusively developed for this purpose. The trope of travel is also employed in connection with going from one country to another, namely, England to Wales within the same island, that is, Britain. Thus isolation in this text functions at a metaphorical as well as at a literal level. Therefore, the temporal disjunction between England in a state of crisis and (post)colonial regions as monuments of the successful empire that nineteenth-century travel narratives assume (Gikandi 1996: 105) can be extended into both a temporal and a spatial disjunction in the case of *The Eyre Affair*. This way the historical novel is equipped with yet another tool to illustrate today's social and political discrepancies.

The book as an institution also owns a very important role in this novel. To reinstate the stolen *Jane Eyre* as a cultic item of English heritage, the Goliath Corporation that manages England is willing to go to war with Wales, hiding the book and the Prose Portal allowing access to it, while Wales asks for its Dylan Thomas poems, sitting in England but constituting Wales's rightful possession, to avoid warfare. The industrial company's main interest lies in the Prose Portal to enhance its profits, yet it utilizes cultural tools to reach its aims: it employs literary detectives and influences political situations with the help of literary works. The (dis)possession of certain texts may lead to political frictions or even the possibility of war, and since these political, economic and cultural organizations interact, this (dis)possession does not only serve as a camouflage for acquiring important patents, but also affects national and cultural identity narratives. In this process, an edition of *Jane Eyre* saves the life of the novel's protagonist by absorbing a bullet. In addition to its political, cultural and individual fate-changing qualities, the book *Jane Eyre* by Charlotte Brontë also functions as an object of desire and as a protective shield saving lives, thus assuming commodity and strongly material, even military functions. Most importantly, through the literary detective's interaction with Rochester and thus the plot of the Victorian novel, the book also adopts a dialogic function, changing its status from a silent cultural memento to one that actively engages in influencing present-day events by utilizing its potential as a historical narrative. Consequently, through its multiple roles, the book as an institution also offers possibilities of reading within the framework of identity discourses.

From a social aspect the novel shows both utopian and dystopian characteristics: perceptions of love reproduce romance clichés in a criminal society governed by corrupt global industrial powers. Thursday and Landen's union in the twentieth-century plot reproduces Jane and Rochester's marriage with unlikely interventions and coincidences, while England features as an Orwellian police state full of crimes triggered by literature, cloning and time travel as everyday realities, and wars with ex-colonies and other island countries provoked for profits in the weapon industry by global economic powers. The fact that literary works are at the center of attention, influencing political decisions and events as well as provoking violence, could be read as an attempt to reinstate literature as a powerful political tool and, certainly, further underlines the political power of books. Relations are quite the opposite in Miranda Miller's *Nina in Utopia* (2010), another post–Victorian novel, where the protagonist, Nina, temporarily disappears into the future from Victorian London to experience an alternative reality. In this text, her relationship with her husband deteriorates and he, not open to her new experiences, finally puts her into an asylum. The only possibility for her to establish a satisfactory relationship is in the imaginary twenty-first century, where she meets Jonathan, with whom she forms a short but strong attachment. So, in contrast to the utopian marriage solutions in *The Eyre Affair*, in Miller's text, happy liaisons can be formed only in a utopian setting. This utopian place is present-day London, which from a Victorian perspective, again opposing the dystopian location in Fforde's novel, "may be a dreamland or the Garden of Eden. All here are young and free. Some glide past sitting on wheels, and others have wheels attached to their feet. Strangely dressed or half-naked, they run and shout and chatter like birds in a hundred tongues [...]. Many have dark skins, and I think they must be freed slaves like the one we saw at the Exhibition" (Miller 2010: 14–15). Had Jane or, for that matter, Bertha, been accorded a narrative voice in Fforde's work, they may have reported a similar understanding of today's London with a nineteenth-century eye.

It always proves difficult to discuss feminist legacies when a male author revises texts by female authors, especially when the protagonist is also female. Examining *The Eyre Affair*, one also confronts the feminist-postfeminist dilemma. Besides pointing out that Thursday and Rochester interact as equals throughout the novel (Wells 2007: 205), feminist scholars also underline that even if Jane largely features as a silent background figure because of the author's fear of intervening in a popular canonical text, Fforde nevertheless "pays tribute to the boldness and originality of Brontë's fictional creation" by reinventing Jane as Thursday (199). On the contrary, postfeminist critics claim that while the original ending of *Jane Eyre* provided at the beginning of *The Eyre Affair*, where, differently from Charlotte Brontë's version, Jane starts a career in India that makes her a role model for Thursday, would be a feminist move, the fact that this ending is reversed by the twentieth-century protagonist, followed by her own utopistic marriage, validates the ending of the Victorian novel: "It emphasises the continuous importance of love, marriage, and family *even* for a strong, independent woman" (Wehrmann 2007: 162–163, emphasis added). This emerging strange contrast of the needs of women with careers to those without probably stems from the unclear definition of postfeminism.

Initially, Wehrmann depicts postfeminism as a pluralist and dynamic amendment to the second wave of feminism in the eighties (Wehrmann 2007: 150), which view he modifies in his conclusion to regarding it as an ambiguous concept. In terms of *The Eyre Affair*, this means that the novel is evaluated as a highly regressive fantasy at the same time as it is judged radical for raising "legitimate questions about feminist assumptions and limiting gender roles propagated by the movement" (163). The author finally concludes that Fforde's text still demonstrates the difficulty of reconciling women's families and careers, which partly explains his use of "even" in the above quote but renders his postfeminist reading less convincing. The other delicate item in this respect seems to be Bertha's fate. Her death is caused by the interference of Jane's abductor setting Thornfield on fire, changing Bertha's last suicidal act of revenge into her coincidentally becoming the victim of a murder. Scholars note the thus emerging revision of her rage advocated by feminists, but they interpret it as a proof of *The Eyre Affair*'s purpose being entertainment and not correction, in contrast to that of *Wide Sargasso Sea* (Berninger and Thomas 2007: 189, footnote 20). Not accepting this argument so willingly, I think there may be a connection between the comic mode and the inattention to, or rejection of, the feminist agenda, possibly putting the novel into a postfeminist or even antifeminist theoretical framework.[10]

The Eyre Affair is characterized as genre-busting (Fforde 2003a: blurb). It shows resemblances to comedy and film scripts, especially observable in Fforde's writing style and plot moves, some of which seem like film cuts. Some critics compare the different fictional worlds of *The Eyre Affair* with the split realities in film production as well (Berninger and Thomas 2007: 192). The novel also blends elements of the Gothic, realism, romance and the fairy tale. Still, it is mostly categorized as detective and science fiction (Wehrmann 2007: 149, Berninger and Thomas 2007: 186). The text appropriates the typical dark urban scenery of Victorian London as a well-defined period landscape, and its plot is based on unraveling mysteries and bloody crimes, amply confirming critics' claim that in such rewritings killing is cute (Sweet 2001: 74). With the action happening simultaneously in the alternative world of Britain in the 1980s and the fictional world of the novel *Jane Eyre*, aided by motifs like time travel and genetic engineering, the text reads as an alternative history fantasy. It certainly also has many comic moments that trivialize nineteenth-century romance and Gothic elements. Thursday's intervention in the plot of *Jane Eyre* provides one such example, supplying a parodic explanation to the scene generally perceived as melodramatic. She reveals the supernatural call that makes Jane return to Rochester as her imitation: "I had found her at the Riverses' house, gone to her window and barked: 'Jane, Jane, Jane!' in a hoarse whisper the way that Rochester did. It wasn't a good impersonation but it did the trick. I saw Jane start to fluster and pack almost immediately" (Fforde 2003a: 347). Rochester as a Byronic hero receives a similarly comic bent, when it turns out that in Jane's absence from Thornfield he guides twentieth-century literary tourists through the house to make some extra money. The Christian tradition gets equally questioned, as a vampire politely warns Thursday that satanic creatures do not dread the Christian cross any more since they come from a multicultural background (Rubik 2007: 175–178, Berninger and Thomas 2007: 188–189). Such novelistic conventions that were popular in the nineteenth century become at once reinforced and revised in current adaptations.

An Endless Source: Charles Dickens

Charles Dickens and his work have been imprinted in cultural memory as *the* representations of Victorian times, explaining the abundance of literary, filmic and stage adaptations as well as the ongoing critical engagement with his oeuvre. This celebrity status not only lives on in novelistic refashionings, where, for example, his fictionalized figure modestly refers to himself as "The One and Only" (Arnold 2008: 138), but also through the operation of the theme park Dickens World. This place of edutainment offers fun for visitors by letting them experience sights, sounds and smells of the Victorian age, by way of participating in simulated events related to Dickens and his novels. In the course of "The *Great Expectations* Boat Ride," for example, they can follow events of the nineteenth-century novel, especially Magwitch's journey. At the same time, the facility provides educational packs on the famous author and his age, which interactively relate one of Dickens' texts, or set up an interview with a Dickensian character whom pupils can ask questions about correspondences of the Victorian times to the twenty-first century.

Based on these multiple translations of the writer, his works, and related popular cultural associations, Marty Gould and Rebecca N. Mitchell interpret Dickens World as a site of literary and cultural encounter that can be framed by adaptation theory, focusing on core adaptive issues including structure, nostalgia, spectacle, narrative and commodification.

In "The *Great Expectations* Boat Ride," for instance, instead of a coherent narrative, visitors are offered its separate elements only. While maintaining the theme of crime, the referents get mixed up and the plot moves are distorted, thus highlighting difficulties adaptation involves. The authors argue that in this process, meaning-making largely depends on the readers/visitors' agency (Gould and Mitchell 2010: 159–161), which is a process I have already pointed out in the case of *The Eyre Affair*, where the novel's website and especially organized commercial events function as forums for such practices. Baudrillard's concept of simulation I have utilized in describing the heritage centers of the 1980s and '90s also applies to today's theme parks. Ann Heilmann and Mark Llewellyn maintain that Dickens's characterization technique grounded in exaggeration assists in perceiving the actors embodying fictional figures in Dickens World as authentic (Heilmann and Llewellyn 2010: 214), and they point out that in this context "the hyperreal world begins to assert a claim to be a visualization of the real" (220). The theme park's scope of activities has been expanded to an international event, including festivals, exhibitions and conferences, for the 200th anniversary of Dickens's birth[11] in 2012 ("Dickens 2012"), which combines academic, popular and commercial interests. This approach of the bicentenary celebrations of the Dickens phenomenon also supports the conciliatory cultural argument concerning the function of Dickens World: rather than dividing critics and consumers into serious readers and those who buy into the Disneyfication of the historical author, the theme park can be viewed as a site that eventually connects high and low culture (Earl 2008, Gould and Mitchell 2010: 149–150).

Enjoying such immense popularity with professional and nonprofessional audiences, the figure and works of Charles Dickens constitute a prolific research source for examining contemporary responses to the Victorian era. Derivatives from Dickens's life and texts, commonly called Dickensiana, constitute a complex web of adaptations. These texts utilize and often mix the author's biographical data with his novels, mainly focusing on the current aspects of revision emphasized throughout this book: literary, social and political factors in general, and authorial, feminist, postcolonial and postimperial issues in particular. Perhaps Peter Ackroyd is the best known Dickens appropriator. His repertoire of refashionings ranges from rewriting one of the Victorian author's texts into a novel (*Little Dorrit* in *The Great Fire of London*, 1982), through referring to numerous of his texts in one chapter of a novel (*English Music*, 1992), to creating a monumental all-integrative biography of the nineteenth-century classic (*Dick-

ens, 1990). Due to its saturation in the Dickens experience, Charles Palliser's *The Quincunx* (1989) is regarded as an attempt to reproduce all Dickens novels (Malone 1990: 12).There are adaptations which qualify the Victorian author's life from a feminist point of view: Anne-Marie Vukelic's *Far Above Rubies* (2010), by fictionalizing the autobiography of Catherine Dickens, and Gaynor Arnold's *Girl in a Blue Dress* (2008), through getting the life of an invented nineteenth-century writer, Alfred Gibson's, modeled on Dickens's, narrated by his neglected wife, mixing biographical records with information taken from his fictional texts. In what follows, I focus on two postcolonial refashionings of mainly one source text from the adaptive map of Dickensiana: Peter Carey's *Jack Maggs*, published in 1997, and Lloyd Jones's *Mister Pip*, short-listed for the Man Booker Prize in 2006. Titled after fictional characters in Dickens's *Great Expectations* (1861), the nineteenth-century original they rewrite, both novels closely combine the concept of the author with British imperial and colonial legacies, providing literary and cultural responses to the conflicting process of exporting and re-importing Dickens.

Jack Maggs is set in the Dickensian London that is full of crimes, prostitution and corruption. Maggs arrives here in search of his ward, Henry Phipps, and meets the writer, Tobias Oates, who promises to help him. The eccentric Oates conducts medical experiments and séances of mesmerism without expertise, which result in his accidental killing of people. He is equally adventurous and careless in his private life: he cheats on his wife with her sister and then kills the sister through an overdose of pills given to her to get rid of her baby from their affair. Similarly to Oates, Henry Phipps turns out to be a conceited character. He lives off the money Jack deposits on his account, but instead of meeting his benefactor, he tries to kill Maggs so that he can keep his house. It becomes clear that the phantom haunting Jack who occurs during the mesmeric sessions, dreams and Jack's emerging memory fragments is Henry Phipps himself: "There, in the firelight, he beheld his nightmare: long straight nose, fair hair, brutal dreadful uniform of the 57th Foot regiment. The Phantom had broken the locks and entered his life. The apparition held a heavy pistol" (Carey 1997b: 385). The Pip of *Great Expectations* reappears in the dystopian shape of an aggressive British soldier threatening the population of invaded territories. Jack escapes from these corruptive crime scenes and offensive images of the colonizer country and exchanges his unsuccessful stay in England for a peaceful, prosperous life in the colony, eventually dying in Australia as an acknowledged president of his district.

Jack Maggs is perceived to be writing back to *Great Expectations* as *Wide Sargasso Sea* writes back to *Jane Eyre*: most of the original situations are reversed, disfavoring the dominant Anglocentric discourse and rehabilitating the Australians (Letissier 2004: 124, Humpherys 2005: 450). Even Maggs's handwriting recording his life bears the sign of this reversal, as it can only be read by applying a mirror, offering an alternative perspective on events, thus constituting another fictional example of the refracting qualities of glass, discussed in connection with Carey's earlier novel, *Oscar and Lucinda*. As in *Oscar and Lucinda*, relations between England and Australia are surveyed by the motivation to understand the past through ancestry. Georges Letissier interprets the ending of the novel, letting Maggs return to Australia, as a shift in the possibility of identifications: instead of the English readership of *Great Expectations*, this way the Australian audience of *Jack Maggs* is able to experience itself as "a whole nation of convicts' descendants" (Letissier 2004: 126). Dianne F. Sadoff reads *Jack Maggs* within the framework of trauma theory, viewing Jack as a return of the repressed underclass, criminalized population of Britain "to re-cognise — and transfigure/transcend — his trauma through (re)writing" (Sadoff 2010: 178); and his way of putting pen to paper can, of course, also be read as Jack's traumatic means of revealing and reliving his experience. However, as Simon Joyce also describes, Maggs has a torn identity, that of an Englishman in England and in New South Wales when he consciously constructs it, and one that oscillates between a Cockney criminal's and an Australian's when he is unconscious or unreflexive. The critic concludes that it belongs to imperial legacies that former colonies continue to be partially defined by the British mindset or cultural tenets (Joyce 2007: 163–165), which would explain Jack's behavior as an individual subjected to those legacies. Another point of unease in reading this novel is the fact that, as Louisa Hadley points out, even if the novel counters the nineteenth-century bildungsroman form and shifts its focus to a marginal figure, Maggs's account on its own does not prove sufficient for the story. It can only be pieced together from more narratives and, in the end, his letters do not survive into the future, in contrast to Oates's adaptation of his narrative (Hadley 2010: 40–44).

I think that in addition to the ex-convict's problematic self-identification, and the endurance of the version of Jack's tale which is narrated by an agent of the dominant culture, in Carey's novel the act of writing back is also qualified by the powerful re-imagining of the author figure, testing the success of the postcolonial narrative (not the success of the postcolonial fictional figure, however). Maggs's letters are not deciphered by his addressee, the convict's ward, Phipps, but by Oates, who compromises the authority of his exquisite mediator position and uses Jack's diary and letters to enhance his own career as a writer. Tobias Oates writes about anything for money, prioritizes writing over life, and perceives all his interactions with others in the service of his great work. On meeting Maggs, Oates wants to find out who the mysterious man is, and mesmerizes him, gaining access to a memory he "can enter, and leave" (Carey 1997b: 87). Oates's relationship to Maggs during these sessions is parasitic, which he maintains later as well by writing the material he gathers this way into an account that will make him famous. Once he learns that the Australian man is a convict, Oates wants to write Jack's story into a groundbreaking novel: "But in all of English literature there was nothing like the dark journey he now planned to take inside the Criminal Mind" (Carey 1997b: 214), which sounds as boastful as Edward Casaubon's venture to find the Key to All Mythologies in George Eliot's *Middlemarch* (1871). As Joyce also observes, in this exercise Oates maintains his colonizer position as he is utterly disinterested in the convict's experience in the colony, providing "insights into the processes by which a figure such as Dickens might have written *Great Expectations*, with little knowledge of or interest in Magwitch's experience between his transportation and return" (Joyce 2010: 164–165). In Oates's novel, titled *The Death of Jack Maggs*, the writer imagines Jack's death in a fire, which is the end he himself finally meets. Maggs reads the manuscript and "[h]e knew his life and death were not his own" (Carey 1997b: 324),[12] so he forces the writer to burn it. However, Oates reproduces the text again, establishing his great fame, which happens chronologically and methodologically in parallel to Dickens's 1859–61 publication of *Great Expectations* in a serial and then a volume format.[13]

Such appropriations of others' lives or letters for narrative purposes problematizes the ethics of writing, that is, the nineteenth-century dichotomy of truth and decency, which translates into the postmodern questioning of "the possibility of accurately narrating the past" (Hadley 2010: 41), and, perhaps, even into the indecency of the power to abuse the past. Oates's empowerment to acquire knowledge about Maggs, through gaining exclusive access to his past by colonizing his brain and stealing his property for his own purposes, resembles the post–Victorian process of appropriating Victorian material and piecing various fragments together into an arbitrary story. The figure of Oates also provides an intriguing example of how the nineteenth-century importance of the writer appears in today's reconstructions of literary authors as celebrities. He reads as a parody of Dickens, mocking the myth surrounding the Victorian author's cultic personality. Such a refashioning can also be understood as an ironic opinion of the dubiousness of current literary endeavors that revive the Victorian age through a fictionalized nineteenth-century account of acquiring literary fame. The claim that the identities of the convict and the author merge—"The novel identifies the writer as criminal and the criminal as writer" (Sadoff 2010: 180)—also seems to underline the ambiguous nature of this project. The authorial chain of Carey rewriting Dickens/Oates rewriting Maggs implies contemporary authors' symbolic move of reinstating authorship, just as I have argued earlier in the case of similar authorial appropriations of Henry James. In this biographical process the Australian writer gets equally implicated (Hadley 2010: 53, Sadoff 2010: 180). Power relations within the novel are just as telling: the ex-convict can prosper only if he transports himself back to the colony, and it is exclusively the text of the metropolitan rewriter that survives.

Carey's *Jack Maggs* and Lloyd Jones's *Mister Pip* are usually connected within a postcolonial framework, as this is the discourse through which their revisionary moves can best be established. By transporting its criminals and exploiting them in the colonies in the long nineteenth century, Britain managed to safely distance its metropolis from the rest of the empire. To use Catherine Hall and Sonya Rose's term, it became an "island nation," which expresses the colonizer's deliberate escapism from difficulties caused by its own actions (Hall and Rose 2006: 20–21). Sadoff reads *Great Expectations* as a novel saturated with traumatic experience, which comes to light through the protagonist's hauntedness by suppressed memories, dreams and hallucinations. This repressed aspect of Dickens's novel returns in the forms of psychic, physical, national, imperial and historical traumas in its postcolonial rewritings, including Carey's Australian and Jones's New Zealand perspectives. In describing what these two adaptations do to the Victorian text, the author uses the terms "argue" and "claim" (Sadoff 2010: 164), which also proves my point that post–Victorian texts can be and, indeed, are read as criticism. Jennifer Gribble even seems to forge a sequel-like relationship between the two rewritings, when she argues that "Carey creates an Australian way of seeing, but Australian ways of seeing are subjected to powerful indictment in *Mister Pip*" (Gribble 2008: 183). In addition, in Jones's adaptation, the privileging of the speaker gets a further twist. The English boy's narrative lead of *Great Expectations*, accorded to the Australian patriarchal man in *Jack Maggs*, is transferred to a young indigenous girl, Mathilda, in *Mister Pip*. Hence, the Victorian text and context are put to an even more complex use in this latter revision.

In *Mister Pip* it is the Australians who try to gain more power over the island of Papua New Guinea in the 1990s, by provoking ethnic and civil conflicts among the inhabitants, which shows how British imperial practices are inherited further in the ex-colonies. Pip's story is doubly rewritten into twentieth-century narratives: it is interwoven with Mr. Watts's account of his life, who, in the course of events, identifies himself both with Pip and Charles Dickens; and it becomes the indigenous character-narrator Mathilda's breakout from the war-stricken Bougainville, New Zealand. In her autobiography, Mathilda retrospectively recounts her village school years, where together with their teacher, Mr. Watts, the students read a version of Charles Dickens's *Great Expectations*. The pupils go home and share their learning experience with their parents, and the name Mr. Pip spreads around the island so rapidly that some rioters, not trained to differentiate between fictional and real characters, start looking for him. Trying to stop the troubles his teaching material has caused, Mr. Watts first assumes the identity of Mr. Dickens, taking responsibility for the creation of Mr. Pip, but once he realizes that the attackers want a Mr. Pip who is alive, he identifies himself as that. The atrocities claim the lives and homes of numerous natives, Mathilda's mother being one of them: she is first raped and then killed. Mr. Watts tries to pacify the rioters by recounting his autobiography, to which they listen for a while, but then suddenly kill him and feed him to the pigs. In addition to the civil war to which the repeating conflicts have amounted, there is a flood in which Mathilda almost dies, an ending that echoes the solution of George Eliot's *Mill on the Floss* (1860). However, a log finally saves her, which she, remembering Pip's benefactor in *Great Expectations*, christens Mr. Jaggers. She then lands in Australia, reads Dickens's complete works and writes her thesis on *Great Expectations*. After visiting the British Library and Dickens heritage sites in London, she disappointedly returns home and, instead of pursuing an academic career, sets to writing her autobiography.

Just like Carey's Maggs, Mathilda embodies a positive bildungsroman figure, and similarly to Tobias Oates, who suffers the death he envisions for Jack, Mr. Watts gets killed in his efforts to claim authority through the Victorian writer and his character. Both novels feature an appropriative writer figure, but the mocking of Dickens's life in *Jack Maggs* takes on a more serious tone when transposing the historical author into the twentieth-century setting of Jones's text, not to mention the closer proximity to the nineteenth-century writer by literally naming him, instead of just modeling a character on his persona. Mr. Watts, as the only white man on the island, becomes the victim of his own project, using an emblematic author and book of the British Empire for the establishment of a Western male cultural influence on a conquered, repeatedly colonized island of the past. In addition, as Mathilda later finds out from his first wife in Australia, Mr. Watts abandoned his family before moving to Bougainville. This character trait can again be paralleled to Dickens's neglecting behavior towards his family, underlined by feminist rewritings of his life, like the following quote from *Far Above Rubies* shows: "I [Catherine Dickens] stood for a moment, waiting for some sign of gratitude or acknowledgment, but instead, he picked up his pen, dipped it in the inkwell and became engrossed once more in his writing. It was as if I was not there at all" (Vukelic 2010: 64). Her readings also make Mathilda realize that Dickens was a character who ruthlessly got rid of his family: "The man who writes so touchingly and powerfully about orphans cannot wait to turn his own kin out the door" (Lloyd Jones 2006: 212). In this capacity, the teller of Dickens's stories is comparable to the Victorian writer, making Watts's life analogous to Dickens's, and his death an end the nineteenth-century author could also have met. Hence, just as in *Jack Maggs*, in *Mister Pip*, the figure of the author possibly rewriting Dickens is controversial and suffers a brutal death, indicating alternative fates for the historical author. This implies further potentials in writing literary biographies, just as the possibility of the rewriting of Charlotte Brontë does in Thomas's *Charlotte* and that of Henry James does in Hollinghurst's *The Line of Beauty*.

One could claim that through its double ending *Great Expectations* has itself delivered its first adaptation.[14] John Bryant, however, counters this, by claiming that even if the more optimistic conclusion means a complete reconception of the original story, the confidence of the second version cannot be comprehended without the pessimism of the first one (Bryant 2002: 87). In my view, this still does not exclude reading the latter version as an adaptation of the former, especially in Bryant's framework, which promotes a flexible understanding of rewriting based on textual fluidity. As we have seen, the controversial ending reappears in the two discussed post–Victorian revisions, since they offer both positive and negative bildungsroman stories for the main characters they rewrite. In *Mister Pip* there is also an emphasis on how Dickens's novel works in a different context. The book functions as a British cultural memento or "portable property" (Gribble 2008: 187) with various repercussions. Due to its strong but foreign influence on children, it incites conflicts between the native parents and Mr. Watts. For one of these children, Mathilda, the text provides a source of identification. Her closeness to the idealized but distant English boy, Pip, and his story resembles the way Antoinette is drawn to the English painting *The Miller's Daughter* in *Wide Sargasso Sea*. Just as the novels *Jane Eyre* and *Wide Sargasso Sea*, together with their authors, feature as central determinants of Miranda's life and narrative in *Charlotte*, *Great Expectations* and Dickens/Mr. Watts also influence Mathilda's fate and account in *Mister Pip*. The Victorian text functions as a narrative of empowerment for her, assisting in creating her own identity, even if she later learns that the real *Great Expectations* is different from the children's version she first knew: "She is able to place her story of emergence within a wider history of exploitation, genocide and slavery. She discovers that stories are subject to interpretation, bearers of ideology" (Gribble 2008: 190–191). Once she acquires enough information about Dickens and his text in the course of her studies and travels, she develops the ability to contextualize her readings. As Sadoff phrases it, "Imitating Dickens's characters and identifying with the author function, Matilda has begun to learn about the place and utility of literary criticism" (Sadoff 2010: 183). Weighing all this knowledge about the production, manipulation and reception of literary texts, Mathilda finally decides that instead of writing her dissertation on Dickens's orphans she will embark on the narrative of her own life. This is where the novel returns to its beginning: the reader becomes conscious that s/he is reading Mathilda's story, the narrator has found her own voice.

The novel has a strong political potential as well: it provokes wars among various ethnicities and civil entities, saving and ruining lives. In a postcolonial and postimperial framework, the fate of *Great Expectations* illustrates how the inheritance of Victorian imperial practices causes warfare among islands of the Pacific at the end of the twentieth century, proving that the discourse of imperialism is still sustained. The function of the book can also be compared to the novel *Jane Eyre* in *Charlotte*, where it means a source of escape for Miranda from herself and the life which she dislikes. In *Mister Pip*, Dickens's text also provides safety, but not in terms of escapism as it would in the metropolis; rather, as a means to diminish fears that arise in the actual real war-context: "Our only consolation was that by reading it a second and a third time we would still have another country to flee to. And that would save our sanity" (Lloyd Jones 2006: 80). Yet, very much like in *The Eyre Affair*, it is precisely the fight over the ownership of the nineteenth-century novel that causes political tensions, so in this case the book as a historical document and a memory object actively participates in engendering events as well. The worshipping of the only copy of *Great Expectations* in Jones's text resembles Miranda's father's enthusiasm for the faked *Jane Eyre* manuscript in *Charlotte* and the protection of the manuscript of the Brontë novel in *The Eyre Affair*. In *Mister Pip*, the book gets lost, stolen, burnt and recreated, and displays multiple roles reviving personal and collective memories of the past; in other words, it is an object whose materiality and fictional content undergo a series of changes. Hence, just like in *The Eyre Affair*, the focalization of a literary text confirms the political potential of literature.

The ongoing reinterpretation of canonized literary characters and texts in new adaptations results in a never-ending novelistic production, reviving the novel sequence. This seems to be a paradoxical postmodern venture whereby nineteenth-century literary conventions are reinforced at the same time as they get deconstructed. Such duplicity of interpretation also informs opinions on post–Victorian fiction's impact on the literary canon. It conserves the canon by making people reread Victorian novels, while simultaneously (re)discovering, revaluing and transforming it (Letissier 2004: 112). Post-Victorian novels affect the canon in an oxymoronic way, namely, by the nostalgic subversion/reinforcement of the Victorian era and its texts (Gutleben 2001: 192). Some even claim that rewriting itself is the main thing responsible for enhancing the actual survival of the canon, especially among nonprofessional readers, and therefore advocate its more intensive research (Lefevere 1992: 7).[15] One way to do this would be to follow the suggestion Linda K. Hughes and Michael Lund make in the conclusion of their book, *The Victorian Serial*, namely, to experience historical reading and meaning-making strategies by reintroducing nineteenth-century serialized reading, thereby not only "situating the literary canon in its cultural context," but also interrogating literary pieces in new ways (Hughes and Lund 1991: 276). In turn, new narratives or new sequences would be summoned, like Mr. Watts's eclectic postimperial account or Mathilda's emerging postcolonial autobiography in *Mister Pip*. In fact, the reintegration of nineteenth-century cultural values Hughes and Lund attribute to the serial as "a central literary form of the era," representing episodes of the human lifespan from birth do death (1), is double-faced, as it triggers new readings at the same time as reinforcing old narratives of human evolution.

Experiments at various levels of readership, from leisurely reading clubs to professional university classes of Victorian and post–Victorian fiction, are conducted to reintroduce the reading of long novels in serial format, as was common in the nineteenth century. This enterprise betrays complex cultural considerations. David Barndollar and Susan Schorn, for example, propose that with the reintroduction of serialized reading, audiences would refocus their attention to text and context, re-establishing a relationship between reading, literature, and aspects of life more generally. They report on their experiments of subjecting groups of people to reading Charles Dickens's *Little Dorrit* and *A Tale of Two Cities* in monthly and weekly installments, respectively, and explain the relevance and possible success of reading in serial format by relating it to methods of consumption audiences employ for digesting today's media soaps (Barndollar and Schorn 2002: 168–169). Iris Kleinecke provides an actual example of this analogy: she compares serialized readings and showings of Dickens's texts with the television series *EastEnders*, concluding that the reader or viewer utilizes the same method of perception and, interestingly, that the two products also correspond topically (Kleinecke 2007). Heilmann and Llewellyn further discuss television adaptations of Dickens's novels with a particular focus on Andrew Davies, who "has built a reputation for the reinvigoration of the classic serial format" (Heilmann and Llewellyn 2010: 237). They describe the reception of Davies's recent adaptations of *Bleak House* (2007) and *Little Dorrit* (2008), which exploit the nineteenth-century installment structure and merge it with today's soap opera techniques, and also argue that this showing method as well as the weeknight time slot, mimicking *EastEnders*,' assists the audience in establishing parallels between the Victorian age and today's realism (ibid.). The authors interpret this generic return to nineteenth-century forms of production and reception as a desire for "a more 'authentic' experience of the Victorian text" (215).

The creation of suspense through the installment structure and the thus accentuated subgenres of sensation and detective fiction also connect these two serial modes of cultural production (Sanders 2006: 122). The immensely popular television series *House, M.D.*, with its protagonist solving a mysterious case in each episode, serves as an example of this connection, the production being inspired by the similarly serialized investigations of Sherlock Holmes, not to mention that the BBC started rebroadcasting the Sherlock Holmes series anew in 2010.[16] In Julian Barnes's fictional biography, *Arthur and George* (2005), the installment format of serializing fiction also receives metacommentary, by tracing Arthur Conan Doyle's thoughts during the creation process and acclaim of his Sherlock Holmes series:

> Magazines published two kinds of stories: either lengthy serialisations which ensnared the reader week by week and month by month; or single, free-standing tales. The trouble with the tales was that they often didn't give you enough to bite on. The trouble with the serializations was that if you happened to miss a single issue, you lost the plot. Applying his practical brain to the problem, Arthur envisaged combining the virtues of the two forms: a series of stories, each complete in itself, yet filled with running characters to reignite the reader's sympathy or disapproval [Barnes 2005: 47–48].

Later, Conan Doyle is shocked by the fact how much art can overwrite life: the newspapers do not devote any space to his father's death but are full of protests against the death of Holmes "whose popularity had begun to embarrass and even disgust his creator" (69). Once he learns how the market works, "He also knows that in the end the reader is king" (213), so he brings Holmes back to life (which is precisely the dilemma the third series of the BBC adaptation has to solve as well). Hence, the engagement with the creative process and authorial intentionality that Hutcheon encourages critics to focus on (Hutcheon 2006: 94–95), as mentioned earlier, is already happening on a fictional level. The invention and later reinvigoration of the figure of Sherlock Holmes thus influenced by the literary market resulted in a series of fifty-six short stories, four novels and a number of adaptations. In *Arthur and George*, the Holmes story is doubled, as Arthur himself becomes his own creation, engaged in researching the case of the wrongly sentenced solicitor, while his assistant gets put into the role of Dr. Watson, which they both reflect on. This encounter could also be serialized as another detective sequel with the author assuming the role of his character.

In the opening remarks of his book *Charles Dickens in Cyberspace*, Jay Clayton argues that the Victorian author qualifies as one of the best candidates for survival in the present technological age, underlining how Dickens promoted innovations of his time, for example, by playing a major role in inventing the serialization of fiction (Clayton 2003: 3–4). *Mister Pip* features a fictional example of serialized comprehension, interpreted as the reiteration of Dickens's own legendary readings (Gribble 2008: 188). A simplified version of *Great Expectations* serves as a successful teaching tool: children's instruction consists of joint reading and discussion of the novel's installments, intermingled with parents' speeches on their most important wisdoms of life. The difficulty in conveying a literary product in a different culture is amply illustrated in the comprehension problems native readers experience. Their lack of matching referents for some phenomena addressed in the novel, such as "a rimy morning" and "metropolis" (Lloyd Jones 2006: 195), hinders their understanding and, in some cases, leads to their discarding of the novel as "fancy nancy English talk" (ibid.). Yet, the text remains popular enough for warriors to search for a real Mister Pip whom their imagination has created from the fictional character, in the process of which the only copy of the novel gets burnt. Thereafter the teacher and his pupils have to recreate *Great Expectations* from their memories, which they do with the help of their detailed knowledge of the serial installments. Atrocities continue until Mr. Watts identifies himself as Mr. Pip to stop the killings. He promises to tell his story to his capturers in seven installments, mixing *Great Expectations* and his own biography — later referred to as "his Pacific version of *Great Expectations*. As with the original, Mr. Watts' version was also serialized, parceled out over a number of nights" (Lloyd Jones 2006: 149), — which he cannot finish because he gets killed as well. When Mathilda eventually becomes a university lecturer in Australia, she repeats Mr. Watts's teaching method and reads *Great Expectations* to her students, who are just as spellbound by the installments as she was earlier.

Mister Pip exemplifies how earlier authors, texts and even modes of reading are employed to (re)write cultural memory, which legitimizes the method of activating various memory objects, such as books, photographs or buildings, as interpretive tools in understanding the past. Contemporary critics of post–Victorian texts tend to consciously embrace multiple perspectives of reading as well as interdisciplinary survey techniques when exploring rewritings. Lena Steveker, for example, bases her research of cultural memory in Byatt's fiction on Jan and Aleida Assmann's theories of remembering, focusing both on verbal and non-verbal media, especially the function of the high canon of British literature constructing British cultural memory (Steveker 2010: 5). Byatt's work is indeed a bank of British classics, and her Booker-winning novel, *Possession*, mostly engages with Victorian material. Similarly to *The Eyre Affair* and *Charlotte*, the finding, stealing, reacquiring and forging of manuscripts, especially the correspondence of the two Victorian authors, gains a central, plot-organizing function, let alone that the greatness of the English nation or primacy of English culture depends on the possession of such original texts, which count as important relics that should be kept in a safe place and not revealed or sold to others. The brooch that provides the proof of family lineage between the twentieth-century researcher Maud and her nineteenth-century research subject Christabel La Motte also functions as an important object for individual memory.

The two immensely popular classics *Jane Eyre* and *Great Expectations*, the impact of which on post–Victorian fiction has been a central focus in this chapter, appear together in Gail Jones's *Sixty Lights* (2004), aiding the acts of personal remembering and mourning. Lucy Strange, the migrant orphan protagonist of the novel, recalls her mother through her favorite reading. Honoria Brady, Lucy's mother, shares the story of *Jane Eyre* like an honorable secret with everyone dear to her, which Lucy in her turn hands down to some of her companions, after having found a copy of the novel with underlined passages among the objects she inherited, and remembering her mother by this memento. Imparting these aspects of the Brontë novel is always connected to important life events whose detailed account is usually missing from Victorian fiction, such as sexual intercourse, the deaths of husbands, and children at childbirth: Honoria tells her future husband about Jane and Rochester's harmonious relationship on an important date before their marriage; then she relates the whole plot of *Jane Eyre* to her housekeeper, Molly Minchin, who has just been widowed; and Lucy reads from the "sentimental novel" *Jane Eyre* to Violet after her friend loses her child. As Kate Mitchell also points out, Lucy's brother, Thomas, finally faces the loss of his sister and is capable of experiencing his grief by rereading *Great Expectations*, the novel they read together in their childhood (Mitchell 2008: 98). By the repeated reading of the novel, he relives the communal experience of reading it with his deceased sister and uncle, which helps him face death and resuscitate personal and collective memories of the past (Mitchell 2010b: 165).

In the same text, photographs equally assist the protagonist's negotiation of self-identity, juxtaposed with dominant narratives of the imperial nation. Apart from serving as a means to construct the orphan's origin linked to her missing mother (Mitchell 2010b: 153–156), photography also assists in rewriting nineteenth-century imperial identity into a multicultural one, based on the travels of an imperial subject. Lucy Strange's visual imagination aids this process by approximating traumatic moments into sixty (mental) snapshots. Having lived in Australia, England and India, Lucy searches for a narrative of identification that synthesizes her experiences. "Lucy now found her own culture a shock. After eight weeks in England she was still thinking of India and feeling misplaced and dislocated" (Gail Jones 2004: 184). Therefore, watching a propaganda film about how the British Empire put down the Indian Mutiny does not awaken the reaction her compatriots expect of her: "I am disgusted," said Lucy loudly, "by National Spirit" (185). Rejecting the binaries in which national and cultural characteristics are commonly perceived, she finally visualizes her identity as a tripod when thinking about her journey back to England: "Australia, England and India all held her — upheld her — on a platform of vision, seeking her own focus. These were the zones of her eye, the conditions of her salutary estrangement" (212). These sentences already account for the attitude of the photographer that she has become, zooming in at certain perspectives of vision and always remaining a constructive outsider. This attitude becomes desirable by another rebellious youth, Lucy's companion Jacob Webb, who expresses a strong wish to be strange (note how, by emphasizing this characteristic, the heroine's surname receives an explanation), that is, foreign enough to have a good basis of comparison for perceiving things (214–215). This example demonstrates how photographs can yield productive memory objects through which remembrances are visualized and refracted.

In my earlier discussions of recontextualizations of the Crystal Palace and the Great Exhibition in some post-Victorian texts, such as Peter Carey's *Oscar and Lucinda* (1988) and Clare Boylan's *Emma Brown* (2003), I have demonstrated how the refraction of memory accounts takes place by utilizing architectural monuments. These stories mark the discordance between individual identities and reigning national and cultural narratives of identity in both the nineteenth and the twentieth centuries. As it emerges from the analyses, post-Victorian novels activating various memory objects yield a range of possible readings. One group of such interpretations offers narratives of ongoing attempts to define and promote national and cultural identities largely dependent on political ideologies, as in *Oscar and Lucinda*, the imperial practices on colonies, as in *Sixty Lights*; or the inheritance and application of these practices by the ex-colonies for gaining local territories, as in *Mister Pip*. While acknowledging this understanding, the other, more recent group of critical analyses focuses more on individual and collective cultural memories that the outcast protagonists of the novels activate. These characters often travel between England and its various (ex)-colonies, experience a number of cultural influences, and are at pains to integrate those to form their own identities. While Oscar fails in this journey as he sinks with the glass church in *Oscar and Lucinda*, Lucinda makes her way into the labor movement. Lucy in *Sixty Lights* dies of consumption, yet her mode of vision and her photographs survive her and have the power to influence the thinking of those who live on. Mathilda's narrative in *Mister Pip* seems a success story: she is able to emerge as a richer person, eventually finding her own voice. All three texts seem to insist on new attitudes to remembering, forming identities that are complex, individual and multiple.

Conclusion: Ways Forward in Researching Post-Victorian Fiction

This final section is devoted to the reiteration of the most important foci of my study and to discussing questions that may require additional inquiry, pointing towards further research directions in mapping out the post–Victorian phenomenon. In this monograph, I have examined texts and contexts of post–Victorian fiction, aiming to situate this increasing body of novels in contemporary literary and cultural criticism, as well as to investigate the theoretical and ideological debates they incite or join. Emphasizing the complexity of these rewritings, I have carried out their discussion at the cross-section of different discourses and cultural practices. I have contextualized them in the generic-literary historical discourse of the historical novel intersecting with contemporary, non-teleological perceptions of history, as well as the theoretical and cultural historical discourse of the literary postmodern, in particular, postmodern prose in English and the accompanying changes in its cultural function and institutional system. As a result of the cultural turn in literary theory and studies, I have also concentrated on framing post–Victorian fiction in the discourse of the continuous re-evaluation of the Victorian age, which advocates emerging analytical perspectives like cultural memory and trauma studies.

Within this discourse, I have addressed the prevalent issue of identity in the critical frameworks of postimperialism and postcolonialism that permanently feature in (re)constructions of the English/British past and pasts in English, by examining narratives of national, cultural, and self-identities via contexts of race, sex, gender, class, authorship, heritage, nostalgia, enterprise, and material culture.

The occasion of drawing up and reflecting on the post-Victorian canon presents itself as an opportunity to establish some transparency in the scholarship of the field as well. In the process of situating this body of novels in various discourses, the ideological deliberations behind the utilized critical frameworks would also merit further examination. For example, while contextualizing the production and reception of post-Victorian reworkings in current theoretical, social, and political discourses, terminological and definitional divergences, as well as ensuing nuances in critical praxes in approaching these texts, have repeatedly been addressed in the course of this book. The variation of respective denominations, such as retro- or post-Victorian, neo or reverse colonization, or transcultural, prefixed retro-, post-, neo-, reverse-, or trans- and the differences in their semantic fields denoting ideological perspectives from recuperative to revisionary could be further theorized with regard to their generic, temporal, and wider cultural connotations. Such thorough investigations may not only assist in the harmonization of the differences in delimiting the post-Victorian phenomenon, but also in clarifying current changes of any noteworthy theoretical consequence in critical discourses per se, perhaps, pointing towards new analytical frameworks with new terms and apparatus.

The generic and topical diversities of adaptations also have important repercussions in their reading: apart from the observable hybridity of genres typical of contemporary rewritings, post-Victorian novels prioritize certain types of fiction, both reinforcing and revising Victorian novelistic conventions and topoi. These foci also emerge in critical literature. Earlier collections surveying post-Victorian fiction, such as John Kucich and Dianne F. Sadoff's *Victorian Afterlife* (2000) and Christian Gutleben's *Nostalgic Postmodernism* (2001), were organized around the paradox of novels mystifying and subverting Victorianism, influenced by modernist and postmodernist tenets. Recent scholarly literature, however, like Cora Kaplan's *Victoriana* (2007) and Louisa Hadley's *Neo-Victorian Fiction and Historical Narrative* (2010), orient their analyses more along the lines of genre, reviewing biographies and industrial novels, as well as crime, detective, and Gothic fiction. A parallel trend followed by contemporary publications discussing the subject is a topical arrangement of their surveys, as in Ann Heilmann and Mark Llewellyn's *Neo-Victorianism: The Victorians in the Twenty-First Century* (2010) and Marie-Luise Kohlke and Christian Gutleben's *Neo-Victorian Tropes of Trauma* (2010), where essays are organized into broader sections on the family, sexuality, and spectrality, as well as the history and legacies of the empire. In my study on rewriting the nineteenth century, the emphasis has neither been on genre nor on topic exclusively; I have rather fostered an integrative approach of the two by indexing utilized novelistic genres to featured topoi. My grouping of subchapters reflects this principle: Biofiction is analyzed in its relation to the literary scene, and island fiction gets connected to prevalent social and political contexts of post–Victorian reworkings. The findings of these surveys regarding the author, the reader, criticism, and the market, as well as various narratives of identity, have then been combined in the diachronic and synchronic case studies of the later chapters, to reveal further insights at both the historical and the contemporary levels.

An area of research that would broaden our horizon of the literary scene and provide a wider scope of current social and political contexts as well is a more in-depth reading of the post–Victorian graphic novel. The multiple ways of publishing and accessing such fiction, as well as its potential audience, ranging from teenagers to academics, may provide input for fresh insights in adapting the Victorian era. The diversity this genre can offer is alluring to both the popular and the academic ends of the literary market, which means that graphic novels are utilized for various purposes. Kaja and Phil Foglio's *Girl Genius* cycle has all entertaining features for maintaining an enthusiastic young group of readers, including adventure and romance fiction, as well as material goods for sale connected to the sequence (Studio Foglio LLC *Girl Genius* 2001). Graphic reworkings of classic fiction in the *Classics Illustrated* series mostly resolve the length and language constraints of Victorian novels, through adapting them into short, image-dominated pieces, and, by supplying some teacher's resources to a selection of these texts, they aim for an educational contribution as well ("Classic Comic Store Ltd"). Scholars underline the fact that graphic novels are often anti-establishment, thereby adding to the subversive body of post–Victorian fiction (Böehnke 2008), yet, since they work with canonical pieces of literature, they subvert as well as reinforce the canon. Refashioning the myth of Jack the Ripper into a conspiracy assisted by the royal family, and thus attacking the aggression of celebrity culture as well as the British monarchy, Alan Moore and Eddie Campbell's epic *From Hell* (1999) exhibits such paradoxical qualities. Expressing dystopian visions of social ills through the medium of graphic novels may thus enrich existing fictional revisions of Victorian times and their critical perceptions.

As a subgenre of historical fiction, the post–Victorian novel is mostly engaged in issues connected to the production and consumption of historical knowledge, and since it is at the same time concerned with the nineteenth, the twentieth, and the twenty-first centuries, it acutely depicts the process of (the impossibility of) acquiring this knowledge as a series of historical experiences. Accordingly, novelistic refashionings of the nineteenth century reflect diverse ideological processes at work in interpretations of historical persona and texts, fact and fiction, or political, social, and ethical legacies. I think it is important to provide a close reading of these processes, for which the diachronic case study of the *Jane Eyre–Wide Sargasso Sea–Charlotte* novelistic sequence has provided a particularly fruitful plane. This adaptive chain of intimately related texts, where the later items contain all the previous ones, has proved productive for such a detailed investigation, to demonstrate how fictional texts and their criticism have evolved between the Victorian and the postmodern era. In the course of this analysis, especially in connection with Jean Rhys, modernism emerges as a point of reference both in terms of constructions of authorship and writing techniques, mostly in comparison with postmodernist perceptions of the same notions. These aspects also appear in the survey of Henry James adaptations, in this case at the other end of the chronology as a transition between late Victorian and early modernist concerns. As my main research focus in this monograph has been how post–Victorian fiction intersects with postmodernist discourses and practices, I have not devoted substantial attention to modernist rewritings of the Victorian era; nevertheless, along with other scholars (Joyce 2007, Wilson 2008, Beaumont 2009, Heilmann and Llewellyn 2010), my definition and contextualization of post–Victorian novels allows for their inclusion into post–Victorian research as well.

Such an opening up towards responses to the nineteenth century immediately after, or even shortly before, the queen's death may also reveal further insights concerning themes, generic conventions, and historical legacies in post–Victorian adaptations at both the historical and the contemporary levels. An interesting issue in this regard could be the exploration of the connections of self, time, and space in more detail. In my analyses of accounts of national, cultural, and self-identifications in postimperial, postcolonial, and feminist narratives of identity, I have repeatedly underlined the role of temporal and spatial aspects of travel and home in processes of the self's disintegration and dislocation. In addition to such a utilization of the trope of travel, the autoethnographic reading of fictionalizations of urban and rural spaces, as well as a further scrutiny of other types of spatialization of personal and historical experience, such as time and book travel in Jasper Fforde's *The Eyre Affair*, may point towards possible new (re)interpretations of modernist concerns.[1] If future appropriations of historical material shift to an interest in modernist authors, topics, and techniques, how will it inform post–Victorian scholarship and its intersections with the modern and the postmodern? The quality of later literary eras revising earlier ones, a parasitic feature highlighted in connection with postmodernism in particular, invites further research, possibly yielding interesting ideological and aesthetic consequences as well as future directions for understanding the phenomenon of rewriting as such, with repercussions for surveying post–Victorian fiction as well.

In terms of adaptive modes and approaches employed in refashioning earlier times, I have aimed to offer a glimpse of the wide scale of trends engendered by popular Victorian authors like Charlotte Brontë and Charles Dickens. As we have seen in the case of *The Eyre Affair*, some adaptations use historical source texts and their topoi for revisionary purposes, as well as starting points for the establishment of their own, new fictional worlds. Thus Fforde's novel has inspired a dialogue with the nineteenth century from a twentieth-century perspective, at the same time as acquiring its own consumer-oriented, market-driven status in the twenty-first-century world of sequels, resulting in further items which constitute a whole adaptive series of novels. The post–Victorian responses to Dickens's life and work, inspiring the generic denomination "Dickensiana," are constantly expanding in their range as well: in addition to the literary reworkings, film adaptations, and theme parks discussed in this work, computer games, songs, websites, illustrations, comics, and cultural mementoes are increasingly included into interpretations of the Victorian author as well.[2] The thus created adaptive maps, incorporating textual, audio-visual, and interactive refashionings of cultic nineteenth-century writers and their texts, point toward further fruitful prospects of responding to Victorian times in contemporary forums and media, thereby pinning down the popularity, importance, and potential of the post–Victorian phenomenon.

This multiplicity of adaptive modes also has repercussions on scholarship in the field, by widening its critical horizons and interpretive frameworks, and further enhancing interdisciplinary research as its working method, through advocating the integration of various fields of studies. The post–Victorian event, attracting an abundance of critical perspectives and methodologies, may even be symptomatic of current potentials and challenges which the diversity of interpretation involves for scholarly research. The sometimes markedly close connections between rewritings and criticism, which could spring from the overlap between creative authors and scholars, as well as the intertextual, integrative, and revisionary nature of the adaptation process itself, may assist in generating a better understanding and critical context of the post–Victorian canon and its discourses. After thorough discursive appraisals and comprehensive contextualizations of post–Victorian fiction, it remains to be seen how these texts can be repositioned into the larger bodies of both the historical novel and contemporary fiction in English. Comparative studies that weigh the findings of works like this monograph against the wider context of current historical fiction[3] are also worth conducting, to find explanations for the popularity of post–Victorianism in an international context, as well as to establish which cultures rewrite which eras and why. What seems quite certain, however, is that the future increasingly belongs to the rewrites of the rewrites. As Linda Hutcheon phrases it, "In the workings of the human imagination, adaptation is the norm, not the exception" (Hutcheon 2006: 177).

Chapter Notes

Introduction

1. In *Neo-Victorian Studies* (also referred to as *NVS*), there is a list of 17 novels of this type published within just a few months of the 2008-09 season (*NVS* 2.1: 196–197). The corpus of this monograph is limited to the most prominent or representative items of the abundance of texts, items that can best indicate the trends and tendencies in focus within this field of study.

2. In this book, I mainly concentrate on the post–Victorian output of the past thirty years, also incorporating these two prominent texts from the end of the 1960s, which post–Victorian scholarship generally considers as the first two items of such fiction. This periodization of post–Victorian novels is, however, debatable, since the determination of a starting point for critically revising the nineteenth century is problematic, as I discuss in more detail in Chapter 1.

3. The Booker Prize became the Man Booker Prize in 2002, when the Man Group plc started sponsoring it. For more information see the relevant section of the Man Booker Prize website ("Sponsor"). References to the prize in this monograph are used accordingly.

4. Malcolm Bradbury already saw signs of this intermingling of fiction and criticism in the early nineties, but still phrased it as a desirable future step: "Literary theory or criticism may well begin striving to recover its intimacy with the creative, with the experimental nature of writing and its exploration of things imagined, or fictive" (Boylan 1993: 61).

5. Other thematic foci of post–Victorian research are also in the process of emerging: science, technology and the immensely popular fashion of steampunk are devoted a special issue of *NVS* (3.1), topical editions of the same journal are planned for visual and material culture as well as the child in neo–Victorian discourse, and Marie-Luise Kohlke and Christian Gutleben have been preparing further collections of studies for their neo–Victorian series, the first of which concentrates on families: *Neo-Victorian Families: Gender, Sexual and Cultural Politics* (2011).

Chapter 1

1. A previous version of this chapter titled "(Re-)workings of Nineteenth-Century Century Fiction: Definitions, Terminology, Contexts" was published in *NVS* 1.1 (2008): 53–80. I have updated that version, in general, through the integration of the most recent critical material and, in particular, by extending the *neo–Victorian* versus *post–Victorian* part of the terminological debate as well as the "Contexts and Critical Discourses of Post-Victorian Fiction" section.

2. Critics of nineteenth-century British literature engage in a similar terminological debate: they call the attention to the inappropriateness of the term *Victorian studies* to denote research that disregards the queen's period of reign and disproves of the colonizing associations of the term *Victorian* (Llewellyn 2008: 166). *Victorian* is also employed with a chronological uncertainty in American studies. Some scholars advocate its usage for the last four decades of

the queen's reign, to denote the invention of the tradition of British royalty, others apply it to denote the middle of the nineteenth century, when the cultural transformations of the era started to gain ground and extend their boundaries (Mills 1992: x).

3. Reflecting on heritage film, which often recruits its subject matter from the long nineteenth century, Hadley also warns that such "aestheticization of the Victorian past" threatens an erasure of the Victorian historical context (Hadley 2010: 11).

4. For a relevant feminist analysis that puts the queen's attempt to harmonize her private and public lives in parallel with similar difficulties faced by today's feminist academics, see Laurie Langbauer's "Queen Victoria and Me" (2000).

5. As Steven Connor acutely phrases it: "No revision can entirely avoid reversion; no attempt to rework the myths of self-possessed beginning can entirely avoid becoming possessed by the desire for self-possession on which it lays hands" (Connor 1994: 97). This is a very valid observation concerning both the writers and the critics of contemporary fiction that reworks Victorian tenets.

6. As my work mostly concentrates on the UK, I have not considered any comparative aspects of interpreting Victorianism. Surveying the convergences and divergences between British and American cultural, social, and economic trends of the nineteenth century, the collection *Victorianism in the United States: Its Era and Its Legacy* (1992), edited by Steve Ickringill and Stephen Mills, could expand this research focus.

7. The coinage of *historiographic metafiction* was preceded by the introduction of *metafiction*, denoting a self-reflexive mode of constructing postmodern novelistic texts. The term *metafiction* was coined by William Gass in the late 1960s, and defined by Robert Scholes and Patricia Waugh in the 1970s and 80s, respectively.

8. See Hayden White's *Metahistory: The Historical Imagination in Nineteenth-Century Europe* (1973) or Francis Fukuyama's *The End of History or the Last Man* (1992) versus a prevalent historical consciousness and an interest in establishing various new historical approaches in current theoretical movements like new historicism, neo-Marxism and cultural studies.

9. Brian McHale partakes in this dialogue in the 1990s, which can best be traced in how he amends his analysis of historical fiction from his 1987 study *Postmodernist Fiction*, to incorporate new generic insights into his 1992 *Constructing Postmodernism*. One of these changes seems to be the employment of Hutcheon's term *historiographic metafiction*, instead of the earlier *postmodern (revisionist) historical fiction*, to denote contemporary examples of historical novels with metafictional input.

10. Hadley uses the term *pseudo–Victorian* to refer to texts that are written by contemporary authors but ascribed to fictional Victorian ones, in order to distinguish the integration of original Victorian excerpts from ventriloquized material into present-day refashionings of nineteenth-century texts. Thus *pseudo–Victorian* seems to be treated as a subcategory of the *neo–Victorian* which the author uses for terming contemporary adaptations of Victorian texts (Hadley 2010: 159–161).

11. Personal communication with Susana Onega: Onega, whose clarification of Hutcheon's definition is widely used, claimed that she had also convinced Christian Gutleben, another prominent researcher in this field, of the application of this term.

12. Unfortunately, this publication has been out of print and unavailable in most libraries for the last few years.

13. Similarly to *postmodern Victoriana*, a duplicity of terms also applies when referring to scholars of contemporary rewrites of the nineteenth century: the term *Victorianist* is used by those who tend to use *Victoriana* to depict this group of novels as postmodern fiction (Kaplan 2007: 4, Krueger 2002: xiii) and its modified versions, such as *progressive Victorianist, contemporary Victorianist*, or the even more specific *nostalgic new Victorianist*, are used by those who are unsure about the meaning of *Victorian* or feel the need to qualify the term to point out up-to-date relevancies. (Joyce 2002: 4, 15, 12, respectively).

14. See Ansgar Nünning's *Von historischer Fiktion zu historiographischer Metafiktion. Teil I: Theorie, Typologie und Poetik des historischen Romans* [*From Historical Fiction to Historiographic Metafiction. Part I: The Theory, Typology and Poetics of the Historical Novel*] (1995) and *Von historischer Fiktion zu historiographischer Metafiktion. Teil II: Erscheinungsformen und Entwicklungstendenzen des historischen Romans in England seit 1950.* [*From Historical Fiction to Historiographic Metafiction. Part II: Realizations and Tendencies of Development of the Historical Novel in England since 1950*] (1995). Nünning has done valuable research in the fields of genre theory and the historical novel.

15. Instead of providing a specific definition of *neo–Victorian*, Shiller distinguishes three

categories within this subgenre: the first revises individual Victorian texts, the second creates new adventures for known Victorian characters (fictional and historical figures are not differentiated, however), and the third imitates Victorian literary conventions (Shiller 1997: 558). This third category is termed *"new" Victorian fiction*, and is also used by Hilary M. Schor when analyzing the postmodernist revisions of formal aspects of the Victorian novel (Schor 2000: 235). *Neo-sensation novel* is considered as another a subtype of neo–Victorian fiction, practiced by those who "have returned to a nineteenth-century form to express their scepticism concerning the effect of this particular system of belief [the postmodern] on our understanding of concepts like morality, ethics, responsibility and culpability" (Marsh 1995: 119). Though it is claimed that this type of fiction is complementary to theories of postmodernism (120), the argument seems nostalgically inclined, judged by its critics as reconstructive, contrasting postmodern valuelessness with nineteenth-century values (Kucich and Sadoff 2000: xxix).

16. For example, Kate Mitchell's *History and Cultural Memory in Neo-Victorian Fiction: Victorian Afterimages* (2010), Rosario Arias and Patricia Pulham's (eds.) *Haunting and Spectrality in Neo-Victorian Fiction: Possessing the Past* (2010), Marie-Luise Kohlke and Christian Gutleben's (eds.) *Neo-Victorian Tropes of Trauma: The Politics of Bearing After-Witness to Nineteenth-Century Suffering* (2010) and *Neo-Victorian Gothic: Horror, Violence, and Degeneration in the Re-Imagined 19th Century* (forthcoming).

17. Dianne F. Sadoff retains the term *post–Victorian* in her later publication on filmic adaptations, *Victorian Vogue: British Novels on Screen* (2009) as well, and her work includes the Victorian, the modernist, and the postmodernist perspectives alike: "Playing off the 1930s and the 1940s against the 1980s and 1990s, I restore the historical situation of heritage film — and the dialogue these films undertake with the decades during which their source narratives were created" (Sadoff 2009: xi).

18. Hadley rejects my argument, which leads to another debate concerning different perspectives of scholarly interpretation. The critic claims that through blending the Victorian and the postmodern contexts, their individual historical actualities would be lost, especially by way of the postmodern cannibalizing the Victorian (Hadley 2010: 3). Since post–Victorian fiction is perceived to be a subcategory of the historical novel that is conscious of aspects of the present as much as the past (as the author herself confirms as well; Hadley 2010: 6), I do not envision such a danger. Rather, I see this anxiety as a symptom of the recent debate between scholars who argue for putting more emphasis on Victorian aspects in researching contemporary rewritings of the nineteenth century and critics who insist more on the postmodernist approach, which naturally influences their choice of terminology as well.

19. This is the only sense in which some scholars employ the term: "our post–Victorian present" (Llewellyn 2008: 165) signifying current times; "radical post–Victorian phenomenon" (Mills 1992: xxi) and "post–Victorian cultural turn" (Kohlke 2008: 3) referring to modernist reactions immediately after the Victorian age. On some occasions, the terms *late Victorian*, *neo–Victorian* and *post–Victorian* are even used synonymously to denote the era that follows the 1880s (Parish 1992: 2).

20. The popularity of producing such conventional texts is manifest in the vast list of works collected on a specific website devoted to historical romance writing. Here one can search not only by author or title, but also by historical era, hero/heroine, or even character type ("Historical Romance Writers").

21. See Kate Flint's "Plotting the Victorians: Narrative, Post-Modernism, and Contemporary Fiction" (1997), Robin Gilmour's "Using the Victorians: the Victorian Age in Contemporary Fiction" (2000), and Anne Humpherys's "The Afterlife of the Victorian Novel: Novels about Novels" (2005).

22. "Retuning *The Piano*" (Kaplan 2007: 119–153).

23. See Kirsten Stirling's "Dr. Jekyll and Mr. Jackass: *Fight Club* as a Refraction of Hogg's *Justified Sinner* and Stevenson's *Dr. Jekyll and Mr. Hyde* (2004), Celestino Deleyto Alcalá's "Return to Austen: Film Heroines of the Nineties" (2004), Nicole Boireau's "To *Hamlet* and back with *Humble Boy* by Charlotte Jones (2001)" (2004), and William Christie's "'Trifling Deviation'": Stage and Screen Versions of Mary Shelley's Monster" (2008).

24. John Madden's movie *The Best Exotic Marigold Hotel* (2012) seems an interesting British reappropriation of both the Hollywood and the Bollywood ambiance, in which an illustrious British cast travels to a retirement home in India, and ends up helping the naïve but industrious Indian owner build and manage his hotel and marry his Indian (and not English or American) girlfriend, while loosening their English ways and discovering a new life for their old age.

25. See, in particular, Andrew Higson's paper "English Heritage, English Literature, English Cinema: Selling Jane Austen to Movie Audiences in the 1990s" (2004), which explicitly attacks the overestimation of fidelity aspects in adaptation criticism, as well as Sadoff's second chapter, "Being True to Nineteenth-Century Narrative," where she argues that, since it is historically situated, the concept of fidelity is itself subject to shifts (Sadoff 2009: 47–99).

26. Hutcheon also reads adaptation as evolution, elaborating the parallel in a very becoming manner: "Evolving by cultural selection, travelling stories adapt to local cultures, just as populations of organisms adapt to local environments" (Hutcheon 2006: 177).

27. Some scholars even argue for the explicit return of realism into novelistic production after the experimental period of the 1960s. In his seminal work *The Novelist at Crossroads and Other Essays,* David Lodge openly campaigns for the realist novel as a legitimate novelistic form at the end of the twentieth century: "This brings me to my conclusion, which is a modest affirmation of faith in the future of realistic fiction. In part this is a rationalisation of personal preference. I like realistic novels, and I tend to write realistic fiction myself. The elaborate code of literary decorum that governs the composition of realistic fiction — consistency with history, solidity of specification [...] is to my mind a valuable discipline and source of strength" (Lodge, 1971: 32).

28. *Memory text* is used in accordance with other scholars' application of the term to denote historical fictions which aid in constructing historical periods as part of our cultural memory. See Annette Kuhn's "Memory and Textuality" (2005) for a general context, or Kate Mitchell's "Ghostly Histories and Embodied Memories: Photography, Spectrality and Historical Fiction in *Afterimage* and *Sixty Lights*" (2008) for a specifically post–Victorian one.

29. *Memory objects* are understood as material items or their records (in the case of already demolished objects) that transmit and mediate individual and collective cultural memories. See Peter Stallybrass's "Worn Worlds: Clothes, Mourning, and the Life of Things" (1999), which refers to cloth in this sense.

30. The author uses the term *memory work* to denote ways of processing cultural events, such as mourning (also referred to as grief work), commemorative practices and creating public and private memory (Kohlke 2008: 9). My use of the term coincides with this definition.

Chapter 2

1. "The reception of new writing has in fact probably never been more obsessively author-centered than it is today, not only in reviewing, but in supplementary forms of exposure through the media — interviews and profiles in the press and on TV, prizes, public readings and book launches and so on. All this attention is focused on the author as a unique creative self, the mysterious, glamorous origin of a text" (Lodge 1990: 15–16).

2. A recent example for prefabricated reality quiz shows would be Danny Boyle's *Slumdog Millionaire* (2008), a movie about a young Indian boy winning the lottery-wheel, where the game was debunked as highly manipulative, ruining many people's lives.

3. Their diminishing authority has seemingly also pushed the members of the royal family into a more popularistic celebrity status, summoning further forums of engagement that increase their vulnerability, such as Stephen Frears's movie, *The Queen* (2006), which is harshly critical of their behavior during the scandals around Princess Diana's death, or news items and tabloid articles that report on the deeds of Princes William and Harry.

4. Such reading guides would be worth examining, in order to establish different interests (or interest groups) that influence readers. In this case, apart from the general questions of examining characters' relation to love, religion and science, more questions encourage readers to compare the nineteenth century with the present in a wide range of subjects from plot development to literary achievement (especially questions 2, 8 and 14), the final one asking them to speculate on figures' future. All these queries point towards the importance of historical consciousness and adaptation.

5. Louise Yelin criticizes Byatt for this plot move by calling attention to its homophobic implications (Yelin 1992: 39).

6. Hadley does not contrast scholarly endeavors with an emotional attachment to the past but combines them, and constructs the ideal reader on that basis, who then for her is only Maud (Hadley 2010: 28, 129–130).

7. Armstrong, Gillian. *Oscar and Lucinda* (film). United States, Australia, United Kingdom: Fox Searchlight Pictures, 1997.

8. LaBute, Neil. *Possession* (film). United States, United Kingdom: Focus Features, Warner Bros., 2002.

9. In addition to visual culture, the application of cultural objects, such as architectural mementoes, photographs and books, provides similarly productive sites of interpreting post–Victorian fiction, as I discuss in later chapters.

10. Due to their ever-emphasized achievements in identity formation, especially concerning postcolonial and postimperial identities, other important Booker-winning novels, such as Ruth Prawer Jhabvala's *Heat and Dust* (1975), Salman Rushdie's *Midnight's Children* (1981), and Kazuo Ishiguro's *The Remains of the Day* (1989), also belong to the list of texts actively concerned with the legacies of the empire as well as with narratives of identity. It is important to acknowledge that these items would have a place in this list; however, since I exclusively focus on post–Victorian fiction in my monograph, they are not discussed in more detail.

11. The post–Victorian status of Hollinghurst's work is debatable, as it is set in the 1980s, and its focus on the nineteenth-century author constitutes just one aspect of the novel, yet I reason for it as one below.

12. A shorter version of this section was presented as part of the paper "The Future of the Post-Victorian Novel: A Speculation in Genre" at the Adapting the Nineteenth Century: Revisiting, Revising and Rewriting the Past Conference at the University of Wales, Lampeter, UK, in August 2008, and published in *HJEAS* 17.2 (2011): 351–70.

13. The increasing theoretical interest in (re)defining the subject and subjectivity has, perhaps, also assisted in its return to (discussions about) literature. An example for such a debate is Deborah Knight and Toril Moi's in the mid-nineties (Knight 1995: 39–56, Moi 1995: 57–62, Knight 1995: 63–70). What emerges from their dialogue is not only the necessity to revisit the critical terminology related to the subject, but the existence of a direct connection between subjectivity and "the popularity of all kinds of biographies, letters, and diaries" as well, which Moi establishes (60) and Knight agrees with (69).

14. Henry James inspired numerous other novels, both prior to 2004 and after, such as Carol de Chellis Hill's *Henry James's Midnight Song* (1993), Kathryn Kramer's *Sweet Water* (1998), Edmund White's *Hotel de Dream* (2007), Cynthia Ozick's *Dictation* (2008) and *Foreign Bodies* (2010), and Paula Marantz Cohen's *What Alice Knew: A Most Curious Tale of Henry James and Jack the Ripper* (2010), which indicates the nineteenth-century author's ongoing appeal.

15. Gilbert and Gubar (1984). From this perspective, Woolson's battle "is not against her (male) precursor's reading of the world but against his reading of *her*. In order to define herself as an author she must redefine the terms of her socialization" (Gilbert and Gubar 1984: 49).

16. Term taken from Saunders (Saunders 2008: 126).

17. Lodge's author-narrator criticizes the use of the term "bestsellers" itself on the basis of its etymology in *Author, Author*, obviously a non-bestseller: he points out that this compound carries with it a confusion of quality and quantity, consequently one cannot have more than one bestseller (Lodge 2005: 326).

18. Heyns recorded one of these visits, in the course of which Tóibín, Lodge and Heyns all appeared at Lamb House for their research. His account, echoing reverence at the same time as fear of the master, sounds like the first chapter of a Gothic novel (Heyns "The Curse of Henry James" 2004).

19. James's rivalry with Constance Fenimore Woolson and George Du Maurier, both of whom were more successful during their lifetime than the author himself, is fictionalized in *Felony* and *Author, Author*, respectively.

20. By rewriting Henry James as well as criticizing this endeavor, Lodge confronts the anxiety of influence both as author and as critic. As the coiner of this notion, Harold Bloom argues that "[p]oets' misinterpretations of poems are more drastic than critics' misinterpretations or criticism, but this is only a difference in degree and not at all in kind" (Bloom 2001: 1804).

Chapter 3

1. Shuttleworth includes various texts by Graham Swift and A. S. Byatt in her analysis, similarly to Daniel Bormann, who focuses on *Waterland* and *Possession* by the same authors while examining the role of science in neo–Victorian fiction, in his *The Articulation of Science in the Neo-Victorian Novel: A Poetics (and Two Case-Studies)* (2002).

2. Neo/post–Victorian studies pays considerable attention to Darwinism and neo-Dar-

winism. At the Neo-Victorianism: The Politics and Aesthetics of Appropriation Conference (University of Exeter, UK, September 2007) there was a roundtable devoted to the topic, examining intersections of Darwinism, literature and biology and their possible theoretical consequences; Gutleben dedicates a section of his book to the discussion of the evolution-revolution dichotomy in post–Victorian fiction (Gutleben 2001: 204–216); and post–Victorian novels themselves reanimate Darwin(ism) in various ways, in particular A. S. Byatt's *Possession* (1990) and *Angels and Insects* (1992), Alasdair Gray's *Poor Things* (1992), Graham Swift's *Ever After* (1992), Beryl Bainbridge's *Master Georgie* (1998), Liz Jensen's *Ark Baby* (1998) and Matthew Kneale's *English Passengers* (2000).

    3. A similarly divertive attempt of national self-definition promoted by dominant political narratives is exposed in Beryl Bainbridge's *Master Georgie* (1998), where photos of dead Englishmen presented as pictures of living heroes of the Crimean War, published in the British press to impress readership, become unveiled by the narrators.

    4. An earlier version of the analysis of "Post-Victorian Narratives of the Crystal Palace: The Case of Peter Carey's *Oscar and Lucinda*" was presented at the British Literature and Cultural Memory Conference at ELTE, Budapest, Hungary, in September 2010. Proceedings: *Confrontations and Interactions: Essays on Cultural Memory*, edited by Bálint Gárdos, Ágnes Péter, Natália Pikli, Máté Vince, 393–407. Budapest: L'Harmattan, 2011.

    5. This essay offers exceptional insights on the topic in a highly ironic tone. See, for example, the passage that further describes the relationship indicated in the title: "Mrs Thatcher's rhetoric of Victorian Values was, on the face of it, a remarkable example of a 'political attitude' struck for purely symbolic rewards. Except for the restoration of hanging — something for which she voted consistently whenever the issue of Capital Punishment came before the House of Commons— Mrs Thatcher showed no signs of wanting to translate it into legislative enactment or administrative practice" (Samuel 1999: 341). The fact that Margaret Thatcher still remains a controversial figure is best illustrated by the reviews of Phyllida Lloyd's *The Iron Lady* (2011), the most recent screen adaptation of Thatcher's life and political career. Some of the voices, including the director's, emphasize the personal over the political history of the only female prime minister in the history of Britain, while others say the two are inseparable. The acclaim of the movie, which earned numerous awards, is accompanied by heated criticism. Opinions range from protective ones accusing the film of being an "over-emotional left-wing fantasy" inaccurately portraying the politician's character (Khalil "The *Iron Lady* Movie Criticized as 'Over-Emotional Left-Wing Fantasy'" 2012), and insensitively focusing on her dementia while she is still alive ("British PM Criticizes Timing of *The Iron Lady*" 2012), to more confrontational ones that find fault with using Thatcher's current state of health to mask her past wrongdoings, or constituting her as a feminist politician in spite of her disregard for women's issues during her premiership ("Review: *The Iron Lady*" 2012).

    6. Even scientific measurements were subject to political pacts. For example, Greenwich mean time was acclaimed as zero point, in return for the establishment of the French metric system as the international standard (Ronald R. Thomas 2002: 24).

    7. Strongman devotes two sections in his examination of Booker-winning novels to the question of insularity, one concerning English identities in their domestic environment (Strongman 2002: 143–146) and the other examining the same in the context of the English abroad (195–196).

    8. The same is true for authors such as South Americans and Indians, and maybe for authors in general who live in exile, so the exclusively Caribbean perspective introduced here can be expanded to various other post–Victorian and non–post–Victorian but postcolonial novels that fictionalize similar changes of location.

Chapter 4

    1. I have developed this chapter from the paper "The *Jane Eyre*–Chain: Tailor-Made Aesthetics and Politics in Appropriations of Victorian Fiction" presented at the Neo-Victorianism: The Politics and Aesthetics of Appropriation Conference, at the University of Exeter, UK, in September 2007.

    2. These extremes also appear in post–Victorian novelistic reactions to her texts: some, as Honoria's opinion in Gail Jones's *Sixty Lights* proves, put them on a pedestal for their romantic qualities, while others, as Sugar's musings in Michel Faber's *The Crimson Petal and the White* suggest, discard them for the same reason.

3. Autoethnography engages in devoting a three-dimensional attention to novels. This process entails a metaphorization of life into culture, of culture into place and of spatialized culture into the textual space of the novel. Employing this reading method, the author, James Buzard, aims to prove that through its narrative nineteenth-century fiction manages to give a picture of the insider's exclusion (Buzard 2005: 12).

4. Of course, this identity is ambiguous, too, since, as Susan Meyer argues (1996), Jane writes against oppression with the aid of a commodity (the India ink) acquired by oppression. Since the figures of the author and the narrator often intersect in the above analysis, Charlotte Brontë's background deserves a brief look as well. Due to her Irish ancestry, the author of *Jane Eyre* also counts as a slightly marginal figure in terms of internal colonization. The analysis of the possible effects of the Brontë sisters' origin on their writing would add an additional dimension to the postcolonial and postimperial discussion of their work. In his *Heathcliff and the Great Hunger: Studies in Irish Culture*, Terry Eagleton does this for Emily Brontë, reading the figure of Heathcliff as a fragment of the Irish famine (Eagleton 1996: 1–26).

5. By independent textual contribution I mean narrative items that are not directly embedded in other narratives. The sum of Bella/Victoria's letters exceed the author-editor's contribution in amount, however, most of her correspondence, except for the letter she writes after Archibald's death, is framed by Archibald's narrative, so in this sense it does not feature as an independent contribution.

6. Not only fictional texts produce such critiques of authorial intention, but similar opinions are advanced in Brontë scholarship as well. Patricia Duncker reads *Jane Eyre* and other texts by Brontë in terms of the author revenging herself on men by maiming or killing them, like blinding Rochester in *Jane Eyre*, getting Robert shot by the workers in *Shirley* or sinking M. Paul on his return trip from the West Indies in *Villette* (Duncker 2008).

7. For a good summary of the feminist critical history of *Jane Eyre*, see Kaplan 2007: 23–29.

8. Edward W. Said provides a convincing analysis of this by focusing on such a transformation attempt in Jane Austen's *Mansfield Park* (1814) in his *Culture and Imperialism* (Said 1994: 80–96).

9. Nostalgia has recently been reevaluated as a possibly constructive interpretive device by other authors as well, see Mitchell 2010: 4–6, Arias and Pulham 2010: xi–xiv.

10. Later in *Guerrillas,* Roche himself muses on England and arrives at a similarly divergent conclusion: "England, Roche thought: it was so hard to get away from England here [in the Caribbean]. And there were so many Englands: his, Jane's, Jimmy's, Lloyd's and the England—hard to imagine—in that old woman's head [a local woman]" (Naipaul 1976: 108). As an Englishman he does not deny the country's existence in any form but acknowledges the possibility of its multiple imaginings.

11. This remark, contrasting academic career to creative writing, can be read as an authorial metacommentary on the increasing split between academic and non-academic contexts at the same time as an ironic self-judgment, considering that many authors of post–Victorian fiction, including D. M. Thomas, have degrees in English literature. Miranda's contrast of creativity and higher education is echoed by her father as well, who could be read as the author's mouthpiece: "Ah, yes—schools! She [Miranda] knows what I [her father] think of that. They drain all the life, all the originality, out of you; I thank God I avoided them, and taught myself, surrounded by Dickens, Thackeray, Trollope, and so on, in my uncle's library" (D. M. Thomas 2000: 140). Ironically, the self-educated antiquarian father does not recognize the fake manuscript, and the institutionally educated daughter whose Ph.D. presupposes that she has a certificate of good conduct engages in faking a manuscript and creating a web of lies around it.

12. For a more detailed description of the parallels of Rhys's and D. M. Thomas's novels, see Sue Thomas 2007: 103–104.

13. This is the title of a novel by Elizabeth Wurtzel, which was presented by Marta Miquel-Baldellou as an example for rethinking female hysteria in post–Victorian fiction. According to the presenter, today's hysteria, called depression, arises from women's realization that it is existentially impossible to acquire a unified self-identity in postmodern culture (Miquel-Baldellou 2008). *Charlotte* was not discussed by the speaker, but fits the concept.

14. The account of a personal meeting with Jean Rhys and the acclaim of her text could also be read as an authorization for further adapting *Jane Eyre*, on the one hand, and for doing this by utilizing *Wide Sargasso Sea*, on the other.

15. As a decipherer of Flaubert's life and work, the narrator of Julian Barnes's *Flaubert's Parrot* (1984) explains why he thinks many people privilege fiction over the empirical reality

of their lives: "My wife: someone I feel I understand less well than a foreign writer dead for a hundred years. Is this an aberration, or is it normal? Books say: She did this because. Life says: She did this. Books are where things are explained to you; life is where things aren't. I'm not surprised some people prefer books. Books make sense of life. The only problem is that the lives they make sense of are other people's lives, never your own" (Barnes 1990: 168).

16. This instance provides a good example of a context where nostalgia could be utilized for reading as a constructive tool, as introduced earlier.

17. The picture is titled *In Dublin Bay: Portrait of the Artist's Wife*, and was painted by Sir William Orpen, R.A., R.H.A. (Stillgoran 1878–1931 London) in 1908. It is an interesting choice for a cover image, and has many aspects that can be related to these texts. Considering publication dates, it was painted between the writing of *Jane Eyre*, *Wide Sargasso Sea* and *Charlotte*; Orpen had a strong Irish national identity, which can be paralleled to the Brontës' Irish ancestry; and the artist's wife was called Grace, which can be related to Grace Poole's role as a mediator in the novels and their adaptations.

18. Jane also tries to drown herself in the pond where Grace's son and many other people have died, but Grace saves her.

19. The strong control of the father over his daughter's life is reminiscent of Shakespeare's *The Tempest*, of which *Charlotte* is also a rewriting, as the daughter's name, Miranda, indicates. It is out of the focus of this book to engage with correspondences between these two texts; however, reading them together may also yield interesting analogies.

20. There are hints at the legacies of English slavery in Jane's narrative but they are left unreflected. Jane expresses pride about the English abolition (D. M. Thomas: 2000: 163), yet French slaves appear freer and more content to her in their manners. According to a Frenchman, this is due to the French colonizers' respect towards the slaves' families, in contrast to the English ones, who split them up (112).

21. Had Jane been able to live in the West Indies longer and immerse in local communities better, she would most probably have developed a similar sensibility towards slavery and its legacies to Emily Cartwright's in Caryl Phillips's *Cambridge* (1991), discussed earlier.

Chapter 5

1. It is interesting how bodily incapable the spiritually possibly matching St. John must become, literally expecting his death, to make him unsuitable for Jane. In this context, on the level of the plot, the novel's last passages clearly indicate that if Jane had followed St. John, she might have met death as well, so she obviously made a wise choice in rejecting him.

2. Though it does not feature in Detmers's analysis, Daphne Du Maurier's *Rebecca* (1938) is a successful early rewriting of *Jane Eyre* in this respect, repeating the paradigm of marrying a plain young woman to a rich old man with a house haunted by a "mad" wife. The 1940 movie version, directed by Alfred Hitchcock, further underlines its uncanny aspects. For more critical engagement with *Rebecca*, see Barbara Schaff's "The Strange Afterlives of *Jane Eyre*" (2007) and Verena-Susanna Nungesser's "From Thornfield Hall to Manderley and Beyond: *Jane Eyre* and *Rebecca* as Transformations of the Fairy Tale, the Novel of Development, and the Gothic Novel" (2007).

3. Similarly to *Adèle*, in Boylan's version, discussed above, Rochester also gets involved in a duel in Paris, and he goes back to Paris after his marriage with Jane to continue his adventures with women. This is how he eventually meets his end.

4. A shorter version of this analysis of *The Eyre Affair* was presented as part of the paper "The Future of the Post-Victorian Novel: A Speculation in Genre" at the Adapting the Nineteenth Century: Revisiting, Revising and Rewriting the Past Conference at the University of Wales, Lampeter, UK, in August 2008, and published in *HJEAS* 17.2 (2011): 351–370.

5. The name Thursday Next and her supportive role to Rochester are reminiscent of the name and function of Friday in Defoe's *Robinson Crusoe* (1719).

6. Fforde's novelistic solution positions him on the popular side of the argument, which could be read as his literary testimony to what he always underlines in his interviews, namely, his lack of university training and the claim that "classics had become stuffy through being academized." (Wells 2007: 198 footnote 4).

7. Fforde's Thursday Next series consists of the following titles: *Lost in a Good Book* (2002), *The Well of Lost Plots* (2003b), *Something Rotten* (2004), *First Among Sequels* (2007), *One of our Thursdays is Missing* (2011) and *The Woman Who Died a Lot* (2012).

8. Term taken from Berninger and Thomas (Berninger and Thomas 2007: 183).

9. Hay-on-Wye is a symbolic location in terms of books, with the possession of which the literary detectives in the novel are constantly occupied. The Welsh town is known for its abundance of secondhand bookshops, even claiming to be the place that has the most books per square mile in the world (Henry "Wales Travel: Hay-on-Wye Bookshops" 2010).

10. The question whether the connection between male authorship and the trivialization of feminist issues implies an ideological authorial bias, a yield to the demand of popular entertainment, or has other reasons, is a topic out of the scope of this book but definitely worth exploring. This problem also acquires relevance in reading D. M. Thomas's *Charlotte*.

11. The draft of this subchapter on "Adapting Dickens in Post-Victorian Fiction" was prepared for this Dickens anniversary and presented at the HUSSE 10 Lit Cult Conference, University of Piliscsaba, Piliscsaba, Hungary, January 2011. Proceedings: *HUSSE 10 Lit Cult*, edited by Kinga Földváry et al., 127–135. Piliscsaba: Institute of English and American Studies, Faculty of Humanities, PPCU, 2011. A revised version of this paper specifically focusing on two contemporary adaptations of *Great Expectations*—*Jack Maggs* and *Mister Pip*—was presented as "Dickens and his *Great Expectations* in Post-Victorian Fiction" at The Other Dickens Conference, University of Portsmouth, UK, July 2012.

12. Catherine Dickens perceives her husband in very similar terms in Vukelic's rewriting: "It's just that sometimes I think he [Dickens] forgot the distinction between truth and fiction. He treated us as though we were all characters in his books, as if he could control our thoughts, and words and actions" (Vukelic 2010: 217).

13. Correspondences between Oates and Dickens are further outlined by Joyce (2007: 162) and Sadoff (2010: 180).

14. For more on the original ending, see the commentary on the novel at "Great Expectations Facsimile Now Available" 2011.

15. André Lefevere had already promoted rewriting as an alternative tool to critical interpretation in an article seven years earlier (Lefevere 1985: 222).

16. The first two series, with three episodes each, were shown in the last two years, and a third series of another three episodes is planned for 2013. The major figures and topoi of the original story have been kept, but it is set in the twenty-first century.

Conclusion

1. This interest in spatializing personal and historical experience seems to be happening on a wider scale than post–Victorian fiction. A number of contemporary texts, from Peter Ackroyd's *London: The Biography* (2000) or *Thames: Sacred River* (2007) to the German Klaus Böldl's *Die fernen Inseln* [*The Distant Islands*] (2003) or *Drei Flüsse* [*Three Rivers*] (2006), connect remembering and space, by fictionalizing the history of cities, islands or rivers, not to mention the theoretical interest in the visualization and verbalization of historical and lived spaces, which is focalized in various genres and disciplines, from travel writing through ethnography to urban studies.

2. In her paper, at The Other Dickens Conference at the University of Portsmouth, UK, in July 2012, Shari Hodges Holt moved into this direction, by surveying intertextual connections between illustrations of a Dickens text, one of its adaptations into a graphic novel, and various film and television adaptations, as well as children's cartoons, to show the Victorian author's cultural presence and impact in our times (Holt 2012).

3. For example, Bényei outlines the possibilities of a comparison between contemporary British and Hungarian historical novels (2005), and there is equally great potential in reading today's German historical fiction, especially works by the already mentioned Daniel Kehlmann, and Uwe Tellkamp's *Der Turm* [*The Tower*] which won the German Book Prize in 2008.

Works Cited

Ackroyd, Peter. 1982. *The Great Fire of London*. London: Hamish Hamilton.
———. 1983. *The Last Testament of Oscar Wilde*. London: Abacus.
———. 1985. *Hawksmoor*. London: Hamish Hamilton.
———. 1987. *Chatterton*. London: Hamish Hamilton.
———. 1990. *Dickens*. London: Mandarin.
———. 1992. *English Music*. London: Hamish Hamilton.
———. 2000. *London: The Biography*. London: Chatto & Windus.
———. 2007. *Thames: Sacred River*. London: Chatto & Windus.
Adaptation. "About the Journal." Oxford: Oxford University Press. http://www.oxfordjournals.org/our_journals/adaptation/about.html.
Alcalá, Celestino Deleyto. 2004. "Return to Austen: Film Heroines of the Nineties." In *Refracting the Canon in Contemporary British Literature and Film*, edited by Susana Onega and Christian Gutleben, 95–110. Amsterdam & New York: Rodopi.
Arias, Rosario, and Patricia Pulham, eds. 2010. *Haunting and Spectrality in Neo-Victorian Fiction: Possessing the Past*. Basingstoke & New York: Palgrave Macmillan.
Armstrong, Gillian. 1997. *Oscar and Lucinda* (film). United States, Australia, United Kingdom: Fox Searchlight Pictures.
Armstrong, Isobel. 1993. *Victorian Poetry: Poetry, Poetics and Politics*. London: Routledge.
———. 2008. *Victorian Glassworlds: Glass Culture and the Imagination 1830–1880*. Oxford: Oxford University Press.
Armstrong, Nancy. 1992. "Imperialist Nostalgia and *Wuthering Heights*." In *Emily Brontë's* Wuthering Heights: *Case Studies in Contemporary Criticism*, edited by Linda H. Peterson, 428–49. Boston: Bedford.
Arnold, Gaynor. 2008. 2009. *Girl in a Blue Dress*. Birmingham: Tindal Press. Toronto: McClelland & Stewart.
Ashcroft, Bill. 2001. *On Post-Colonial Futures: Transformations of Colonial Culture*. London: Continuum.
Bainbridge, Beryl. (1998) 1999. *Master Georgie*. London: Abacus.
Barndollar, David, and Susan Schorn. 2002. "Revisiting the Serial Format of Dickens's Novels." In *Functions of Victorian Culture at the Present Time*, edited by Christine L. Krueger, 157–70. Athens: Ohio University Press.
Barnes, Julian. (1984) 1990. *Flaubert's Parrot*. New York: Vintage.
———. 1987. "Diary." *London Review of Books* 9.20 (12 November): 21. http://www.lrb.co.uk/v09/n20/julian-barnes/diary.
———. 1998. *England, England*. London: Jonathan Cape.
———. 2005. *Arthur and George*. New York: Knopf.
Bassnett, Susan. 2001. "Afterword." In *British Cultural Studies: Geography, Nationality and Identity*, edited by David Morley and Kevin Robins, 495–502. Oxford: Oxford University Press.
Baudrillard, Jean. (1981) 1994. *Simulacra & Simulations*. (Translated by Sheila Faria Glaser).

Ann Arbor: University of Michigan Press. http://www9.georgetown.edu/faculty/irvinem/theory/Baudrillard-Simulacra_and_Simulation.pdf

Beaumont, Matthew. 2009. "Cutting up the Corpse: Agatha Christie, Max Ernst, and Neo-Victorianism in the 1930s." *Literature Interpretation Theory. Neo-Victorianism: The Politics and Aesthetics of Appropriation.* Guest edited by Rebecca Munford and Paul Young. 20.1–2: 12–26.

Bényei, Tamás. 2003. *Az ártatlan ország. Az angol regény 1945 után* [The Innocent Country: The English Novel after 1945]. Debrecen: Kossuth.

———. 2005. "Történelem és emlékezés a kortárs történelmi regényben [History and Remembering in the Contemporary Historical Novel]." *Alföld* (March): 37–47.

———. 2006. "A szajha útja (Michel Faber: *A bíbor szirom és fehér*) [The Prostitute's Progress (Michel Faber's *The Crimson Petal and the White*)]." *Élet és Irodalom.* (14 April): 28.

———. 2008. "Skanzen (Julian Barnes: *Anglia, Anglia*) [Theme Park (Julian Barnes's *England England*)]." *Élet és Irodalom* (2 May): 24.

Berninger, Mark, and Katrin Thomas. 2007. "A Parallelquel of a Classic Text and Reification of the Fictional — The Playful Parody of *Jane Eyre* in Jasper Fforde's *The Eyre Affair*." In *A Breath of Fresh Eyre: Intertextual and Intermedial Reworkings of* Jane Eyre, edited by Margarete Rubik and Elke Mettinger-Schartmann, 181–96. Amsterdam: Rodopi.

Bertens, Hans. 1986. "The Postmodern Weltanschauung and Its Relation with Modernism: An Introductory Survey." In *Approaching Postmodernism: Papers Presented at a Workshop on Postmodernism, 21–23 September 1984, University of Utrecht*, edited by Douwe Fokkema and Hans Bertens, 9–51. Amsterdam & Philadelphia: John Benjamin's Publishing.

Bhabha, Homi K. 1994. *The Location of Culture.* London: Routledge.

Bloom, Harold. 2001. "From the Anxiety of Influence." In *The Norton Anthology of Theory and Criticism*, edited by Vincent B. Leitch, 1797–1805. New York: Norton.

Böehnke, Dietmar. 2008. "V for Victorian: The Victorian Age in Comics and Their Film Versions." Paper presented at the Adapting the Nineteenth Century: Revisiting, Revising and Rewriting the Past Conference, University of Wales, Lampeter, UK, August.

Boireau, Nicole. 2004. "To *Hamlet* and Back with *Humble Boy* by Charlotte Jones (2001)." In *Refracting the Canon in Contemporary British Literature and Film*, edited by Susana Onega and Christian Gutleben, 231–45. Amsterdam & New York: Rodopi.

Böldl, Klaus. 2003. *Die Fernen Inseln* [The Distant Islands]. Frankfurt am Main: Fischer.

———. 2006. *Drei Flüsse* [Three Rivers]. Frankfurt am Main: Fischer.

Bormann, Daniel Candel. 2002. *The Articulation of Science in the Neo-Victorian Novel: A Poetics (and Two Case-Studies).* Frankfurt am Main: Peter Lang.

Boylan, Clare. 1990. "*Jane Eyre* Revisited: An Alternative Ending." *Good Housekeeping*, January, 136–41.

———, ed. 1993. *The Agony and the Ego: The Art and Strategy of Fiction Writing Explored.* London: Penguin.

———. *Emma Brown.* (2003). 2004. London: Abacus.

Boyle, Danny. 2008. *Slumdog Millionaire* (film). United Kingdom: Pathé (UK), Fox Searchlight Pictures and Warner Bros. Pictures (U.S.).

Brantlinger, Patrick, and William B. Thesing, eds. (2002) 2005. *A Companion to the Victorian Novel.* Oxford: Blackwell.

"British PM Criticizes Timing of *The Iron Lady*." 2012. *CBC News* (6 January). http://www.cbc.ca/news/arts/story/2012/01/06/cameron-iron-lady-criticism.html.

Brontë, Charlotte. (1847) 1999. *Jane Eyre.* Hertfordshire: Wordsworth.

Brontë, Emily. 1992. "*Wuthering Heights* (1847)." In *Emily Brontë's* Wuthering Heights: *Case Studies in Contemporary Criticism*, edited by Linda H. Peterson, 15–285. Boston: Bedford.

Bryant, John. 2002. *The Fluid Text: A Theory of Revision and Editing for Book and Screen.* Ann Arbor: University of Michigan Press.

Budra, Paul, and Betty Schellenberg, eds. 1998. *Part Two: Reflections on the Sequel.* Toronto: University of Toronto Press.

Bullen, J.B., ed. 1997. *Writing and Victorianism.* London & New York: Longman.

Burke, Seán. (1992) 1993. *The Death and Return of the Author: Criticism and Subjectivity in Barthes, Foucault and Derrida.* Edinburgh: Edinburgh University Press.

Butler, Christopher. 2002. *Postmodernism: A Very Short Introduction.* Oxford: Oxford University Press.

Buzard, James. 2005. *Disorienting Fiction: The Autoethnographic Work of Nineteenth-Century British Novels.* Princeton: Princeton University Press.

Buzard, James, Joseph W. Childers, and Eileen Gillooly, eds. 2007. *Victorian Prism: Refractions of the Crystal Palace*. Charlottesville: University of Virginia Press.

Byatt, A. S. (1990) 2002. *Possession*. New York: Vintage.

———. 1992. *Angels and Insects*. London: Chatto & Windus.

Carey, Peter. (1988) 1997a. *Oscar and Lucinda*. New York: Vintage.

———. 1997b. *Jack Maggs*. Queensland: University of Queensland Press.

Carroll, Samantha J. 2010. "Putting the 'Neo' Back into Neo-Victorian: The Neo-Victorian Novel as Postmodern Revisionist Fiction." *Neo-Victorian Studies* 3.2: 172–205.

Cartmell, Deborah, and Imelda Whelehan. 1999. *Adaptations: From Text to Screen, Screen to Text*. London: Routledge.

Chavanelle, Sylvie. 1998. "Caryl Phillips's *Cambridge*: Ironical (Dis)Empowerment?" *The International Fiction Review* 25.1–2. http://journals.hil.unb.ca/index.php/IFR/article/view/7598/8655.

Childers, Joseph W. (2002) 2005. "Victorian Theories of the Novel." In *A Companion to the Victorian Novel*, edited by Patrick Brantlinger and William B. Thesing, 406–23. Oxford: Blackwell.

Christie, William. 2008. "'Trifling Deviation': Stage and Screen Versions of Mary Shelley's Monster." In *Victorian Turns, NeoVictorian Returns: Essays on Fiction and Culture*, edited by Penny Gay, Judith Johnston, and Catherine Waters, 158–70. Newcastle: Cambridge Scholars Publishing.

Ciolkowski, Laura E. 1997. "Navigating the Wide Sargasso Sea: Colonial History, English Fiction, and British Empire." *Twentieth Century Literature* 43.3 (Fall). http://linksource.ebsco.com AN 436523.

"Classic Comic Store Ltd." http://www.classiccomicstore.com.

Clayton, Jay. 2003. *Charles Dickens in Cyberspace: The Afterlife of the Nineteenth Century in Postmodern Culture*. Oxford: Oxford University Press.

Coetzee, J. M. 1986. *Foe*. London: Penguin.

Cohen, Paula Marantz. 2004. "The Quest for a Necessary Shell." *Times Literary Supplement* (28 March). http://www.powells.com/review/2004_03_28.html.

———. 2010. *What Alice Knew: A Most Curious Tale of Henry James and Jack the Ripper*. Naperville, IL: Sourcebooks, Landmark.

Connor, Steven. 1994. "Rewriting Wrong: On the Ethics of Literary Reversion." In *Liminal Postmodernisms: The Postmodern, the (Post)Colonial and the (Post)Feminist*, edited by Theo D'haen and Hans Bertens, 79–97. Amsterdam: Rodopi.

Corner, John, and Sylvia Harvey. 1991. "Mediating Tradition and Modernity: The Heritage/Enterprise Couplet." In *Enterprise and Heritage: Crosscurrents of National Culture*, edited by John Corner and Sylvia Harvey, 45–75. London & New York: Routledge.

Corner, John, and Sylvia Harvey, eds. 1991. *Enterprise and Heritage: Crosscurrents of National Culture*. London & New York: Routledge.

Cunningham, Valentine. 1994. *In the Reading Gaol: Postmodernity, Texts, and History*. Oxford: Blackwell.

Deane, Bradley. 2003. *The Making of the Victorian Novelist: Anxieties of Authorship in the Mass Market*. New York & London: Routledge.

De Chellis Hill, Carol. 1993. *Henry James's Midnight Song*. New York: Poseidon Press.

Defoe, Daniel. 1719. *Robinson Crusoe*. London: W. Taylor.

Deirdre, David. (2002) 2005. "Empire, Race, and the Victorian Novel." In *A Companion to the Victorian Novel*, edited by Patrick Brantlinger and William B. Thesing, 84–100. Oxford: Blackwell.

Dentith, Simon. 2007. "The Workhouse: The Afterlife of a Victorian Institution." Paper presented at the Neo-Victorianism: The Politics and Aesthetics of Appropriation Conference, University of Exeter, UK, September.

Detmers, Ines. 2007. "'The Second Mrs. Rochesters': Telling Untold Stories of Jane Eyre's (Im-)Possible Married Lives." In *A Breath of Fresh Eyre: Intertextual and Intermedial Reworkings of Jane Eyre*, edited by Margarete Rubik and Elke Mettinger-Schartmann, 81–99. Amsterdam: Rodopi.

"Dickens 2012." 2011. http://www.dickens2012.org/.

Dickens, Charles. (1861) 1958. *Great Expectations*. London: Collins.

Dickens World. http://www.dickensworld.co.uk/.

Du Maurier, Daphne. 1938. *Rebecca*. London: Victor Gollancz.

Duncker, Patricia. 2008. "Victorian Fictions: Historical Imagination and Heritage Industry."

Paper presented at the Adapting the Nineteenth Century: Revisiting, Revising and Rewriting the Past Conference, University of Wales, Lampeter, UK, August.
Eagleton, Terry. (1995) 1996. *Heathcliff and the Great Hunger: Studies in Irish Culture*. London & New York: Verso.
Earl, Ben. 2008. "Theming Dickens: Dickens World and Issues of Taste and Distinction." Paper presented at the Adapting the Nineteenth Century: Revisiting, Revising and Rewriting the Past Conference, University of Wales, Lampeter, UK, August.
Easthope, Antony. 1991. *Literary into Cultural Studies*. London: Routledge.
———. 1999. *Englishness and National Culture*. London: Routledge.
Eliot, George. 1860. *The Mill on the Floss*. London & Edinburgh: William Blackwood and Sons.
———. 1871. *Middlemarch*. London & Edinburgh: William Blackwood and Sons.
"Enduring Love." 2007. *The Mail on Sunday* (26 August): 14–15.
English, James F. 2006. *A Concise Companion to Contemporary British Fiction*. Oxford: Blackwell.
———, and John Frow. 2006. "Literary Authorship and Celebrity Culture." In *A Concise Companion to Contemporary British Fiction*, edited by James F. English, 39–57. Oxford: Blackwell.
Faber, Michel. (2002) 2003. 2010. *The Crimson Petal and the White*. New York: Harvest. Edinburgh: Canongate.
Fforde, Jasper. (2001) 2002. 2003a. *The Eyre Affair*. New York: Viking. New York: Penguin.
———. 2002. *Lost in a Good Book*. New York: Penguin.
———. 2003b. *The Well of Lost Plots*. London: Hoder and Stoughton.
———. 2004. *Something Rotten*. New York: Penguin.
———. 2007. *First Among Sequels*. New York: Penguin.
———. 2011. *One of Our Thursdays Is Missing*. New York: Penguin.
———. 2012. *The Woman Who Died a Lot*. New York: Penguin.
———. "Beginnings." http://www.jasperfforde.com/beginnings.html#beginnings.
———. "Ffiesta." http://www.ffordeffiesta.co.uk/.
———. "Sovietreppage." http://www.jasperfforde.com/sovietreppage2.html.
———. "Thursday." http://www.jasperfforde.com/reader/thursday.html.
Flint, Kate. 1997. "Plotting the Victorians: Narrative, Post-Modernism, and Contemporary Fiction." In *Writing and Victorianism*, edited by J. B. Bullen, 286–305. London & New York: Longman.
Fowles, John. (1969) 1996. *The French Lieutenant's Woman*. London: Vintage.
Frears, Stephen. 2006. *The Queen* (film). France, United Kingdom, Italy: Pathé Pictures, Miramax Films.
Friedman, Paula. 2000. "Humor, Horror in the Voyage of Sincerity." *Los Angeles Times* (13 April). http://international.westlaw.com WLNR 8336375.
Fukuyama, Francis. 1992. *The End of History or the Last Man*. New York: Penguin.
Garrett, Stewart. 1996. *Dear Reader: The Conscripted Audience in Nineteenth-Century British Fiction*. Baltimore & London: Johns Hopkins University Press.
Gasiorek, Andrzej. 1995. *Post-War British Fiction: Realism and After*. London: Edward Arnold.
Gay, Penny, Judith Johnston, and Catherine Waters, eds. 2008. *Victorian Turns, Neovictorian Returns: Essays on Fiction and Culture*. Newcastle: Cambridge Scholars Publishing.
Gibson, Andrew. 1999. *Postmodernity, Ethics and the Novels: From Leavis to Levinas*. London & New York: Routledge.
Gikandi, Simon. 1996. *Maps of Englishness: Writing Identity in the Culture of Colonialism*. New York: Columbia University Press.
Gilbert, Sandra M., and Susan Gubar. 1984. *The Madwoman in the Attic*. New Haven & London: Yale.
Gillies, Mary Ann. 1998. "The Literary Agent and the Sequel." In *Part Two: Reflections on the Sequel*, edited by Paul Budra and Betty Schellenberg, 131–43. Toronto: University of Toronto Press.
Gilmour, Robin. 2000. "Using the Victorians: The Victorian Age in Contemporary Fiction." In *Rereading Victorian Fiction*, edited by Alice Jenkins and Juliet John, 189–200. Basingstoke: Macmillan.
Good Housekeeping. http://www.goodhousekeeping.com/.
Gould, Marty, and Rebecca N. Mitchell. 2010. "Understanding the Literary Theme Park: Dickens World as Adaptation." *Neo-Victorian Studies* 3.2: 145–71.
Gray, Alasdair. *Poor Things*. (1992). 2002. London: Bloomsbury.

"Great Expectations Facsimile Now Available." 2011. http://www.wisbechmuseum.blogspot.com/2011/12/great-expectations-facsimilie-now.html.
Green-Lewis, Jennifer. 2000. "At Home in the Nineteenth Century: Photography, Nostalgia, and the Will to Authenticity." In *Victorian Afterlife: Postmodern Culture Rewrites the Nineteenth Century*, edited by John Kucich and Dianne F. Sadoff, 29–48. Minneapolis: University Press of Minnesota.
Gribble, Jennifer. 2008. "Portable Property: Postcolonial Appropriations of *Great Expectations*." In *Victorian Turns, Neovictorian Returns: Essays on Fiction and Culture*, edited by Penny Gay, Judith Johnston, and Catherine Waters, 182–92. Newcastle: Cambridge Scholars Publishing.
Gutleben, Christian. 2001. *Nostalgic Postmodernism: The Victorian Tradition and the Contemporary British Novel*. Amsterdam & New York: Rodopi.
_____. 2002. "Palinodes, Palindromes and Palimpsests: Strategies of Deliberate Self-Contradiction in Postmodern British Fiction." *Miscelánea: A Journal of English and American Studies* 26: 11–20.
Gutleben, Christian, and Julian Wolfreys. 2010. "Postmodernism Revisited: The Ethical Drive of Postmodern Trauma in Neo-Victorian Fiction." In *Neo-Victorian Tropes of Trauma: The Politics of Bearing After-Witness to Nineteenth-Century Suffering*, edited by Marie-Luise Kohlke and Christian Gutleben. Amsterdam & New York: Rodopi.
Hadley, Louisa. 2010. *Neo-Victorian Fiction and Historical Narrative: The Victorians and Us*. Basingstoke & New York: Palgrave Macmillan.
Hall, Catherine, and Sonya Rose, eds. 2006. *At Home with the Empire: Metropolitan Culture and the Imperial World*. Cambridge: Cambridge University Press.
Haralson, Eric. 2003. *Henry James and Queer Modernity*. Cambridge: Cambridge University Press.
Harris, Jane. 2006. 2007. *The Observations*. London: Faber & Faber. New York: Penguin.
Harrison, Sophie. 2004. "'The Portrait of a Layabout': *Author, Author* by David Lodge." *The New York Times* (10 October). http://query.nytimes.com/gst/fullpage.html?res=9C04E1D61538F933A25753C1A9629C8B63.
Heilmann, Ann. 2010. "The Haunting of Henry James: Jealous Ghosts, Affinities, and *The Others*." In *Haunting and Spectrality in Neo-Victorian Fiction: Possessing the Past*, edited by Rosario Arias and Patricia Pulham, 111–30. Basingstoke & New York: Palgrave Macmillan.
Heilmann, Ann, and Mark Llewellyn. 2010. *Neo-Victorianism: The Victorians in the Twenty-First Century, 1999–2009*. Basingstoke & New York: Palgrave Macmillan.
Henry, Lori. 2010. "Wales Travel: Hay-on-Wye Bookshops." (8 April). http://lorihenry.ca/04/wales-travel-hay-on-wye-bookshops-and-festival-in-the-uk/.
Hewison, Robert. 1991. "Commerce and Culture." In *Enterprise and Heritage: Crosscurrents of National Culture*, edited by John Corner and Sylvia Harvey, 162–77. London & New York: Routledge.
Heyns, Michiel. 2004. "The Curse of Henry James." *Prospect* (26 September). http://www.prospectmagazine.co.uk/magazine/thecurseofhenryjames/, http://linksource.ebsco.com AN RN154825163.
_____. 2005. *The Typewriter's Tale*. Jeppestown: Jonathan Ball.
Higson, Andrew. 2004. "English Heritage, English Literature, English Cinema: Selling Jane Austen to Movie Audiences in the 1990s." In *Janespotting and Beyond: British Heritage Retrovisions Since the Mid-1990s*, edited by Eckart Voigts-Virchow, 35–50. Tübingen: Narr.
"Historical Romance Writers." http://historicalromancewriters.com/timeperiods.cfm?genreID=24.
Hochschild, Adam. 2000. "The Floating Swap Meet." *New York Times Book Review* (28 May): 26.
Hollinghurst, Alan. 2004. *The Line of Beauty*. London: Picador.
Holt, Shari Hodges. 2012. "Will the 'Real' Dickens Please Stand Up? The 'Other Dickens' of Adaptation." Paper presented at the The Other Dickens Conference, University of Portsmouth, UK, July.
Hoving, Isabel. 2001. *In Praise of New Travelers: Reading Caribbean Migrant Women Writers*. Stanford, CA: Stanford University Press.
Hughes, Linda K., and Michael Lund, eds. 1991. *The Victorian Serial*. Charlottesville: University Press of Virginia.
Humpherys, Anne. (2002) 2005. "The Afterlife of the Victorian Novel: Novels About Novels."

In *A Companion to the Victorian Novel*, edited by Patrick Brantlinger and William B. Thesing, 442–57. Oxford: Blackwell.
Hutcheon, Linda. (1988) 1995. *A Poetics of Postmodernism*. London: Routledge.
———. 2006. *A Theory of Adaptation*. London: Routledge.
Ickringill, Steve, and Stephen Mills, eds. 1992. *Victorianism in the United States: Its Era and Its Legacy*. Amsterdam: VU University Press.
Ishiguro, Kazuo. 1989. *The Remains of the Day*. London: Faber & Faber.
Jacobson, Howard. 1984. *Peeping Tom*. London: Chatto & Windus.
Jaffe, Audrey. (2002) 2005. "Modern and Postmodern Theories of Prose Fiction." In *A Companion to the Victorian Novel*, edited by Patrick Brantlinger and William B. Thesing. Oxford: Blackwell.
Jameson, Fredric. (1991) 1996. *Postmodernism, or the Cultural Logic of Late Capitalism*. London & New York: Verso.
Jenkins, Alice, and Juliet John, eds. 2000. *Rereading Victorian Fiction*. Basingstoke: Macmillan.
Jensen, Liz. 1998. *Ark Baby*. London: Penguin.
Jhabvala, Ruth Prawer. 1975. *Heat and Dust*. London: John Murray.
Johnston, Judith, and Catherine Waters. 2008. "Introduction." In *Victorian Turns, Neovictorian Returns: Essays on Fiction and Culture*, edited by Penny Gay, Judith Johnston, and Catherine Waters, 1–11. Newcastle: Cambridge Scholars Publishing.
Jones, Gail. 2004. *Sixty Lights*. London: Harvill.
Jones, Lloyd. 2006. *Mister Pip*. London: John Murray.
Jones, Sally Mair. 2008. "Naturally Not Selected: Anita Brookner's Writing Protagonists." Paper presented at the Adapting the Nineteenth Century: Revisiting, Revising and Rewriting the Past Conference, University of Wales, Lampeter, UK, August.
Joyce, Simon. 2002. "The Victorians in the Rearview Mirror." In *Functions of Victorian Culture at the Present Time*, edited by Christine L. Krueger, 3–17. Athens: Ohio University Press.
———. 2007. *The Victorians in the Rearview Mirror*. Athens: Ohio University Press.
Kaplan, Cora. 2006. "Imagining Empire: History, Fantasy and Literature." In *At Home with the Empire: Metropolitan Culture and the Imperial World*, edited by Catherine Hall and Sonya Rose. Cambridge: Cambridge University Press.
———. 2007. *Victoriana: Histories, Fictions, Criticism*. Edinburgh: Edinburgh University Press.
Kehlmann, Daniel. 2005. *Die Vermessung Der Welt* [*Measuring the World*]. Reinbek: Rowohlt.
Kermode, Frank. 1966. *The Sense of an Ending: Studies in the Theory of Fiction*. Oxford: Oxford University Press.
Khalil, Yasmin Pascual. 2012. "The *Iron Lady* Movie Criticized as 'Over-Emotional Left-Wing Fantasy.'" (6 January). http://www.toonaripost.com/2012/01/entertainment/the-iron-lady-criticized-as-over-emotional-left-wing-fantasy/.
Kirchknopf, Andrea. 2008. "(Re-)Workings of Nineteenth-Century Century Fiction: Definitions, Terminology, Contexts." *Neo-Victorian Studies* 1.1: 53–80.
———. 2011. "Post-Victorian Narratives of the Crystal Palace: The Case of Peter Carey's *Oscar and Lucinda*." In *Confrontations and Interactions: Essays on Cultural Memory*, edited by Bálint Gárdos, Ágnes Péter, Natália Pikli, Máté Vince, 393–407. Budapest: L'Harmattan. Paper presented at the British Literature and Cultural Memory Conference, ELTE, Budapest, Hungary, September 2010.
———. 2011. "The Future of the Post-Victorian Novel: A Speculation in Genre." *HJEAS* 17.2: 351–70. Paper presented at the Adapting the Nineteenth Century: Revisiting, Revising and Rewriting the Past Conference, University of Wales, Lampeter, UK, August 2008.
———. 2011. "Adapting Dickens in Post-Victorian Fiction." In *HUSSE 10 LitCult.*, edited by Kinga Földváry et al., 127–135. Piliscsaba: Institute of English and American Studies, Faculty of Humanities, PPCU. Paper presented at the HUSSE 10 LitCult Conference, University of Piliscsaba, Piliscsaba, Hungary, January 2011. A revised version of this paper titled "Dickens and his *Great Expectations* in Post-Victorian Fiction" was presented at The Other Dickens Conference, University of Portsmouth, UK, July 2012.
Kleinecke, Iris. 2007. "Imagining Victoriana: *Bleak House* and the Shifting Interest in the Victorian on Current British Television." Paper presented at the Neo-Victorianism: The Politics and Aesthetics of Appropriation Conference, University of Exeter, UK, September.
Kontou, Tatiana. 2009. *Spiritualism and Women's Writing: From the Fin de Siècle to the Neo-Victorian*. Basingstoke & New York: Palgrave Macmillan.

Kneale, Matthew. 2000. *English Passengers*. London: Hamish Hamilton.
Knight, Charmian, and Patsy Stoneman, eds. 2004. *The Brontë Influence*. Haworth: Brontë Society.
Knight, Deborah. 1995. "Women, Subjectivity, and the Rhetoric of Anti-Humanism in Feminist Film Theory." *New Literary History* 26.1: 39–56.
_____. 1995. "The Rhetoric of Theory: Responses to Toril Moi." *New Literary History* 26.1: 63–70.
Kohlke, Marie-Luise. 2008. "Introduction: Speculations in and on the Neo-Victorian Encounter." *Neo-Victorian Studies* 1.1: 1–18.
Kohlke, Marie-Luise, and Christian Gutleben, eds. 2010. *Neo-Victorian Tropes of Trauma: The Politics of Bearing After-Witness to Nineteenth-Century Suffering*. Amsterdam & New York: Rodopi.
_____. 2011. *Neo-Victorian Families: Gender, Sexual and Cultural Politics*. Amsterdam & New York: Rodopi.
_____. *Neo-Victorian Gothic: Horror, Violence, and Degeneration in the Re-Imagined 19th Century*. Amsterdam & New York: Rodopi, forthcoming.
Kramer, Kathryn. 1998. *Sweet Water*. New York: Knopf.
_____. 2008. "The Secrets of the Master." *The Henry James Review* 29.2 (Spring). http://muse.jhu.edu/journals/henry_james_review/v029/29.2.kramer.html.
Krueger, Christine L., ed. 2002. *Functions of Victorian Culture at the Present Time*. Athens: Ohio University Press.
Kucich, John, and Dianne F. Sadoff, eds. 2000. *Victorian Afterlife: Postmodern Culture Rewrites the Nineteenth Century*. Minneapolis: University of Minnesota Press.
Kuhn, Annette. 2005. "Memory and Textuality." In *Inventing the Past: Memory Work in Culture and History*, edited by Otto Heim and Caroline Wiedmer, 15–23. Basel: Schwabe.
Kurnick, David S. 1993. "Middle Passages: Caryl Phillips's Fiction Traces the Consequences of Empire." *The Harvard Crimson* (15 April). http://www.thecrimson.com/article/1993/4/15/middle-passages-pbibn-caryl-phillips-work.
Kuurola, Mirja. 2007. "Caryl Phillips's *Cambridge*: Discourses in the Past and Readers in the Present." *NJES Special Issue: Literature as Communication* 6.2: 129–44.
LaBute, Neil. 2002. *Possession* (film). United States, United Kingdom: Focus Features, Warner Bros.
Langbauer, Laurie. 2000. "Queen Victoria and Me." In *Victorian Afterlife: Postmodern Culture Rewrites the Nineteenth Century*, edited by John Kucich and Dianne F. Sadoff, 211–33. Minneapolis: University Press of Minnesota.
Langland, Elisabeth. (2002) 2005. "The Receptions of Charlotte Brontë, Charles Dickens, George Eliot, and Thomas Hardy." In *A Companion to the Victorian Novel*, edited by Patrick Brantlinger and William B. Thesing, 387–405. Oxford: Blackwell.
Lefevere, André. 1985. "Why Waste Our Time on Rewrites? The Trouble with Interpretation and the Role of Rewriting in an Alternative Paradigm." In *The Manipulation of Literature: Studies in Literary Translation*, edited by Theo Hermans, 215–13. London: Croom Helm.
_____. 1992. *Translation, Rewriting and the Manipulation of Literary Fame*. London: Routledge.
Letissier, Georges. 2004. "Dickens and Post-Victorian Fiction." In *Refracting the Canon in Contemporary British Literature and Film*, edited by Susana Onega and Christian Gutleben, 111–28. Amsterdam & New York: Rodopi.
_____. 2010. "Trauma by Proxy in the 'Age of Testimony': Paradoxes of Darwinism in the Neo-Victorian Novel." In *Neo-Victorian Tropes of Trauma: The Politics of Bearing After-Witness to Nineteenth-Century Suffering*, edited by Marie-Luise Kohlke and Christian Gutleben, 73–98. Amsterdam & New York: Rodopi.
Levine, George. 1981. *The Realistic Imagination: English Fiction from Frankenstein to Lady Chatterley*. Chicago: Chicago University Press.
Lindner, Christoph. 2003. *Fictions of Commodity Culture: From the Victorian to the Postmodern*. Burlington, VT: Ashgate.
Literature Interpretation Theory. Neo-Victorianism: The Politics and Aesthetics of Appropriation. 2009. 20.1–2. Guest edited by Rebecca Munford and Paul Young.
Llewellyn, Mark. 2008. "What Is Neo-Victorian Studies?" *Neo-Victorian Studies* 1.1: 164–85.
_____. 2008/2009. "On the Turn: Review of Penny Gay, Judith Johnston, and Catherine Waters, eds., *Victorian Turns, NeoVictorian Returns*." *Neo-Victorian Studies* 2.1: 153–58.
_____. 2010. "Spectrality, S(p)ecularity, and Textuality: Or Some Reflections in the Glass." In

Haunting and Spectrality in Neo-Victorian Fiction: Possessing the Past, edited by Rosario Arias and Patricia Pulham, 23–42. Basingstoke & New York: Palgrave Macmillan.

Lloyd, Phyllida. 2011. *The Iron Lady* (film). United Kingdom, France: The Weinstein Company (U.S.), 20th Century–Fox (UK), Pathé (International).

Lodge, David. 1971. *The Novelist at the Crossroads and Other Essays*. London: Routledge.

_____. 1990. *After Bakhtin: Essays on Fiction and Criticism*. London: Routledge.

_____. (2004). 2005. *Author, Author*. London: Penguin.

_____. 2006. *The Year of Henry James: The Story of a Novel*. London: Penguin.

"Looking for Eden." 2000. *The Economist* (25 November): 107. http://www.economist.com/node/434700.

Lundén, Bo. 1999. *(Re)Educating the Reader: Fictional Critiques of Poststructuralism in Banville's Dr. Copernicus, Coetzee's Foe and Byatt's Possession*. Göteborg: Acta Universitatis Bothoburgensis.

Macfarlane, Robert. 2007. *Original Copy: Plagiarism and Originality in Nineteenth-Century Literature*. Oxford: Oxford University Press.

Madden, John. 2012. *The Best Exotic Marigold Hotel* (film). United Kingdom: Fox Searchlight Pictures.

Malone, Michael. 1990. "The Spirit of Dickens Present." *New York Times Book Review* (4 March): 12.

Mardorossian, Carine M. 2005. *Reclaiming Difference: Caribbean Women Rewrite Postcolonialism*. Charlottesville: University of Virginia Press.

Marguerite, Alexander. 1990. *Flights from Realism: Themes and Strategies in Postmodernist British and American Fiction*. London: Edward Arnold.

Marsh, Kelly. 1995. "The Neo-Sensation Novel: A Contemporary Genre in the Victorian Tradition." *Philological Quarterly* 74.1: 99–123.

McDonald, Rónán. 2007. *The Death of the Critic*. London: Continuum.

McGowan, John. 2000. "Modernity and Culture, the Victorians and Cultural Studies." In *Victorian Afterlife: Postmodern Culture Rewrites the Nineteenth Century*, edited by John Kucich and Dianne F. Sadoff, 3–28. Minneapolis: University Press of Minnesota.

McHale, Brian. (1987) 1999. *Postmodernist Fiction*. London & New York: Routledge.

_____. 1992. *Constructing Postmodernism*. London & New York: Routledge.

Meyer, Susan. 1996. *Imperialism at Home: Race and Victorian Women's Fiction*. Ithaca, NY: Cornell University Press.

Miller, Lucasta. (2001) 2002. *The Brontë Myth*. London: Vintage.

Miller, Miranda. 2010. *Nina in Utopia*. London: Peter Owen.

Mills, Stephen F. 1992. "Introduction." In *Victorianism in the United States: Its Era and Its Legacy*, edited by Steve Ickringill and Stephen F. Mills, ix–xxi. Amsterdam: VU University Press.

Miquel-Baldellou, Marta. 2008. "From the Madwoman to a Prozac Nation: Rethinking Female Hysteria in Neo-Victorian Texts." Paper presented at the Adapting the Nineteenth Century: Revisiting, Revising and Rewriting the Past Conference, University of Wales, Lampeter, UK, August.

Mitchell, Kate. 2008. "Ghostly Histories and Embodied Memories: Photography, Spectrality and Historical Fiction in *Afterimage* and *Sixty Lights*." *Neo-Victorian Studies* 1.1: 80–109.

_____. 2010a. "Australia's 'Other' History Wars: Trauma and the Work of Cultural Memory in Kate Grenville's *The Secret River*." In *Neo-Victorian Tropes of Trauma: The Politics of Bearing After-Witness to Nineteenth-Century Suffering*, edited by Marie-Luise Kohlke and Christian Gutleben, 253–82. Amsterdam & New York: Rodopi.

_____. 2010b. *History and Cultural Memory in Neo-Victorian Fiction: Victorian Afterimages*. Basingstoke & New York: Palgrave Macmillan.

Moi, Toril. 1995. "'Am I That Name': Reply to Deborah Knight." *New Literary History* 26.1: 57–62.

Moore, Alan, and Eddie Campbell. 1999. *From Hell*. London: Knockabout Comics.

Naipaul, V. S. *Guerrillas*. (1975) 1976. Harmondsworth: Penguin.

Neo-Victorian Studies (NVS). 2008. 1.1. http://www.neovictorianstudies.com/.

_____. 2009/2010. 2.2. *Adapting the Nineteenth Century: Revisiting, Revising and Rewriting the Past*. Guest edited by Alexia L. Bowler and Jessica Cox. http://www.neovictorianstudies.com/.

_____. "Aims and Scope." http://www.neovictorianstudies.com/aims_scope.htm.

_____. 2010. 3.1. *Steampunk, Science, and (Neo)Victorian Technologies*. Guest edited by Rachel A. Bowser and Brian Croxall. http://www.neovictorianstudies.com/.

_____. 2008/2009. 2.1. *Special Issue: "Swing Your Razor Wide...": Sweeney Todd and Other (Neo)Victorian Criminalities*. http://www.neovictorianstudies.com/.

Nicol, Bran. 2004. *D. M. Thomas*. Tavistock: Northcote House in association with the British Council.

"Novel Approach to the Roots of Racism." 2001. *African Business* (October). 01413929.269. http://linksource.ebsco.com DB Business Source Complete AN 5369288.

Nungesser, Verena-Susanna. 2007. "From Thornfield Hall to Manderley and Beyond: *Jane Eyre* and *Rebecca* as Transformations of the Fairy Tale, the Novel of Development, and the Gothic Novel." In *A Breath of Fresh Eyre: Intertextual and Intermedial Reworkings of Jane Eyre*, edited by Margarete Rubik and Elke Mettinger-Schartmann, 209–26. Amsterdam: Rodopi.

Nünning, Ansgar. 1995. *Von historischer Fiktion zu historiographischer Metafiktion. Teil I: Theorie, Typologie und Poetik des historischen Romans* [*From Historical Fiction to Historiographic Metafiction. Part I: The Theory, Typology and Poetics of the Historical Novel*]. Tier: Wissenschaftlicher Verlag Trier.

_____. 1995. *Von historischer Fiktion zu historiographischer Metafiktion. Teil II: Erscheinungsformen und Entwicklungstendenzen des historischen Romans in England seit 1950* [*From Historical Fiction to Historiographic Metafiction. Part II: Realizations and Tendencies of Development of the Historical Novel in England Since 1950*]. Tier: Wissenschaftlicher Verlag Trier.

Oates, Joyce Carol. 2006. "Romance and Anti-Romance: From Brontë's *Jane Eyre* to Rhys's *Wide Sargasso Sea*." In *Charlotte Brontë's* Jane Eyre: *A Casebook*, edited by Elsie B. Michie, 195–208. Oxford: Oxford University Press.

Onega, Susana. "Ethics and Trauma in Contemporary Narrative in English." http://cne.literatureresearch.net/Research-projects/competitive-research-projects-carried-out-by-the-team.html.

Onega, Susana, and Christian Gutleben, eds. 2004. *Refracting the Canon in Contemporary British Literature and Film*. Amsterdam & New York: Rodopi.

Oxford World's Classics Complete List. 2008. Oxford: Oxford University Press.

Ozick, Cynthia. 1982. "The Lesson of the Master." *The New York Review of Books* (12 August). http://www.nybooks.com/articles/archives/1982/aug/12/the-lesson-of-the-master/?pagination=false.

_____. 2008. *Dictation: A Quartet*. New York: Houghton Mifflin Harcourt.

_____. 2010. *Foreign Bodies*. New York: Houghton Mifflin Harcourt.

Palliser, Charles. 1989. *The Quincunx*. Edinburgh: Canongate.

Parish, Peter J. 1992. "Confidence and Anxiety in Victorian America." In *Victorianism in the United States: Its Era and Its Legacy*, edited by Steve Ickringill and Stephen F. Mills, 1–18. Amsterdam: VU University Press.

Parrinder, Patrick. 2006. *Nation and Novel: The English Novel from Its Origins to the Present Day*. Oxford: Oxford University Press.

Perosa, Sergio. 1992. "The Case of Henry James: From Victorianism to the Avant-Garde." In *Victorianism in the United States: Its Era and Its Legacy*, edited by Steve Ickringill and Stephen F. Mills, 61–77. Amsterdam: VU University Press.

Phillips, Caryl. 1991. *Cambridge*. London: Bloomsbury.

Pillitz, Christopher. 1993. "Brazil, Rio de Janeiro, Partially Clothed Man and Woman on Beach (B&W)." (photograph) http://www.gettyimages.com/detail/photo/brazil-rio-de-janeiro-partially-clothed-man-high-res-stock-photography/200530438-001.

Renk, Kathleen J. 1999. *Caribbean Shadows & Victorian Ghosts: Women's Writing and Decolonization*. Charlottesville & London: University Press of Virginia.

"Review: *The Iron Lady*." 2012. *BBC Kermode Uncut Filmblog* (11 January). http://www.bbc.co.uk/blogs/markkermode/2012/01/review_the_iron_lady.html.

Rhys, Jean. (1966) 1968. *Wide Sargasso Sea*. London: Penguin.

Rollyson, Carl. 2005. "James & the Zeitgeist." *The New Criterion* 23 (February). http://www.newcriterion.com/articles.cfm/James___the-Zeitgeist-1238.

Rubik, Margarete. 2007. "Invasions into Literary Texts, Re-Plotting and Transfictional Migration in Jasper Fforde's *The Eyre Affair*." In *A Breath of Fresh Eyre: Intertextual and Intermedial Reworkings of* Jane Eyre, edited by Margarete Rubik and Elke Mettinger-Schartmann, 167–79. Amsterdam: Rodopi.

Rubik, Margarete, and Elke Mettinger-Schartmann, eds. 2007. *A Breath of Fresh Eyre: Intertextual and Intermedial Reworkings of* Jane Eyre. Amsterdam: Rodopi.
Rushdie, Salman. 1981. *Midnight's Children*. London: Jonathan Cape.
Sadoff, Dianne F. 2009. *Victorian Vogue: British Novels on Screen*. Minneapolis: University Press of Minnesota.
_____. 2010. "The Neo-Victorian Nation at Home and Abroad: Charles Dickens and Traumatic Rewriting." In *Neo-Victorian Tropes of Trauma: The Politics of Bearing After-Witness to Nineteenth-Century Suffering*, edited by Marie-Luise Kohlke and Christian Gutleben, 163–90. Amsterdam & New York: Rodopi.
Said, Edward W. (1993) 1994. *Culture and Imperialism*. New York: Knopf.
Samuel, Raphael. (1998) 1999. *Island Stories: Unravelling Britain. Theatres of Memory Vol. II*. London: Verso.
Sanders, Julie. 2006. *Adaptation and Appropriation*. London: Routledge.
Saunders, Max. 2008. "Master Narratives." *Cambridge Quarterly* 37: 121–31.
Schaff, Barbara. 2007. "The Strange Afterlives of *Jane Eyre*." In *A Breath of Fresh Eyre: Intertextual and Intermedial Reworkings of* Jane Eyre, edited by Margarete Rubik and Elke Mettinger-Schartmann, 25–36. Amsterdam: Rodopi.
Scherzinger, Karen. 2008. "The Anacoluthic Interruption: Biographical Fiction and the Example of Henry James." Inaugural Address, Department of English, University of Johannesburg (29 October): 1–22. https://ujdigispace.uj.ac.za/bitstream/handle/10210/1635/Scherzinger%20K.pdf?sequence=1
Schor, Hilary M. 2000. "Sorting, Morphing, and Mourning: A. S. Byatt Ghostwrites Victorian Fiction." In *Victorian Afterlife: Postmodern Culture Rewrites the Nineteenth Century*, edited by John Kucich and Dianne F. Sadoff, 234–51. Minneapolis: University Press of Minnesota.
Schorer, Mark. 1972. "Technique as Discovery." In *20th Century Literary Criticism: A Reader*, edited by David Lodge, 387–401. London: Longman.
Schwarz, Daniel R. 1986. *The Humanistic Heritage: Critical Theories of the English Novel from James to Hillis Miller*. Basingstoke: Macmillan.
Séllei, Nóra. 1999. *Lánnyá válik, s írni kezd: 19. századi angol írónők* [Becoming a Woman, She Starts Writing: 19th-Century English Woman Writers]. Debrecen: Kossuth.
_____. 2002. "Autobiography and the Female Voice: Jane Eyre's Telling and Controlling Her Story in Gateshead." *Gender Studies* 1.1: 7–16.
Shaffer, Brian W. 2006. *Reading the Novel in English 1950–2000*. Oxford: Blackwell.
Shiller, Dana. 1997. "The Redemptive Past in the Neo-Victorian Novel." *Studies in the Novel* 29.4: 538–60.
Shuttleworth, Sally. 1998. "Natural History: The Retro-Victorian Novel." In *The Third Culture: Literature and Science*, edited by Elinor Shaffer, 253–68. Berlin and New York: Walter de Gruyter.
Sinha, Sanskrity. 2011. "'The World' Islands in Dubai Sinking, Does It Signal Earth's Future?" *International Business Times* (28 January). http://www.ibtimes.com/articles/106171/20110128/the-world-islands-in-dubai-sinking-does-it-signal-earth-s-future–the-world-sinking-the-world-islands.htm.
Spencer, Richard. 2011. "The World Is Sinking: Dubai Islands 'Falling into the Sea.'" *The Telegraph* (20 January). http://www.telegraph.co.uk/news/worldnews/middleeast/dubai/8271643/The-World-is-sinking-Dubai-islands-falling-into-the-sea.html.
"Sponsor." *The Man Booker Prize*. http://www.themanbookerprize.com/prize/about/sponsors.
Stallybrass, Peter. 1999. "Worn Worlds: Clothes, Mourning, and the Life of Things." In *Cultural Memory and the Construction of Identity*, edited by Dan Ben-Amos and Liliane Weissberg, 27–44. Detroit: Wayne State University Press.
Starling, Belinda. (2006). 2007. 2008. *The Journal of Dora Damage*. London: Bloomsbury.
Stirling, Kirsten. 2004. "Dr. Jekyll and Mr. Jackass: *Fight Club* as a Refraction of Hogg's *Justified Sinner* and Stevenson's *Dr Jekyll and Mr Hyde*." In *Refracting the Canon in Contemporary British Literature and Film*, edited by Susana Onega and Christian Gutleben, 83–94. Amsterdam & New York: Rodopi.
Stoneman, Patsy. 1996. *Brontë Transformations: The Cultural Dissemination of* Jane Eyre *and* Wuthering Heights. London: Harvester Wheatsheaf.
_____. 2006. "*Jane Eyre* in Later Lives: Intertextual Strategies in Women's Self-Definition." In *Charlotte Brontë's* Jane Eyre: *A Casebook*, edited by Elsie B. Michie, 177–94. Oxford: Oxford University Press.

Strongman, Luke. 2002. *The Booker Prize and the Legacy of Empire*. Amsterdam & New York: Rodopi.
Studio Foglio LLC. 2001. *Girl Genius*. http://www.girlgeniusonline.com.
Su, John. 2005. *Ethics and Nostalgia in the Contemporary Novel*. Cambridge: Cambridge University Press.
Sutherland, John. 1997. *Can Jane Eyre Be Happy?: More Puzzles in Classic Fiction*. Oxford: Oxford University Press.
_____. 2006. *How to Read a Novel?* London: Profile.
_____. 2007. "Gaslit Londons: The Neo-Victorian Novel in Modern Times." Paper presented at the Neo-Victorianism: The Politics and Aesthetics of Appropriation Conference, University of Exeter, UK, September.
Sweet, Matthew. 2001. *Inventing the Victorians*. London: Faber & Faber.
Swift, Graham. 1983. *Waterland*. New York: Poseidon.
_____. 1992. *Ever After*. London: Picador.
Tellkamp, Uwe. 2008. *Der Turm [The Tower]*. Berlin: Suhrkamp.
Tennant, Emma. 1993. *Tess*. London: Flamingo.
_____. (2002) 2003. *Adèle: Jane Eyre's Hidden Story*. New York: William Morrow/HarperCollins.
_____. 2002. *Felony: The Private History of the Aspern Papers*. London: Jonathan Cape.
_____. 2006. *The French Dancer's Bastard: The Story of Adele from* Jane Eyre. Columbus, OH: Maia Books.
_____. 2007. *Thornfield Hall: Jane Eyre's Hidden Story*. New York: Harper.
Thomas, D. M. 1981. *The White Hotel*. New York: Viking.
_____. 2000. *Charlotte: The Final Journey of Jane Eyre*. London: Duck.
Thomas, Ronald R. 2002. "The Legacy of Victorian Spectacle: The Map of Time and the Architecture of Empty Space." In *Functions of Victorian Culture at the Present Time*, edited by Christine L. Krueger, 18–33. Athens: Ohio University Press.
_____. 2006. "The Advertisement of *Jane Eyre*." In *Charlotte Brontë's* Jane Eyre*: A Casebook*, edited by Elsie B. Michie, 47–77. Oxford: Oxford University Press.
Thomas, Sue. 2007. "Pathologies of Sexuality, Empire and Slavery: D. M. Thomas's *Charlotte*." In *A Breath of Fresh Eyre: Intertextual and Intermedial Reworkings of* Jane Eyre, edited by Margarete Rubik and Elke Mettinger-Schartmann, 101–14. Amsterdam: Rodopi.
Todd, Richard. 1996. *Consuming Fictions: The Booker Prize and Fiction in Britain Today*. London: Bloomsbury.
_____. 2006. "Literary Fiction and the Book Trade." In *A Concise Companion to Contemporary British Fiction*, edited by James F. English, 19–38. Oxford: Blackwell.
Tóibín, Colm. (2004) 2005. *The Master*. New York: Scribner.
Tsomondo, Thorell Porter. 2007. *The Not So Blank "Blank Page": The Politics of Narrative and the Woman Narrator in the Eighteenth- and Nineteenth-Century British Novel*. New York & Oxford: Peter Lang.
Voigts-Virchow, Eckart, ed. 2004. *Janespotting and Beyond: British Heritage Retrovisions since the Mid-1990s*. Tübingen: Narr.
Vrettos, Athena. (2002) 2005. "Victorian Psychology." In *A Companion to the Victorian Novel*, edited by Patrick Brantlinger and William B. Thesing, 67–83. Oxford: Blackwell.
Vukelic, Anne-Marie. 2010. *Far Above Rubies*. London: Robert Hale.
Watt, Ian. 1957. *The Rise of the Novel*. London: Chatto & Windus.
Waugh, Patricia. 1995. *Harvest of the Sixties: English Literature and Its Background 1960–1990*. Oxford: Oxford University Press.
Wehrmann, Jürgen. 2007. "*Jane Eyre* in Outer Space: Victorian Motifs in Post-Feminist Science Fiction." In *A Breath of Fresh Eyre: Intertextual and Intermedial Reworkings of* Jane Eyre, edited by Margarete Rubik and Elke Mettinger-Schartmann, 149–63. Amsterdam: Rodopi.
Wells, Juliette. 2007. "An Eyre–Less Affair? Jasper Fforde's Seeming Elision of Jane." In *A Breath of Fresh Eyre: Intertextual and Intermedial Reworkings of* Jane Eyre, edited by Margarete Rubik and Elke Mettinger-Schartmann, 197–208. Amsterdam: Rodopi.
Whelehan, Imelda. 2008. "A Simple Twist?: The Genrification of Nineteenth-Century Fiction." Paper presented at the Adapting the Nineteenth Century: Revisiting, Revising and Rewriting the Past Conference, University of Wales, Lampeter, UK, August.
White, Edmund. 2007. *Hotel de Dream*. London: Bloomsbury.
White, Hayden. 1973. *Metahistory: The Historical Imagination in Nineteenth-Century Europe*. Baltimore: John Hopkins.
Williams, Carolyn. 1997. "Closing the Book: The Intertextual End of *Jane Eyre*." In *Contem-

porary Critical Essays: Jane Eyre, edited by Heather Glen, 227–47. London: Palgrave Macmillan.
Wilson, Cheryl A. 2008. "(Neo-)Victorian Fatigue: Getting Tired of the Victorians in Conrad's *The Secret Agent." Neo-Victorian Studies* 1.1: 19–40.
Winterson, Jeanette. 1985. *Boating for Beginners.* London: Methuen.
Wolfreys, Julian. 2001. "Victoriographies: Inventing the Nineteenth Century." (Spring). http://www.english.ufl.edu/courses/undergrad/2001spring_up-d.html#LIT_4930.jw.
Wood, James. 2004. "The Ogee Curve: *The Line of Beauty* by Alan Hollinghurst." *The New Republic* (9 December). http://www.powells.com/review/2004_12_09.html.
_____. 2004. "The Spoils: *Author, Author* by David Lodge." *The New Republic* (21 October). http://www.powells.com/review/2004_10_21.html.
Worpole, Ken. 2001. "Cartels and Lotteries: Heritage and Cultural Policy in Britain." In *British Cultural Studies: Geography, Nationality and Identity,* edited by David Morley and Kevin Robins, 235–48. Oxford: Oxford University Press.
Wyndham, Francis, and Diana Melly, eds. 1984. *The Letters of Jean Rhys.* New York: Viking.
Yates, Louisa. 2009/2010. "'But It's Only a Novel, Dorian': Neo-Victorian Fiction and the Process of Re-Vision." *Neo-Victorian Studies* 2.2: 186–211.
Yelin, Louise. 1992. "Cultural Cartography: A. S. Byatt's *Possession* and the Politics of Victorian Studies." *Victorian Newsletter* 81: 38–41.
Young, Robert. 1994. "Colonialism and the Desiring-Machine." In *Liminal Postmodernisms: The Postmodern, the(Post)Colonial and the (Post)Feminist,* edited by Theo D'haen and Hans Bertens, 11–34. Amsterdam: Rodopi.

Index

academic literary criticism 11, 49, 59–60, 69, 119, 120, 148, 157, 171, 188, 199*n*11, 200*n*6; *see also* literary journalism

Ackroyd, Peter 65, 171; *English Music* 171; *The Great Fire of London* 171; *Hawksmoor* 34; *The Last Testament of Oscar Wilde* 65; *London: The Biography* 201*n*1; *Thames: Sacred River* 201*n*1; *see also* Chatterton; Dickens

Adaptation (journal) 36, 37

adaptation studies 2, 11, 36–38, 46, 50, 72, 73, 78, 94, 104, 148, 150, 170–171, 196*n*25, 196*n*26

adaptive chain 2, 3, 10, 12, 13, 79, 107, 108, 148, 158, 161, 189; *see also* adaptive map; adaptive series; derivative; fluidity; literary continuum; prequel; sequel(ization); source text

adaptive map 2, 3, 10, 13, 14, 147, 148, 149, 161, 172, 190; *see also* adaptive chain; adaptive series; aftering; derivative; fluidity; literary continuum; midquel; parallelquel; paraquel; prequel; sequel(ization); source text

adaptive series 3, 10, 13, 73, 147, 148, 149, 161, 180, 181, 188, 190, 201*n*16; *see also* adaptive chain; adaptive map; aftering; derivative; fluidity; literary continuum; midquel; parallelquel; paraquel; prequel; sequel(ization); serial(ization); source text

Adèle: Jane Eyre's Hidden Story 56–57, 155–156, 163; *see also The French Dancer's Bastard: The Story of Adèle from 'Jane Eyre'*; Tennant, Emma; *Thornfield Hall: Jane Eyre's Hidden Story*

adventure fiction 5, 188

Africa(n) 81, 102, 103

aftering 13, 150; *see also* adaptive map; adaptive series

architecture 8, 55, 146, 197*n*9; monument 20, 88, 90, 184; *see also* Crystal Palace; cultural memento; cultural object; Millennium Dome

Arias, Rosario 9, 45, 195*n*16, 199*n*9

Armstrong, Gillian *see Oscar and Lucinda*

Armstrong, Isobel 19, 93

Armstrong, Nancy 80

Arnold, Gaynor *see Girl in a Blue Dress*

Arthur and George 64, 65, 73, 180–181; *see also* Barnes, Julian

artistic compromise 11, 69; *see also* authorial anxiety; authorial intention; author(ship); James, Henry

Ashcroft, Bill 59, 60–61

Australia 6, 57, 63, 83, 84, 87, 91, 172, 173–174, 175–176, 177, 182, 183–184; *see also Jack Maggs*; *Oscar and Lucinda* (book); *Oscar and Lucinda* (film)

authenticity 11, 12, 50, 64, 110–113, 120, 138, 150, 171, 180; *see also* authorial anxiety; author(ship); historical author; *Jane Eyre*; originality, plagiarism; *Poor Things*

Author, Author 11, 49, 67, 70, 71–72, 73, 75, 197*n*17, 197*n*19; *see also* authorial anxiety; James, Henry, adaptations of; Lodge, David

author-reader interaction 11, 48, 51–52, 148; *see also* author(ship); reader(ship)

authorial anxiety 13, 38, 48, 64, 68, 69, 72, 73, 108, 113–114, 118, 119, 197*n*20; *see also* artistic compromise; authenticity; *Author, Author*; authorial (narrative) authority; author(ship); *Felony*; historical author; *The Line of Beauty*; Lodge, David; *Wide Sargasso Sea*

authorial intention 50, 61, 120–122, 155, 164, 181, 199*n*6; *see also* artistic compromise; author(ship); *Charlotte*

authorial (narrative) authority 11, 50, 64, 67, 109–112, 113, 115, 127, 131, 135, 152, 174; *see also* authorial anxiety;

author(ship); *Charlotte*; *Jane Eyre*; *Poor Things*; *Wide Sargasso Sea*
author(ship) 2, 3, 6, 11, 12, 13, 14, 20–21, 38, 40, 48, 49–76, 79, 82, 100, 105, 116, 117–122, 135–138, 147–149, 154, 161, 163, 171–177, 187, 188, 189, 195n20, 196n1, 199n4, 201n10; as novelistic function 12, 108, 109–113, 114–115, 178, 181; the myth of 11, 50–51, 65, 75–76, 109, 175; *see also* artistic compromise; authenticity; author-reader interaction; authorial anxiety; authorial intention; authorial (narrative) authority; historical author; literary cult; literary market; reader(ship)
autobiography 20, 76, 109, 172, 176, 179, 182; *see also* biography; *Jane Eyre*; *Mister Pip*
autoethnography 110, 189–190, 199n3; *see also* cultural studies; space (concept of)

Bainbridge, Beryl *see Master Georgie*
Barndollar, David 180
Barnes, Julian 62, 65; *see also Arthur and George*; *England, England*; *Flaubert's Parrot*
Bassnett, Susan 95, 165
Baudrillard, Jean 41, 90, 98–99, 171
Beaumont, Matthew 30, 189
Bényei, Tamás 43, 58, 59, 60, 80, 96, 201n3
Berninger, Mark 163, 164, 166, 169, 170, 200n8
Bertens, Hans 32
The Best Exotic Marigold Hotel (film) 195n24; *see also* Madden, John
Bhabha, Homi K. 103, 129
bildungsroman 6, 108, 124, 131–135, 173, 176, 177, 200n2; *see also Charlotte*; *Jack Maggs*; *Jane Eyre*; *Mister Pip*; *Wide Sargasso Sea*
biofiction *see* biographical novel; biographilia; biography; fictional biography; literary biography
biographical novel 2, 48, 66, 73; *see also* biofiction; biographilia; fictional biography; literary biography
biographilia 49, 65, 72, 75; *see also* biofiction; biographical novel; fictional biography; literary biography
biography 20, 66, 70, 73, 75–76, 109, 114, 134, 171; *see also* autobiography; biofiction; James, Henry
biopics 75; *see also* biofiction
Bloom, Harold 68, 197n20
Böehnke, Dietmar 188
book: as an institution 167–168, 178–179; *see also* book cover; book travel; canon(ization); manuscript; *The Eyre Affair*; *Mister Pip*
book cover 11, 49, 55–59, 162; *see also* book as an institution; literary market; visual culture

book travel 56, 166, 190; *see also* book as an institution; *The Eyre Affair*; time travel; travel
Bormann, Daniel Candel 23, 24–25, 26–28, 197n1
Boylan, Clare 153–155, 193n4; *see also Emma Brown*; *Good Housekeeping*; "*Jane Eyre* Revisited: An Alternative Ending"
Boyle, Danny *see Slumdog Millionaire*
Brantlinger, Patrick 7, 59–60
Brazil, Rio de Janeiro, Partially Clothed Man and Woman on Beach (B&W) see Martinique, French West Indies 1999
Britain (British) 12, 27, 37, 42, 51, 57, 61, 62, 69, 77–81, 85, 88, 93, 95, 97–100, 105, 125, 145, 149, 165–166, 169, 172–173, 175, 176, 177, 182, 186, 188, 193n2, 194n6, 195n24, 198n3, 198n5; *see also* British Empire
British Empire 6, 42, 44, 60, 62, 77–82, 84–86, 88, 90, 94–95, 101, 115, 125, 126, 128, 142, 165–166, 175, 177, 184; legacies of 12, 14, 27, 63, 77–78, 82, 84, 90, 93, 105, 125, 138, 142, 145, 149, 172–173, 188, 189, 197n10; *see also* Britain (British); devolution; discovery narratives; isolation; national identity; postcolonialism; postimperialism; slavery; travel narratives
Brontë, Charlotte 75–76, 109, 113–114, 121–122, 124, 125, 134, 135, 144, 145, 152, 154–155, 190, 199n4, 199n6, 200n17; in D. M. Thomas's *Charlotte* 69, 119–122, 133–134, 136–139, 144–145, 164, 177; *Shirley* 199n4; *Villette* 199n4; *see also Jane Eyre*
Brontë, Emily 113, 134, 145, 157, 199n4; *see also Wuthering Heights*
Bryant, John 46, 57, 61, 78, 149, 163, 177
Budra, Paul 52, 147, 157
Bullen, J.B. 7, 19
Burke, Seán 50
Butler, Christopher 40
Buzard, James 92–93, 110, 126, 199n3
Byatt, A.S. 43, 63, 182, 197n1; *Angels and Insects* 198ch3n2; *see also Possession* (book)

Cambridge 12, 77–78, 93, 95, 100–105, 200n21; *see also* Caribbean; Phillips, Caryl; slavery; West Indies
Campbell, Eddie *see From Hell*
canon(ization) 5, 6, 8, 10, 15, 33, 37, 46, 53, 61, 76, 79, 107, 108, 109, 114, 115, 116, 122, 127, 132, 148, 154, 159, 161, 163, 164, 166, 168, 179, 182, 187, 188, 191; *see also* book as an institution; high culture; literary reception; refraction
Carey, Peter 63, 175; *see also Jack Maggs*; *Oscar and Lucinda*
Caribbean 63, 94, 100, 103, 115, 131, 139,

143, 146, 199*n*10; *see also* Cambridge; Charlotte; West Indies; *Wide Sargasso Sea*
Carroll, Samantha J. 7, 29, 33, 46
Cartmell, Deborah 36, 37
case study 10, 12, 79, 96, 107, 108, 147, 161, 189
celebrity culture 11, 12, 48, 50–51, 64–65, 67, 73, 108, 111, 119, 138, 149, 170, 175, 188, 196*n*3; *see also* literary cult; literary market; meet the author culture
Charlotte: The Final Journey of Jane Eyre (*Charlotte*) 12, 13, 37, 69, 89, 107–108, 116, 117, 119–124, 132–146, 148, 155, 156, 157, 159–161, 163, 177, 178, 179, 182, 189, 199*n*13, 200*n*17, 200*n*19, 201*n*10; *see also* authorial intention; authorial (narrative) authority; bildungsroman; Caribbean; Cornwall; Diamond Rock of Martinique; ghostwriting; *Jane Eyre*; manuscript; metropolis; originality; reading process; sexuality; slavery; Thomas, D.M.; West Indies; *Wide Sargasso Sea*; writing process
Chatterton 17, 22, 48, 65, 72, 77, 107, 147; *see also* Ackroyd, Peter
Chavanelle, Sylvie 104, 105
Childers, Joseph W. 78, 92–93
Ciolkowski, Laura E. 127–128, 141
Clayton, Jay 8, 38, 43, 60, 84, 87, 88, 89, 90, 91, 181
Coetzee, J.M. *Foe* 105
Cohen, Paula Marantz 69; *see also What Alice Knew: A Most Curious Tale of Henry James and Jack the Ripper*
comic fiction 105, 188, 190
commemoration 88, 142–143, 145–146; *see also* Crystal Palace; cultural memento; cultural object; memory object; memory text
commodity culture 13, 39, 42, 55, 58, 85, 88, 89, 103, 114, 142, 162, 167, 170, 199*n*4; *see also* consumption (consumerism); cultural production; material culture
consumption (consumerism) 39, 42, 46, 50, 62, 65, 142, 171, 180, 189, 190; *see also* commodity culture; literary market; literary production
Corner, John 84–85
Cornwall 143–145; *see also* Charlotte
crime fiction 2, 46, 54, 171, 187
criminal(ity) 9, 96, 128, 165, 167, 173–175; *see also* England, England; *English Passengers*; *The Eyre Affair*; *Jack Maggs*
Crimean War 6, 130, 165, 166, 198*n*3
The Crimson Petal and the White 52, 56, 58, 83, 123–124, 198*ch*2*n*2; *see also* Faber, Michel
Crystal Palace 2, 12, 83–86, 88–93, 146, 184; *see also* architecture; commemoration; cultural memento; cultural memory; cultural object; glass objects; Great Exhibition; memory object; Millennium Dome; *Oscar and Lucinda* (book); refraction; Scotland (Scottish), Kibble Palace; Wales (Welsh), Wales Millennium Centre
cultural criticism 12, 14, 24–25, 38, 94, 129, 186; *see also* cultural studies
cultural discourse 6, 15, 27, 64, 84, 127, 186; *see also* cultural policy; cultural practice; cultural studies
cultural identity 2, 3, 6, 12, 13, 14, 48, 60, 61–64, 66, 77, 78, 80, 84, 93, 94, 99, 100, 103–104, 105, 108, 124, 127–131, 138, 143, 146, 158, 167, 183–185, 186, 188, 189, 197*n*10, 199*n*4; *see also* dislocation; *England, England*; *English Passengers*; home; national identity; postcolonialism; postimperialism; self-identity
cultural memento 2, 146, 167, 177, 190; *see also* architecture; commemoration; Crystal Palace; cultural object; Diamond Rock of Martinique; memory object; memory text; Millennium Dome; painting; photograph
cultural memory 1, 2, 9, 11, 12, 14, 39, 40, 42–43, 50, 61, 90–92, 102, 104, 145–146, 170, 182–183, 186, 196*n*28; *see also* Crystal Palace; cultural studies; Diamond Rock of Martinique; memory studies; Millennium Dome; postcolonialism
cultural object 14, 55, 108, 129, 138, 197*n*9; *see also* architecture; commemoration; Crystal Palace; cultural memento; memory object; memory text; Millennium Dome; painting; photograph
cultural policy 77, 85, 87–90; *see also* cultural discourse; cultural practice; dominant culture; Millennium Dome; Thatcher(ite)
cultural practice 39, 84, 186; *see also* cultural discourse; cultural policy; Millennium Dome; Thatcher(ite)
cultural production 1, 6, 8, 180; *see also* commodity culture; cultural reproduction; literary market; literary production; literary reproduction; material culture
cultural reproduction 8, 24; *see also* cultural production; literary production; literary reproduction
cultural studies 2, 11, 14, 37, 43, 44, 46, 49, 52, 57, 59–61, 87, 93, 194*n*8; *see also* autoethnography; cultural criticism; cultural discourse; cultural memory; postcolonialism; postimperialism; remembering; trauma studies
Cunningham, Valentine 110–111, 125

Darwin(ism) 19, 41, 80, 197–198*ch*3*n*2; evolution 96, 179, 196*n*26
Deane, Bradley 50–51, 65, 117
De Chellis Hill, Carol *see Henry James's Midnight Song*

Defoe, Daniel *see Robinson Crusoe*
Deirdre, David 126
Dentith, Simon 90
derivative 7, 151, 171; *see also* adaptive chain; adaptive map; adaptive series
detective fiction 2, 46, 54, 74, 152, 161, 169, 180, 181, 187; *see also The Eyre Affair*
Detmers, Ines 152–153, 155, 200n2
devolution 78, 85, 88, 95, 99, 165, 166; British Empire; postimperialism
Diamond Rock of Martinique 145–146; *see also Charlotte*; cultural memento; cultural memory
Dickens 21, 65, 171–172; *see also* Ackroyd, Peter; Dickens, Charles; Dickensiana
Dickens, Charles 3, 21, 50, 69, 149, 170–178, 180–181, 190, 199n11, 201n2, 201n12, 201n13; *see also Dickens*; Dickens World; Dickensiana; *Great Expectations*; *Jack Maggs*; *Mister Pip*
Dickens World 3, 149, 170–171; *see also* Dickens, Charles; Dickensiana; *Great Expectations*; theme park
Dickensiana 3, 13, 64, 149, 171–172, 190; *see also Dickens*; Dickens, Charles; Dickens World; *Great Expectations*
Dictation: A Quartet 74–75, 197n14; *see also* Ozick, Cynthia
discovery narrative 12, 78, 94; *see also* British Empire; travel; travel narratives; trope of travel
dislocation 12, 78, 97–100, 104, 116, 129–130, 156, 189; *see also* cultural identity; home; self-identity; travel
dominant culture 62, 105, 142, 173; *see also* cultural policy

Earl, Ben 171
Easthope, Antony 59–60, 62
Eliot, George 174, 176
Emma Brown 85–86, 111, 131–132, 146, 155, 184; *see also* Boylan, Clare
"Enduring Love" 157
England (English) 6, 13, 43, 62–63, 74, 80, 81, 82, 83, 89, 93–103, 105, 115, 117, 125–132, 137, 139, 142–145, 156, 158, 160, 161, 165, 166–167, 172, 173, 174, 178, 182, 183–184, 186, 195n24, 196n25, 198n3, 198n7, 199n10, 200n20
England, England 89, 95–96, 98–99, 165; *see also* Barnes, Julian; criminal(ity); cultural identity; heritage; national identity; theme park
English, James F. 50–52, 60, 64–65
English Passengers 12, 63–64, 77–78, 93–100, 101, 104, 105, 197–198ch3n2; *see also* criminal(ity); cultural identity; Kneale, Matthew; national identity; Tasmania
enterprise 77, 84, 88, 90, 96, 98–99, 164, 187; *see also* heritage; theme park

escapism 28, 80, 125, 128, 129, 136, 137, 158, 165, 175, 178
ethics 11, 40, 43–45, 61, 64, 68, 118, 128, 174, 189, 194–195n15; *see also* morals; trauma studies
Ever After 36, 135, 198ch3n2; *see also* Swift, Graham
The Eyre Affair 3, 13, 56, 95, 120, 149, 150, 157–158, 160, 161–170, 171, 178, 179, 182, 190, 200n5, 200n6; *see also* book as an institution; book travel; criminal(ity); detective fiction; Fforde, Jasper; manuscript; originality; science fiction; time travel; Wales (Welsh); war(fare)

Faber, Michel 63; *see also The Crimson Petal and the White*
fairy tale 169, 200n5
Far Above Rubies 172, 177, 201n12; *see also* Vukelic, Anne-Marie
Felony: The Private History of the Aspern Papers (Felony) 11, 49, 67–68, 71, 75, 197n 19; *see also* authorial anxiety; James, Henry, adaptations of; Tennant, Emma
feminism 13, 18, 21, 39, 40, 61, 68, 79, 105, 107–108, 114, 117, 124, 126, 127, 152, 161, 168–169, 171–172, 177, 189, 194n4, 198n5, 199n7, 201n10; *see also* narrative of empowerment; postcolonialism; postimperialism; sexuality
Fforde, Jasper 63, 109, 162, 164, 166, 200n7; *see also The Eyre Affair*
fiction in English 5, 14, 40, 41, 44, 60, 62, 78, 105, 186, 191
fictional biography 74, 180; *see also* biofiction; biographical novel; biographilia; literary biography
fictional figure 6, 46, 68, 73, 75, 120, 171, 172, 173–174, 182; *see also Jack Maggs*; *Mister Pip*
film adaptation 2, 3, 7, 8, 13, 24, 28, 36–38, 50, 55–56, 57, 62, 69, 87, 92, 107, 150, 151, 162, 169, 170, 190, 195n17, 195n23, 196n7, 196n2, 197n8, 198n5, 200n2, 201n2; *see also* film studies; heritage film; Hollywood; *The Iron Lady* (film); *Oscar and Lucinda* (film); *Possession* (film); *The Queen* (film); television adaptation
film studies 7, 11, 36–38, 46, 59, 75, 164; *see also* film adaptation; media studies
Flaubert's Parrot 65, 199–200n15; *see also* Barnes, Julian
Flint, Kate 46, 195n21
fluidity 13, 66–67, 103–104, 129, 149, 177; *see also* adaptive chain; adaptive map; adaptive series; identity; transgressiveness
Fowles, John *see The French Lieutenant's Woman*
Frears, Stephen *see The Queen* (film)

The French Dancer's Bastard: The Story of Adèle from 'Jane Eyre' 56–57, 163; *see also Adèle: Jane Eyre's Hidden Story*; Tennant, Emma; *Thornfield Hall: Jane Eyre's Hidden Story*
The French Lieutenant's Woman 5, 26, 52–53, 79, 193*i.n*2; *see also* Fowles, John
Friedman, Paula 97, 100
From Hell 188; *see also* Campbell Eddie; Moore, Alan
Frow, John 50–52, 64–65

Garrett, Stewart 111
Gasiorek, Andrzej 41
Gay, Penny 7, 60
ghostwriting 11, 45, 69, 72, 119, 133–136, 141; *see also* Charlotte; James, Henry, adaptations of; literary ventriloquism
Gibson, Andrew 43
Gikandi, Simon 12, 78, 94–95, 166–167
Gilbert, Sandra M., and Susan Gubar 68, 125, 155–156, 197*n*15
Gillies, Mary Ann 54
Gillooly, Eileen 92–93
Girl in a Blue Dress 5, 56, 64, 170, 172; *see also* Arnold, Gaynor
glass objects 82, 83–87, 91–93, 146, 173, 184; *see also* Crystal Palace; *Oscar and Lucinda* (book); refraction; religion
Good Housekeeping 153, 154; *see also* Clare Boylan; *Jane Eyre*; novel endings
Gould, Marty, and Rebecca N. Mitchell 170–171
Gothic fiction 2, 9, 27, 46, 54, 131, 132, 135, 152, 169, 187, 195*n*16, 197*n*18, 200*n*2; *see also Jane Eyre*; *Possession* (book); *Wide Sargasso Sea*
graphic fiction 54, 188, 201*n*2
Gray, Alasdair 63; *see also Poor Things*
Great Exhibition 83, 86, 88, 90, 92, 184; *see also* Crystal Palace; Millennium Celebrations; Millennium Dome
Great Expectations 14, 69, 147, 149, 170–179, 181–183, 201*n*14; *see also* Dickens, Charles; Dickens World; Dickensiana; novel ending(s); *Sixty Lights*
Green-Lewis, Jennifer 19
Gribble, Jennifer 175, 177, 178, 181
Gubar, Susan 68, 125, 155–156, 197*n*15
Guerrillas 130–131, 199*n*10; *see also* Naipaul, V. S.
Gutleben, Christian 8–9, 23, 26, 35, 36, 40, 42, 44–45, 117, 122, 133, 135, 137, 138, 139–140, 142, 143, 159–160, 179, 187–188, 193*n*5, 194*n*11, 195*n*16, 197–198*ch*3*n*2

Hadley, Louisa 8, 26, 28, 31, 35, 75, 173, 174, 175, 187, 194*n*3, 194*n*10, 195*n*18, 196*n*6
Hall, Catherine, and Sonya Rose 85, 95, 175,

Haralson, Eric 66
Harris, Jane 56, 58
Harrison, Sophie 70
Harvey, Sylvia 84–85
haunting 1, 45, 66, 84, 92, 172; *see also* spectrality
Heilmann, Ann 66
Heilmann, Ann, and Mark Llewellyn 8, 26, 28–33, 36, 58, 171, 180, 187, 189
Henry James's Midnight Song 74, 197*n*14; *see also* De Chellis Hill, Carol
heritage 2, 12, 77, 80, 84, 89–90, 96, 98, 102, 144–145, 167, 171, 176, 187; *see also England, England*; enterprise; heritage film; theme park
heritage film 8, 36, 164, 194*n*3; 195*n*17; 196*n*25; *see also* film adaptation; heritage
Hewison, Robert 85, 99
Heyns, Michiel 66–67, 71–72, 197*n*18; *see also The Typewriter's Tale*
high culture 61, 68, 91, 152, 171, 182; *see also* canon(ization); popular culture
historical author 11, 36, 46, 49, 50–51, 54, 64–66, 67, 69, 70–75, 76, 79, 113–115, 118–121, 122, 133, 134, 141, 144, 149–150, 155, 160, 164, 171, 176, 177, 189, 190, 197*n*11, 197*n*14; *see also* authenticity; authorial anxiety; author(ship)
historical data 19, 70, 75; *see also* historical material
historical era 19, 34, 55, 195*n*20
historical event 81, 118, 143, 146, 165; *see also* Thomas, D.M.
historical experience 189, 190, 201*n*1; *see also* history; historical knowledge; space (concept of)
historical fiction 6, 10, 15, 18, 22–30, 33, 34, 43, 46, 48, 53, 92, 138, 157, 167, 186, 189, 191, 194*n*9, 194*n*14, 195*n*18, 196*n*28, 201*n*3
historical knowledge 11, 41, 46, 189; *see also* history; historical experience
historical material 51, 90, 122, 190; *see also* historical data
historiographic metafiction 22–29, 34, 41, 194*n*7, 194*n*9, 194*n*14
history 11, 12, 14, 15, 23–27, 40, 41–43, 46, 53, 67, 77, 78, 88, 89, 92, 95, 99, 104, 166, 177, 186, 188, 194*n*8, 196*n*27; *see also* historical experience; historical knowledge
Hochschild, Adam 100
Hollinghurst, Alan *see The Line of Beauty*
Hollywood 37, 87, 195*n*24; *see also* film adaptation
home 12, 13, 78, 81, 83, 85, 95–106, 108, 124–131, 138, 142, 144, 156, 176, 189, 195*n*24; *see also* cultural identity; dislocation; island fiction; national identity; self-identity; space (concept of); travel
Hoving, Isabel 94, 100, 106
Hughes, Linda K., and Michael Lund 179

Humpherys, Anne 36, 52, 173, 195*n*21
Hutcheon, Linda 23, 37, 40, 41, 50, 57, 61, 72, 104, 108, 148, 150, 181, 191, 194*n*9, 196*n*26

identity quest 13, 55, 125–127, 135
India 98, 153, 157, 161, 168, 183, 184, 195*n*24, 196*n*2, 198*n*8; *see also* Jane Eyre; Sixty Lights
industrial fiction 6, 187
installment 52, 149, 150, 180–182; *see also* Mister Pip; sequel(ization); serial(ization)
insularity 12, 78, 95, 198*n*7; *see also* isolation; island fiction
interculturation 13, 128, 129; *see also* Wide Sargasso Sea
interdisciplinarity 2, 11, 14, 17, 35, 37, 40, 43, 47, 59, 61, 182, 190
intertextuality 2, 6, 43, 118, 149
Ireland (Irish) 86, 99, 166, 199*n*4, 200*n*17
The Iron Lady (film) 198*n*5; *see also* film adaptation; Lloyd, Phyllida; Thatcher(ite)
island fiction 2, 12, 48, 77, 93–107, 188; *see also* home; insularity; isolation; travel
isolation 12, 59, 80, 94–95, 99, 166; *see also* British Empire; insularity; island fiction

Jack Maggs 14, 75, 149, 172–175, 176, 177; *see also* Australia; bildungsroman; Carey, Peter; criminal(ity); Dickens, Charles; fictional figure; metropolis
Jacobson, Howard: *Peeping Tom* 65
Jaffe, Audrey 54, 60
James, Henry 65–68, 70, 71, 74, 197*n*19; adaptations of 2, 11, 21, 49, 64–77, 175, 177, 197*n*14; *see also* artistic compromise; biofiction; biography; ghostwriting; "The Lesson of the Master"; transgressiveness; writing process
Jameson, Fredric 25, 32, 41, 46
Jane Eyre 2, 12, 13, 20, 21, 37, 56, 57, 79, 107–183, 189, 199*n*4, 199*n*6, 199*n*7, 199*n*14, 200*n*2, 200*n*17; *see also* authenticity; authorial (narrative) authority; autobiography; bildungsroman; Brontë, Charlotte; *Charlotte*; *Good Housekeeping*; Gothic fiction; India; narrative of empowerment; novel ending(s); reading process; Sixty Lights; slavery; Wide Sargasso Sea; writing process
"*Jane Eyre* Revisited: An Alternative Ending" 153–155, 160–161, 200*n*3; *see also* Boylan, Clare
Jenkins, Alice 7, 18
John, Juliet 7, 18
Johnston, Judith 7, 27, 60
Jones, Gail 63; *see also* Sixty Lights
Jones, Lloyd 63; *see also* Mister Pip
Jones, Sally Mair 137

The Journal of Dora Damage 56, 58; *see also* Starling, Belinda
Joyce, Simon 8, 18, 19–21, 29, 38–39, 92, 173, 174, 189, 194*n*13, 201*n*13

Kaplan, Cora 8, 19–20, 24, 36, 42, 64, 65, 66, 69, 73, 75, 100, 125, 166, 187, 195*n*22, 199*n*7
Kehlmann, Daniel 73–74, 201*n*3
Kermode, Frank 45
Kirchknopf, Andrea 31–32, 195*n*18
Kleinecke, Iris 180
Kneale, Matthew 63; *see also* English Passengers
Knight, Charmian 149–150
Kohlke, Marie-Luise 7–9, 19, 27–28, 42, 44–45, 58–59, 187–188, 193*n*5, 195*n*16, 195*n*19, 196*n*30
Kontou, Tatiana 45–46
Kramer, Kathryn 66, 71; *Sweet Water* 197*n*14
Krueger, Christine L. 8, 39, 55, 58–59, 60, 194*n*13
Kucich, John, and Dianne F. Sadoff 8, 24, 31, 39, 45, 46, 59, 60, 148, 187, 194–195*n*15
Kurnick, David S. 103, 104, 105
Kuurola, Mirja 104, 105

LaBute, Neil *see* Possession (film)
Langland, Elisabeth 109
Lefevere, André 46, 53, 59, 149, 179, 201*n*15
"The Lesson of the Master" 68, 74; *see also* James, Henry; Ozick, Cynthia
Letissier, Georges 23, 31, 42, 96, 100, 173
Levine, George 152
Lindner, Christoph 39
The Line of Beauty 11, 49, 64, 67, 69–70, 73, 177, 197*n*11; *see also* authorial anxiety; Hollinghurst, Alan; James, Henry, adaptations of
literary adaptation 1, 2, 3, 11, 13, 18, 24, 28, 30, 34, 36, 37, 40, 72, 83, 108, 107, 157, 159, 170, 179, 189, 190, 198*ch*4*n*2; *see also* literary production; literary reproduction; literary studies
literary award 5, 42, 49, 50, 61–63, 196*n*2, 201*n*3; *see also* literary market; Man Booker Prize
literary biography 5, 11, 21, 49, 64, 65, 69, 75, 177; *see also* biofiction; biographical novel; biographilia; fictional biography
literary continuum 13, 150; *see also* adaptive chain; adaptive map; adaptive series; fluidity
literary cult 11, 12, 13, 50, 64–65, 107, 109, 111, 114, 119, 123, 167, 175, 190; *see also* authorship; celebrity culture; literary market; literary production
literary historical era 59, 66, 116–117; *see also* modernism; Wide Sargasso Sea

literary journalism 11, 49, 59, 119; see also academic literary criticism
literary market 9, 11, 13, 48, 49–51, 52, 55, 59–62, 64–65, 108, 109–111, 122, 162, 181, 188, 190; marketing strategies 1, 42, 51, 55–59, 62, 89, 103, 148; see also author(ship); book cover; celebrity culture; consumption (consumerism); cultural production; literary award; literary cult; literary production; Man Booker Prize; reader(ship)
literary production 2, 5, 15, 39, 46, 49, 50, 62, 67, 69–70, 74, 95, 107, 111, 149, 162, 178, 179, 180, 187, 196n27; see also consumption (consumerism); cultural production; cultural reproduction; literary adaptation; literary cult; literary market; literary reception; literary reproduction
literary reception 2, 12, 13, 15, 36, 39, 49, 52, 60, 61, 71, 73, 74, 107, 108, 111, 114, 149, 151, 162, 178, 180, 187, 196n1; see also canon(ization); literary production; post-Victorian fiction as literary criticism
literary reproduction 39, 150, 151; see also cultural production; cultural reproduction; literary adaptation; literary production; post-Victorian responses to Victorian texts
literary scene 2, 10, 11, 12, 48–76, 108, 109, 148, 188
literary studies 2, 8, 11, 14, 18, 36, 38, 46, 59–60, 186; see also literary adaptation
literary ventriloquism 13, 69, 118, 119, 122, 161, 194n10; see also ghostwriting; manuscript; originality; plagiarism
Literature Interpretation Theory (journal) 9
Llewellyn, Mark 7, 28, 92, 193ch1n2, 195n19
Lloyd, Phyllida see *The Iron Lady* (film)
Lodge, David 49–51, 63, 71–73, 196n1, 196n27, 197n18, 197n20; see also *Author, Author*; authorial anxiety
London 6, 62, 63, 83, 85–86, 88, 91, 102, 129, 155, 165, 168, 169, 171, 172, 176, 201n1
"Looking for Eden" 97
Lundén, Bo 54

Macfarlane, Robert 38, 114
Madden, John see *The Best Exotic Marigold Hotel* (film)
Malone, Michael 172
Man Booker Prize 5, 49, 61–64, 67, 70, 82–83, 118, 172, 182, 193n3, 197n10, 198n7; see also literary award; literary market
manuscript 54, 120, 137–138, 163, 174, 179, 182, 199n11; see also book as an institution; *Charlotte*; *The Eyre Affair*; literary ventriloquism; originality; plagiarism; *Possession* (book)
Mardorossian, Carine M. 103–104, 115, 116, 127, 128, 132, 158

Marguerite, Alexander 40
Marsh, Kelly 152, 194–195n15
Martinique 119, 133, 136, 138–139, 144, 145, 160
Martinique, French West Indies 1847 (map extract) 138
Martinique, French West Indies 1999 (photograph) 138–140
Marxism 110, 124, 194n8; see also psychoanalysis
The Master 11, 21, 49, 64, 67, 68–69, 70, 73; see also James, Henry, adaptations of; Tóibín, Colm
Master Georgie 26, 130, 198ch3n2, 198n3; see also Bainbridge, Beryl
material culture 39, 42, 55, 84, 187, 193n5, 197n9; see also commodity culture; cultural production
McDonald, Rónán 59
McGowan, John 46, 60
McHale, Brian 32, 33, 40, 117, 194n9
media studies 14, 36–38, 51, 180; see also film studies; visual culture
meet the author culture 11, 51, 119; see also celebrity culture
Melly, Diana 113–114, 158, 159
memory object 42, 62, 179, 182, 184, 196n29; see also commemoration; Crystal Palace; cultural memento; cultural object; memory text; painting; photograph; *Possession* (book); *Sixty Lights*
memory studies 41–44, 55, 90, 91, 92, 96, 179, 183–184, 196n30; see also cultural memory; memory object; memory text; remembering; self-identity; trauma studies
memory text 42, 196n28; see also commemoration; cultural memento; cultural object; memory object
metafictional writing techniques 29, 33, 34, 40, 41, 53, 79, 161, 164, 194n9; see also reading process; reading techniques
metropolis 95, 125, 140, 142, 175, 178, 182; see also *Charlotte*; *Jack Maggs*; *Mister Pip*
Mettinger-Schartmann, Elke 150–151, 164, 170
midquel 13, 163–164; see also adaptive map; adaptive series
Millennium Celebrations 77, 88–90; see also Crystal Palace; Great Exhibition; Millennium Dome
Millennium Dome 12, 84, 88–90, 99, 146; see also architecture; Crystal palace; cultural memento; cultural memory; cultural object; cultural policy; cultural practice; Great Exhibition; Millennium Celebrations; Scotland (Scottish), Kibble Palace; Wales (Welsh), Wales Millennium Centre
Miller, Lucasta 75–76, 109, 110

Miller, Miranda *see Nina in Utopia*
The Miller's Daughter (painting) 129, 173
Mills, Stephen F. 194*n*6, 195*n*19
Mister Pip 5, 14, 64, 69, 149, 172, 175–179, 181, 182, 184, 185; *see also* autobiography; bildungsroman; book as an institution; Dickens, Charles; fictional figure; installment; Jones, Lloyd; metropolis; narrative of empowerment; New Zealand; teaching; war(fare)
Mitchell, Kate 9, 32–33, 42, 91, 183, 195*n*16, 196*n*28, 199*n*9
modernism 18, 19, 20, 21, 23, 29–33, 35, 40, 66–67, 70, 107, 109, 115, 116–117, 187, 189–190, 195*n*17, 195*n*19; *see also* literary historical era; *Wide Sargasso Sea*
Moore, Alan *see From Hell*
morals 6, 43, 46, 67, 69–70, 75, 90, 96, 109, 113, 119, 194–195*n*15; *see also* ethics

Naipaul, V.S. *see Guerrillas*
narrative of empowerment 14, 15, 110, 178; *see also* feminism; *Jane Eyre*; *Mister Pip*; postcolonialism
national identity 2, 3, 6, 12, 13, 48, 60, 61–64, 66, 77–89, 90, 91, 93, 94–96, 99, 100, 103–104, 105, 108, 124, 126–131, 138, 142, 143, 144, 145, 146, 158, 165, 167, 173, 183–185, 186, 188, 189, 197*n*10, 198*n*3, 200*n*17; *see also* British Empire; cultural identity; *England, England*; *English Passengers*; home; nationalism studies; postcolonialism; postimperialism; self-identity
nationalism studies 28, 31, 37, 39, 90, 127; *see also* national identity
natural history 25, 77, 80, 81; *see also* natural history novel
natural history novel 80, 83, 190; *see also* natural history; *Waterland*
neo–Victorian fiction 6, 7, 8, 9, 10, 22, 24–34, 35, 36, 40, 44, 45, 117, 187, 193*n*1, 193*n*5, 194*n*10, 194–195*n*15, 195*n*16, 195*n*19, 197*n*1; versus post–Victorian fiction 31–35; *see also* retro–Victorian fiction
Neo-Victorian Studies (*NVS*, journal) 7–8, 9, 27–28, 36, 39, 44, 193*i*.*n*1, 193*ch*1*n*1, 193*n*5
neo–Victorian studies 2, 9, 31, 193*n*5, 197*n*2; *see also* post–Victorian studies; Victorian studies
New Zealand 63, 175–176, 177; *see also Mister Pip*
Nicol, Bran 118–119, 134, 143
Nina in Utopia 168; *see also* Miller, Miranda
nostalgia 25–26, 31, 45, 80, 84, 128–129, 132, 137, 158, 170, 179, 187, 194*n*13, 194–195*n*15, 199*n*9, 199–200*n*15
"Novel Approach to the Roots of Racism" 96, 97

novel ending(s) 3, 13, 20, 105, 110, 112, 120, 121, 123, 126, 137, 141, 147, 148, 151–164, 168, 173, 177, 201*n*14; *see also Good Housekeeping*; *Great Expectations*; *Jane Eyre*; sequel(ization); source text; *Wide Sargasso Sea*
Nünning, Ansgar 24–26, 194*n*14

Oates, Joyce Carol 109, 110–111, 115, 158
Onega, Susana 8, 42, 44, 159–160, 194*n*11
original 13, 14, 37–38, 57, 71, 92, 98, 107, 108, 113, 114, 119, 120, 122, 123, 139, 148, 149, 151, 155, 157, 161, 163–164, 168, 172, 173, 177, 182, 194*n*10, 201*n*14, 201*n*16; *see also* source text
originality 12, 38, 90, 98, 99, 112, 118, 119, 120, 137, 138, 148–149, 161, 163–164, 168, 199*n*11; *see also* authenticity; *Charlotte*; *The Eyre Affair*; literary ventriloquism; manuscript; plagiarism; Rhys, Jean; source text
Oscar and Lucinda (book) 2, 5, 12, 57, 62–63, 77, 82–84, 86–87, 90–91, 104, 127, 146, 173, 184–185; *see also* Australia; Carey, Peter; Crystal Palace; glass objects; *Oscar and Lucinda* (film); war(fare)
Oscar and Lucinda (film) 57, 87; *see also* Armstrong, Gillian; Carey, Peter; film adaptation; *Oscar and Lucinda* (book)
Oxford World's Classics Complete List 137
Ozick, Cynthia 74; *Foreign Bodies* 197*n*14; *see also Dictation: A Quartet*; "The Lesson of the Master"

painting 37, 57, 58, 59, 67, 129, 150, 178, 200*n*17; *see also* cultural memento; cultural object; memory object
Palliser, Charles: *The Quincunx* 172
parallelquel 13, 163–164; *see also* adaptive map; adaptive series
paraquel 163; *see also* adaptive map; adaptive series
Parrinder, Patrick 78, 89, 125–126
Perosa, Sergio 66
Phillips, Caryl *see Cambridge*
photograph 42, 138–139, 182–185, 197*n*9, 198*n*3; *see also* cultural memento; cultural object; memory object
plagiarism 12, 13, 38, 67, 72, 114, 117–118, 119, 120, 137, 139; *see also* authenticity; literary ventriloquism; manuscript; originality; Thomas, D.M.
Poor Things 20–21, 85, 112–113, 197–198*ch*3*n*2; *see also* authenticity; authorial (narrative) authority; Gray, Alasdair; sexuality; Victorian, connotative meaning of
popular culture 8, 36, 119, 138, 152, 157, 170–171, 188, 201*n*10; *see also* high culture
Possession (book) 5, 36, 53–55, 57, 62–63,

182–183, 196n5, 197n1, 198ch3n2; *see also* Byatt, A.S.; Gothic fiction; manuscript; memory object; *Possession* (film)
Possession (film) 57; *see also* Byatt, A.S.; film adaptation; LaBute, Neil; *Possession* (book)
postcolonialism 2, 12, 13, 18, 35, 39, 42, 44, 60, 61, 62–63, 64, 69, 77–79, 82, 85, 87, 93–95, 100, 107–108, 114, 117, 119, 124–125, 127–128, 130–132, 140, 142–145, 146, 148, 152, 161, 165, 166, 171–173, 175, 178, 179, 186, 189, 197n10, 198n8, 199n4; *see also* British Empire; cultural identity; cultural memory; cultural studies; feminism; narrative of empowerment; national identity; postimperialism; self-identity; sexuality; slavery; trauma studies
postimperialism 2, 12, 13, 35, 42, 61, 62–64, 77–78, 93–95, 105–106, 108, 124, 127–128, 146, 161, 165, 166, 171, 178, 179, 186, 189, 197n10, 199n4; *see also* British Empire; cultural identity; cultural studies; devolution; feminism; national identity; postcolonialism; self-identity
post–Victorian fiction as literary criticism 47, 60, 108, 120, 154, 175, 191, 193n4, 201n15; *see also* literary reception; post–Victorian responses to Victorian texts
post–Victorian responses to Victorian texts 1, 8, 9, 10, 13, 28, 30, 35, 39, 79, 92, 112, 116, 150, 171, 172, 189, 190; *see also* literary reproduction; post–Victorian fiction as literary criticism
post–Victorian studies 2, 9, 11, 35, 92, 93, 197n2; *see also* neo–Victorian studies; Victorian studies
prequel 13, 22, 107, 150, 151, 155, 163; *see also* adaptive chain; adaptive map; adaptive series
pseudo-historical fiction 6, 22–23
pseudo–Victorian fiction 22–23, 31, 194n10
psychoanalysis 44, 110, 124; *see also* Marxism; trauma studies
Pulham, Patricia 9, 45, 195n16, 199n9

The Queen (film) 196n3; *see also* film adaptation; Frears, Stephen
Queen Victoria 18, 19, 21, 27, 30, 33, 59, 89, 189, 193–194ch1n2, 194n4

reader(ship) 6, 7, 10, 11, 20, 37, 48, 49–64, 71, 75, 76, 104, 105, 118, 122, 132, 136–138, 154, 157, 161–164, 171, 173, 178, 179–182, 188, 196n4, 196n6, 198n3; as novelistic function 12, 108, 110–113, 116, 122–124; *see also* author-reader interaction; author(ship); literary market
reading process 53, 58, 73, 104, 111, 123, 136, 137, 150, 163; *see also Charlotte*; *Jane Eyre*; metafictional writing technique; reading techniques
reading techniques 48, 52–55, 149–150, 158, 159, 163, 171, 179–182; *see also* metafictional writing techniques; reading process
realist fiction 13, 31, 33, 41, 49, 75, 121, 123, 124, 162, 169, 196n27; *see also* romance fiction
refraction 8, 36, 92–93, 124, 132, 146, 159, 173, 184, 195n23; *see also* canon(ization); Crystal Palace; glass objects; remembering; self-identity
religion 6, 80, 83, 91, 146, 196n4; *see also* glass objects; science
remembering 14, 42, 43, 77, 182, 183, 185, 201n1; *see also* cultural memory; memory studies; refraction; *Sixty Lights*; space (concept of); trauma studies
Renk, Kathleen J. 94, 100
retro-Victorian fiction 6, 10, 22, 25–26, 31, 34–35, 36, 80, 117, 187; *see also* neo–Victorian fiction
Rhys, Jean 13, 38, 63, 113–115, 117, 118, 119, 158, 159, 189; in D.M. Thomas's *Charlotte* 134, 136, 143, 145, 199n14; *see also* originality; *Wide Sargasso Sea*
Robinson Crusoe 93, 200n5; *see also* Defoe, Daniel
Rollyson, Carl 66, 68
romance fiction 5, 13, 33, 34, 54, 105, 121–122, 123–124, 126, 152, 154, 157, 162, 167, 169, 188, 195n20; *see also* realist fiction
Rubik, Margarete 150–151, 164, 170

Sadoff, Dianne F. 36–37, 173, 175, 178, 195n17, 196n25, 201n13
Said, Edward W. 93, 199n8
Samuel, Raphael 84–85, 145, 165–166, 198n5
Sanders, Julie 37–38, 41, 78, 94, 114, 115, 148, 159, 165, 180
Saunders, Max 66, 69, 73, 76, 197n16
Schaff, Barbara 156, 200n2
Schellenberg, Betty 52, 147, 157
Scherzinger, Karen 71, 73
Schorer, Mark 65
Schorn, Susan 180
Schwarz, Daniel R. 60
science 6, 8, 24, 38–39, 73, 80, 193n5, 196n4, 197n1; *see also* religion; technology
science fiction 54, 161, 169; *see also The Eyre Affair*
Scotland (Scottish) 6, 63; Glasgow 20, 86, 90; Kibble Palace 86, 90; *see also* Crystal Palace; Millennium Dome
self-identity 2, 3, 6, 12, 13, 42–43, 44, 48, 53–55, 61–64, 66, 69, 74, 77, 78, 80, 90, 93, 94, 100, 101–104, 105, 106, 108, 110–113, 115, 116, 121, 123, 124–131, 132–135, 138, 141, 143, 155–156, 158, 159, 167, 173,

176, 178, 183–185, 186, 188, 189, 197*n*10, 199*n*4, 199*n*13; *see also* cultural identity; dislocation; home; memory studies; national identity; postcolonialism; postimperialism; refraction
Séllei, Nóra 121, 126–127
sensation fiction 6, 46, 54, 152, 180, 194–195*n*15
sequel(ization) 3, 13, 22, 52, 54, 122, 147–150, 151, 153, 160–163, 175–176, 181, 190, 200*n*7; *see also* adaptive chain; adaptive map; adaptive series; installment; novel ending(s); serial(ization)
serial(ization) 13, 52, 71, 73, 149, 161, 162, 174, 179–182, 200*n*7, 201*n*16; *see also* adaptive series; installment; sequel(ization)
sexuality 19–21, 39, 54, 56, 58, 65–66, 69, 79, 108, 109, 112–113, 118–119, 127, 130, 134–135, 138–145, 155, 160–161, 183, 188, 193*n*; *see also* Charlotte; feminism; *Poor Things*; postcolonialism; slavery; trauma studies; *Wide Sargasso Sea*
Shaffer, Brian W. 23, 62, 78, 114–115, 116–117, 158
Shiller, Dana 25, 27, 194–195*n*15
Shuttleworth, Sally 25, 26, 80, 197*n*1
Sinha, Sanskrity 99
Sixty Lights 123–124, 183–185, 196*n*28, 198ch4*n*2; *see also Great Expectations*; India; *Jane Eyre*; Jones, Gail; memory object; remembering
slavery 96, 100–105, 108, 124–125, 127–128, 141–142, 168, 178, 200*n*20, 200*n*21; *see also* British Empire; *Cambridge*; *Charlotte*; *Jane Eyre*; postcolonialism; sexuality; trauma studies; *Wide Sargasso Sea*
Slumdog Millionaire (film) 196*n*2; *see also* Boyle, Danny
source text 5, 7, 10, 13, 23, 37–38, 55, 76, 108, 118, 138, 148, 154, 155, 158, 172, 190, 195*n*17; *see also* adaptive chain; adaptive map; adaptive series; novel ending(s); original; originality
space (concept of) 13, 43, 64, 80, 81, 85, 90, 91, 94, 100–101, 104, 115, 121, 130, 138, 143–144, 146, 166–167, 189, 190, 199*n*3, 201*n*1; *see also* autoethnography; historical experience; home; remembering; time (concept of)
spectrality 1, 9, 40, 45, 188; *see also* haunting
Spencer, Richard 99
stage adaptation 24, 36, 150, 151, 170, 195*n*23; *see also* theatre studies
Starling, Belinda *see The Journal of Dora Damage*
steampunk 2, 54, 193*n*5
Stoneman, Patsy 115, 127, 137, 149–151, 159
Strongman, Luke 62, 82, 198*n*7
Studio Foglio LLC: *Girl Genius* 188

Su, John 100, 128–129, 132, 158, 159
Sutherland, John 51, 52, 55, 154, 156
Sweet, Matthew 21–22, 55, 169
Swift, Graham 197*n*1; *see also Ever After*; *Waterland*

Tasmania 64, 92, 96–100; *see also English Passengers*
teaching 8, 37, 61, 176, 181, 182; *see also Mister Pip*
technology 8, 38–39, 148, 181, 193*n*5; *see also* science
television adaptation 7, 36, 180, 201*n*2; *see also* film adaptation
Tennant, Emma 157; *see also Adèle: Jane Eyre's Hidden Story*; *Felony: The Private History of the Aspern Papers*; *The French Dancer's Bastard: The Story of Adèle from 'Jane Eyre'*; *Tess*; *Thornfield Hall: Jane Eyre's Hidden Story*
Tess 65; *see also* Tennant, Emma
Thatcher(ite) 20–21, 29, 39, 80, 84–85, 89, 198*n*5; *see also* cultural policy; cultural practice; *The Iron Lady* (film)
theatre studies 36; *see also* stage adaptation
theme park 2, 3, 13, 36, 84, 88, 90, 98, 149, 170–171, 190; *see also* Dickens World; *England, England*; enterprise; heritage
Thesing, William B. 7, 59–60
Thomas, D.M. 117–120; *see also Charlotte*; historical event; plagiarism; *White Hotel*
Thomas, Katrin 163, 164, 166, 169, 170, 200*n*8
Thomas, Ronald R. 88, 90, 110, 198*n*6
Thomas, Sue 121, 123, 134, 138, 139, 142, 145, 199*n*12
Thornfield Hall: Jane Eyre's Hidden Story 56–57, 163; *see also Adèle: Jane Eyre's Hidden Story*; *The French Dancer's Bastard: The Story of Adèle from 'Jane Eyre'*; Tennant, Emma
time (concept of) 43, 88, 97, 104, 132, 138, 166–167, 189, 198*n*6; *see also* space (concept of); time travel
time travel 56, 157, 166, 167, 169, 190; *see also* book travel; *The Eyre Affair*; time (concept of); travel
Todd, Richard 51, 62, 81
Tóibín, Colm 197*n*18; *see also The Master*
tombeau des caraibes 146
transgressiveness 66; *see also* fluidity; James, Henry
trauma studies 1, 9, 11, 14, 40, 42, 43–45, 90–91, 100, 108, 131–133, 137, 145, 173, 175, 183, 186; *see also* cultural studies; ethics; memory studies; postcolonialism; psychoanalysis; remembering; sexuality; slavery
travel 12, 13, 37, 63, 64, 78, 85, 94–96, 100–106, 112, 138, 139, 153, 166, 178, 183–184,

189, 195n24, 196n26, 201n1; *see also* book travel; discovery narratives; dislocation; home; island fiction; time travel; travel narratives; trope of travel
travel narratives 12, 78, 94, 100, 101, 166, 201n1; *see also* British Empire; discovery narratives; travel; trope of travel
trope of travel 12, 78, 94, 104, 105, 166, 189; *see also* discovery narratives; travel; travel narratives
Tsomondo, Thorell Porter 120–121
The Typewriter's Tale 11, 49, 67, 70–71; *see also* Heyns, Michiel; James, Henry, adaptations of

United Kingdom 6, 63, 194n6
United States (American) 57, 62, 63, 70, 98, 99, 157, 193n2, 194n6, 195n24

Victorian: connotative meaning of 10, 18, 19, 20, 22; denotative meaning of 10, 18, 19, 22, 193n2; *see also Poor Things*; Victorian studies
Victorian studies 7, 8, 30, 78, 92, 193ch1n2, 194n13; *see also* neo–Victorian studies; post–Victorian studies; Victorian, connotative meaning of; Victorian, denotative meaning of
Victorian woman in travel outfit 139
Victoriana 8, 10, 22, 24, 28, 34, 36, 39, 55, 187, 194n13
Victoriography 10, 22, 23–24
visual culture 11, 28, 37, 57–59, 92, 138–139, 151, 184, 190, 193n5, 197n9; *see also* book cover; cultural studies; film studies; media studies; painting; photograph
Voigts-Virchow, Eckart 36–37, 38
Vrettos, Athena 158
Vukelic, Anne-Marie *see Far Above Rubies*

Wales (Welsh) 6, 9, 63, 90, 165–166, 167, 201n9; Wales Millennium Centre 90; *see also* Crystal Palace; *The Eyre Affair*; Millennium Dome
war(fare) 14, 82, 87, 165, 167, 176, 178, 182; *see also The Eyre Affair*; *Mister Pip*; *Oscar and Lucinda* (book)

Waterland 77, 80–82, 83, 197n1; *see also* natural history novel; Swift, Graham
Waters, Catherine 7, 27, 60
Watt, Ian 78
Waugh, Patricia 79–80, 117, 149, 194n7
Wehrmann, Jürgen 168–169
Wells, Juliette 164, 168, 200n6
West Indies 6, 13, 69, 100, 101, 105, 115, 119, 125, 130, 132, 136, 137, 138, 139, 141, 143, 144, 145–146, 155, 160, 199n6, 200n21; *see also* Cambridge; Caribbean; *Charlotte*; *Wide Sargasso Sea*
What Alice Knew: A Most Curious Tale of Henry James and Jack the Ripper 74, 197n14; *see also* Cohen, Paula Marantz
Whelehan, Imelda 36, 37, 38
White Hotel 118–119, 120, 137, 143; *see also* Thomas, D.M.
Wide Sargasso Sea 5, 12, 13, 37, 79, 107–108, 114–117, 124, 127–143, 145, 148, 150, 155–160, 163, 169, 173, 178, 189, 199n12, 199n14, 200n17; *see also* authorial anxiety; authorial (narrative) authority; bildungsroman; Caribbean; *Charlotte*; Gothic fiction; interculturation; *Jane Eyre*; literary historical era; modernism; novel ending(s); Rhys, Jean; sexuality; slavery; West Indies; writing process
Williams, Carolyn 152, 153
Wilson, Cheryl A. 30, 189
Winterson, Jeanette 50; *Boating for Beginners* 105
Wolfreys, Julian 23–24, 44, 45
Wood, James 69–70
Worpole, Ken 87, 88
writing process 11, 58, 65, 67, 69, 70, 72, 73, 75, 104, 109, 111, 113, 118, 123, 136, 137, 149, 164; *see also* James, Henry, adaptations of; *Jane Eyre*; *Charlotte*; *Wide Sargasso Sea*
Wuthering Heights 80, 116, 130, 140, 150; *see also* Brontë, Emily
Wyndham, Francis 113–114, 158, 159

Yates, Louisa 29, 33
Young, Robert 141